Coming Out
in Japan

JAPANESE SOCIETY SERIES

General Editor: Yoshio Sugimoto

Lives of Young Koreans in Japan
Yasunori Fukuoka

Globalization and Social Change in Contemporary Japan
J.S. Eades   Tom Gill   Harumi Befu

Coming Out in Japan: The Story of Satoru and Ryuta
by Satoru Ito and Ryuta Yanase

Coming Out in Japan

The Story of Satoru and Ryuta

by Satoru Ito and Ryuta Yanase

Translated by F. Conlan

Trans Pacific Press

Melbourne

First published in 2001 by
Trans Pacific Press
PO Box 120, Rosanna, Melbourne, Victoria 3084, Australia
Telephone: +61 3 9459 3021
Fax: +61 3 9457 5923
E-mail: enquiries@transpacificpress.com
Website: http://www.transpacificpress.com

Copyright © Trans Pacific Press 2001

Set in CJR Times New Roman by digital environs Melbourne
enquiries@digitalenvirons.com

Printed in Melbourne by Brown Prior Anderson

Distributed in North America by
International Specialized Book Services, Inc.
5824 NE Hassalo Street
Portland, Oregon 97213-3644
USA
Telephone: +1 800 944 6190 (toll free)
Fax: +1 503 280 3644
E-mail: orders@isbs.com
Website: http://www.isbs.com

ISSN   1443–9670 (Japanese Society Series)
ISBN   1–876843–02–0

National Library of Australia Cataloging in Publication Data

Ito, Satoru, 1953– .
Coming out in Japan.

ISBN 1 876843 02 0.

1. Homosexuality, Male – Japan. I. Yanase, Ryuta, 1962– .
II. Conlan, F. III. Title.

306.76620952

Contents

Part One: My Gay Pride Declaration

Dedication

This book is dedicated to the memory of Matthew Shepard.

Translator's Preface

In 1974, having completed a 3 year Asian Studies course at Curtin University in Perth, Western Australia, I was fortunate enough to be awarded a Japanese Government Ministry of Education scholarship which enabled me to study the Japanese language at the Tokyo University of Foreign Studies and then pursue subsequent studies at Tokyo Gakugei University. In 1981 I returned to Australia and commenced a career in education, lecturing in the Japanese language. When, in January 1998, I revisited Japan after an absence of some 17 years, two things stood out amongst those which had faded from my memory in the time I had been away from Japan. One was how very early it went dark in Tokyo at that time of year. Coming from a glary Australian summer where the days are as long as a politician is shrewd, it was hard to believe that I had, in the past, acclimatized to life in a city where, in winter, the mantle of darkness spread about 4pm.

The other thing which struck me was the continued existence of television shows which openly pilloried gays. Here were television shows reinforcing the most negative of negative imagery in relation to gays. There were panel shows churning out segments which parodied and denigrated gays in the interest of providing humour for mass consumption. The extraordinarily high level of technology which surrounded me in Japan was juxtaposed with an equally extraordinary willingness on the part of television programmers to exploit those of the minority sexual persuasion as a source of derogatory humour. The imbalance between the levels of development in technology and social attitudes was striking.

I believe that the interests of promoting and fostering international understanding can be furthered by opening windows onto aspects of Japanese society which go beyond the superficial. This book represents such a window. It provides an insight into an aspect of Japanese society which is rarely included in formal courses of study.

Parts One and Two of this book were published separately in Japan, one year apart. Part One was published in 1993 under the title '*Otoko Futari Gurashi*' and Part Two under the title '*Otoko to Otoko no Renai Noto*' in 1994. The two parts of this book, therefore, represent a progression in the events which took place in the lives of the authors. Part One deals with developments which took place in their lives up to the point where they found the courage to personally accept and publicly declare that most profound aspect of their being, their sexual orientation. Part Two picks up from that point and details the progression of events which surrounded their search for a means of leading their lives together as a gay couple in a social environment which provided no positive imagery or reinforcement. Having declared their sexual orientation in the public arena, they were prepared to pioneer a living arrangement outside the comfort zone of the positively sanctioned social structures, fully aware that their search for this lifestyle would be conducted in an environment devoid of any form of encouragement or support from mainstream society.

Acknowledgments

It is a great honour to have had this translated manuscript accepted for publication by Trans Pacific Press. I wish to thank Professor Yoshio Sugimoto for providing the opportunity to bring the story of Satoru and Ryuta to an audience beyond that of the Japanese speaking world, thereby assisting in promoting a better international understanding of the realities of contemporary Japanese society.

I thank the authors, Mr Ito and Mr Yanase, for entrusting me with the English translation of their manuscripts. I have endeavoured to produce a translation which balances the need to faithfully render the message as stated in the original language with the requirement to achieve a finished product which sounds natural in the target language.

I am greatly indebted to Mr Andrew Irvine for his painstaking proof-reading and Ms Rivka Niesten for her technical support. I also acknowledge the ready assistance provided by Professor Francisco Martinez of Kyoto Women's University in completing this project.

Last, but not least, I acknowledge the support and encouragement given by my family, Siew-Lian, Sarah and Grace. Their acceptance of my taking this project on and my monopolizing the computer for months on end has been much appreciated.

Francis Conlan
Perth, Australia
August 2000

Introduction

The traditional linguistic isolation of Japan has worked to foster the image of that country as being a unified social unit, a monolithic juggernaut in which all share not only a common language and nationality but, beyond this, a work ethic and an allegiance to a common value system. In reality there exist within Japanese society, and yet apart from it, numerous minority groupings which are not highly visible. Access to primary language source materials in Japanese increases an awareness of the differences, divisions and tensions existing beneath the appearance of cohesiveness and equanimity at the surface level of Japanese society.

Traditionally the Japanese have shunned those who do not conform to the mainstream. All social minorities have suffered ostracism, with pernicious stereotyping being the order of the day.

Social issues which are seen to be confronting have never been welcomed by the Japanese. Perhaps the question of sexuality represents one of the 'last frontiers' in this regard. It is an issue with which Japanese society doggedly refuses to openly engage. This book aims to give the English speaker, through the first hand experiences of the authors, an appreciation of the difficulties confronting homosexuals in mainstream Japanese society. It details how they are rejected by those of the majority sexual persuasion and ignored by the authorities.

Being highly heteronormative, Japanese society sanctions stereotypical portrayals of homosexuals. They are the constant butt of jokes and jibes in the mass media, particularly in television comedy shows. By way of illustration, let me cite one example of exploitation of the authors in the name of humour. After the appearance of 'My Gay Pride Declaration' and 'Our Partnership' in Japan, the authors were paid an unwelcome visit by a television comedy crew. With cameras rolling they knocked on the authors' door. They brought with them a comedian dressed in children's clothing. Amongst the things that were called out with the aim of obtaining footage which could be overlayed with pre-recorded laughter and used as a skit for a television program for general consumption were comments to the effect that if there were no children in the household one could be provided for the night. Whilst it seems the intention was not to suggest paedophilia, it was undeniably an attempt to profit from the chance to publicly ridicule the authors. In this regard, if mainstream Japan has moved forward at all in the past 25 years, it is by a negligible amount. However, the appearance of these works in Japan marked a watershed in that country's attitude to homosexuality and helped to dispel ignorance in relation to this question. Indeed, a number of mass media outlets have since embarked on a hitherto unchartered path of serious investigative journalism in relation to this subject.

These autobiographies trace the tortuous path the authors travelled through their formative years to the realization that they were homosexual, poignantly describing a lack of both formal and informal education about sexuality. This, coupled with a total lack of gay positive imagery, resulted in a sense of terrible social isolation. This book describes the denial which the authors experienced in the process of coming to terms with their sexuality as well as their eventual acknowledgment and personal acceptance of their sexual orientation. It deals with the mental torment inflicted on Ryuta as a result of his agonizing childhood as a homosexual and the difficulty Satoru faced in coming to terms with the need to break the parental bond he had with his mother. It reports on both the psychological and practical problems the authors faced in seeking to set up their lives together. Furthermore, it describes their 'coming out' to society and subsequent appeals, on both a personal and public level, for the acceptance of homosexuality by Japanese society. It details the influences and events which were personally significant for the authors, those which were character building and those which proved to be turning points in their lives.

The suicide of young Japanese gays, the experience of being blackmailed at work, the decision to 'come out' to family, the search for a partner, the fostering of that relationship, the acceptance of responsibilities in relation to aged parents, the court battle against the City of Tokyo over discrimination...the learning curve involved in handling these and other situations is portrayed in a matter-of-fact, non-sensational way from the personal viewpoint of these remarkable men who have declared their homosexuality in the public arena and – through a personal campaign of public education – dedicated their lives to the cause of promoting an understanding of homosexuality and removing discrimination and prejudice in relation to same sex relationships in Japan.

Francis Conlan

Translator's Notes

There are certain aspects of life in Japan which are considerably different to those with which we are familiar in English speaking societies. An appreciation of some of these will assist in setting the scene for the authors' life experiences, which have been described in the following pages.

Confucianist traditions, especially in regards to family relationships and obligations pertaining thereto, underpin certain aspects of Japanese society. For example, it is generally expected that children (particularly the eldest son) will take on the responsibility of looking after aged parents. Indeed, at least traditionally, it would have been considered a source of disgrace for a son to abrogate responsibility in this regard.

The Confucianist influence in Japan is further seen in the value placed on group consensus and the concomitant expectation that individuals and minority groups will accept the requirement to mould themselves in order to avoid the situation where there is a duality of interests, an absence of consensus. The lack of value placed on opinions which run contrary to the traditionally socially sanctioned mainstream, conservative opinion is a prominent feature of Japanese society. This consensus mentality represented a major obstacle for the authors to negotiate in their search for a place and a sense of belonging in Japanese society. The Confucianist mentality, which favours uniformity and authoritarianism, would appear to be a major cause of Japanese society's outward hostility towards homosexuality. This hostility, in turn, was the cause of much of the authors' self-denial.

The basic Japanese mentality is driven by the perceived validity of rigid hierarchy, conformity and obedience to authority. These values are so deeply rooted that the always difficult job of bringing about social change is even more difficult in Japan than in the West. The mass media and the Japanese Government's Ministry of Education represent two major pillars of the authoritarian culture whose combined forces make heterosexuality virtually a religion in Japan. Traditionally held conservative, mainstream attitudes are so deeply ingrained in the Japanese psyche that they are virtually sacred. Those in positions of authority routinely use the supposed superiority of heterosexuality to shape public attitudes towards homosexuality. This supposed superiority is used to justify the denigration of homosexuals and to ignore their needs. People in positions of authority treat homosexuals as both a perceived challenge to the system and an easy target. This book represents the authors' open challenge to the feudal values that hold non-conformity in contempt in Japan.

The all pervasive and inexorable pressure Japanese society exerts on young adults to get married is surely a modern day expression of feudal values. The popular image of marriage, especially as far as girls are concerned, is one which is equated with happiness. Indeed the Japanese wedding industry goes so far as to use the term for happiness, '*shiawase*', synonymously with the term for marriage.

The popular image of gays as virtual extra-terrestrials is supported by a culture of ignorance. Consequently it is no wonder that young people who experience feelings of same-sex attraction desperately seek to deny these feelings and to dissociate themselves from the omnipresent negative imagery associated with what is perceived, in the popular mind, to be a repulsive world. Derogatory stereotyping of gays is the standard fare served up to the Japanese public by the mass media. An astoundingly negative image of gay men is commonly portrayed and gays are openly pilloried in public arenas. The question of female same-sex relationships is hardly ever encountered. This would appear to be the Japanese response to a social issue which is perhaps thought to be too uncomfortable to deal with any other way.

The reader of this work will realize that city life in Japan involves living in close proximity to neighbours and that consequently there is very little privacy in terms of having visitors or sharing the house with anyone. The density of housing and proximity of neighbours means that living with an awareness of the potential existence of prying eyes is an unavoidable feature of urban life for the Japanese. Leading one's life with complete privacy is well-nigh impossible in a Japanese city.

The life experiences delineated here bring the hierarchical and extremely competitive nature of the Japanese education system into focus. Competition to gain places at kindergartens, primary schools and junior and senior high schools which enhance the prospect of being offered a place at a prestigious university, is a fact of life. At the pinnacle of the academic ladder is the hallowed Tokyo University. A graduate of this institution is virtually guaranteed a secure future within Japanese society. Its corridors are reserved for the *crème de la crème* of the intelligentsia.

As a translator I sympathized with the authors who struggled to find a term in Japanese which equates with the expression 'sexual orientation'. Without a recognized term to express this notion, convincing people of its validity, even its very existence, has clearly proven to be a very challenging exercise for the authors.

Throughout this work the elongated vowel sounds of Japanese words have been indicated using macrons, except where the words in question can be considered to be generally familiar to English speakers. The exceptions are the names Ryuta and Ito. The macronization of these has been avoided as it was felt that it would tend to have a visually unsettling effect, given that these names appear so frequently.

Francis Conlan
April 2000

Foreword to Part One

Fear and prejudice are rooted in the same cause – ignorance. The key to overcoming ignorance is education.

Providing education which will allow us to overcome fear and prejudice is easier said than done. Homophobia, in particular, is difficult to expose and eradicate when mythology about it is deeply ingrained in a nation's psyche. Western and Eastern cultures are no different in this regard, although differing social mores and religious values between these worlds can obstruct the road to community education and understanding of taboo issues in different ways.

The remarkable educative role being played out in Japan by Satoru and Ryuta is testimony to what can be achieved when people are prepared to put themselves in the front line of social reform.

As a former gay rights activist in Australia and now as an elected member of its Federal Senate, I have learned that changing people's hearts and minds is more important than changing laws. This strategy will, however, eventually result in law reform because most politicians follow public opinion rather than lead it.

Only when homosexuality is seen as an issue of personal humanity rather than a theory about human behaviour will the general population begin to understand. Only when lesbian and gay people are seen as normal, human and ordinary will long held misconceptions change.

The remarkable Japanese precedent being set by Satoru and Ryuta is courageous, inspiring and necessary. Without precedent you cannot have progress. Part One of this book is a tribute to their work and a manual for others to follow.

Brian Greig
Australian Democrats
Senator for Western Australia
April 2000

Part One:
My Gay Pride Declaration
by Satoru Ito

Preamble to Part One

I am a homosexual.

It has taken thirty-nine years for me to reach the point where I can put these four words down on paper.

Bravery is not a natural attribute of mine. In fact I must admit that I am basically a coward. There are many things that I am afraid of. I only need a hairy caterpillar to crawl on me and all hell breaks loose. When there is a peal of thunder I put on a show of maintaining equanimity but deep down I start to panic, wondering what I should do if lightning were to strike. Just by taking the window seat of a restaurant in a tall building I start to get unnerved. I can't stand watching horror films or torture scenes for more than a few seconds. There are even times when I find myself afraid to sleep, thinking that I might not wake up in the morning. Looking back over my life to date, I was afraid to take that big step from being a student to entering the work force and I treated a period spanning ten whole years at university and post-graduate school (which I left without completing) as a period of moratorium, putting off taking that step. It is only very recently that I have been able to put my fears aside and stand up to those in positions of authority – people such as school principals, radio station directors, government officials and the like.

At the present time, to publicly declare that you are homosexual in Japan certainly upsets the applecart. In fact it would be more accurate to say such a proclamation unleashes a raging hurricane! Heterosexuals have decided that as far as sexuality is concerned, theirs is the one and only way people should live. And, simply because they represent the majority in society, heterosexuality is considered to be a nonnegotiable absolute. They become disconcerted and alarmed at the appearance of a sexual nonconformist and desperately refuse to sanction the existence of homosexuality. Sometimes they go so far as to try to eliminate those who do not share their sexual preference. Perhaps they fear that by knowing about another world, their understanding of what constitutes normal society – their notion of 'common sense and rationality' – would be in severe jeopardy. When you think of it this way heterosexuals can also be thought of as being afraid of many things and quite cowardly, can they not? Though the treatment I have received has not included attempts to eliminate me as such, I have nevertheless lived my life constantly surrounded by all manner of prejudice-laden gossip. Comments such as 'I wonder if he secretly talks like a drag queen?', 'Is he into anal sex?', 'It is against God's law' etc. abound. I have taken the opportunity to address questions such as these in this book.

If people ask me about the things they want to know I am only too happy to work through their list of queries to put an end to the misconceptions they labour under. But they don't bother to approach me or ask me anything, preferring the simple comforts of their closed mindsets, which assume that 'that is what gays are like, full stop'. Having such a closed mind and lumping all members of a group together – basing your understanding of them and your attitude towards them on a sweeping generalization – is the definition of prejudice. Prejudice is the basis for much of the discriminatory behaviour we homosexuals suffer. I simply can't stand having my personality, my way of thinking, my lifestyle and my abilities misconstrued, undervalued and underestimated because of such prejudices. Even contemplating it is anathema for me.

Despite being afraid of many things, I have unequivocally and explicitly recorded in the very first line of this book that I am a homosexual. The reasons why I came out like this are far from simple, but I can begin by saying, first and foremost, that even without making this pronouncement publicly my life has been hell. Making this pronouncement cannot make things any worse for me. The amount of energy I have had to expend in making sure the fact that I am gay was always concealed has been simply tremendous. When I was in heterosexual company and everyone around me relaxed and chatted about heterosexually oriented topics, I had to take care to ensure that what I said 'fitted' their conversation, choosing words and expressing emotions which I did not feel in my heart. I was ever conscious of the need to keep the topic of conversation from turning towards sweethearts or marriage.

Furthermore, though I might go on a date with a gay partner, I was never able to hold hands with him in public. The only place I felt I could really relax and let my guard down was behind closed doors. This being the case, it became clear to me that it would be better to live my life true to myself, as nature intended for me. The fact that I was placed in a truly hellish situation was due to the dictates of the wider society which abounds with the 'rationality' of heterosexuals. I eventually came to realize that this rationality was flawed and that I would probably never find happiness unless I attempted to bring about a change to the *status quo*. This perhaps sounds as though it is easily said, but to reach the stage where I could find the courage to say it I had to first acknowledge and accept myself as a homosexual and have faith in myself as such. In order for you to appreciate the position I was in it is worth mentioning that for nearly eight years I had thought that homosexuality was a sickness and tried to cure myself of it.

It goes without saying that the process of acknowledgment and acceptance of one's sexual orientation starts with the acquisition of accurate information about sexuality and a proper understanding of the facts pertaining to this.

It has to be appreciated, for example, that homosexuals have existed since the birth of the human race right through to the present day. They have existed everywhere and are neither abnormal, weird nor perverted. Their appearance is simply due to the fact that the human race has been programmed in such a way as to always have a proportion of gays present. Likewise, it has to be understood that the reason why homosexuality is proscribed by most religions is because religious authorities felt it was necessary to encourage the birth of children amongst adherents in order to propagate their own kind. This aspect of religious dogma was taught to followers in order to expand the sphere of influence the various religions commanded in the world.

What gave me the confidence to live my life as a homosexual was the emotional support offered by my homosexual friends and my partner, Mr Ryuta Yanase. This was a confidence which welled up from within. Notwithstanding the fact that we have had almost continuous arguments, sometimes on a grand scale, Ryuta and I have provided support for each other for 7 years. We have steadily and painstakingly built up a relationship of mutual respect, paying no heed whatsoever to the dictates of the heterosexual majority (mainstream society) nor their pronouncements regarding societal expectations in terms of how males 'should' behave. Even a coward like me has found a person I can trust and in whom I can confide. I have a partner who is strict with me, yet who lovingly envelops me. We have proven that even homosexuals can find happiness in life. We have successfully formed a new kind of loving relationship, one which is different to that of heterosexuals, and as a result I have the courage to meet the challenges of life!

In this book you will find a record of the whole gamut of the feelings and emotions I have experienced as a homosexual, expressed candidly and without exaggeration. This book represents a re-discovery of myself. It details the process by which I came to terms with my homosexual self and analyzes that process. It is my life history. In it my soul is revealed. This is my personal story told honestly, my public coming out. It is a declaration by which I hope to live openly and proudly as a homosexual. It is also an acknowledgment that this declaration is a major turning point in my life.

I believe this book is relevant to the way all minorities, not only homosexuals, are treated in Japan. There are common elements to be found amongst all the social minorities which exist in Japanese society. Accordingly, I could find no greater happiness than if, through reading the story of Ryuta and me, you were to gain an insight into both the agony that comes about as a result of being a member of a social minority in Japan and the even greater joys that can be borne out of this.

In particular I hope to draw your attention to the new kind of partnership Ryuta and I are attempting to forge – one which surely is difficult to appreciate for those who exist as members of the mainstream society – and I quietly take pride in the thought that perhaps this might provide an opportunity for us, together, to put thought into just how we all might make our way through the uncertainties of the tumultuous 1990s.

Let me repeat – I am, without doubt, a homosexual: a homosexual such as can be found anywhere in the world.

Satoru Ito

1 Jottings Notebook

The Path I Walked Until I Was Able to Admit that I Like What I Like.

1 The courage to admit that I like what I like[1]

The practice of accepting students for who they are ('I like you fine just as you are') leads to my being branded a 'deviant teacher'.

Events in my life developed such that ten years ago I became a part-time instructor at a private high school. During the past ten years I depended on the school system for my livelihood, though I also did stints at other jobs, including being a radio disc-jockey. At the moment I am an instructor at Kashiwa Preparatory School, which is located in a sub-centre of the city of Tokyo.

I feel profoundly that the school system represents a 'lost world' which is eons behind the times. Let's look at arithmetic, for example. The explanations given by the program *The Heisei Education Committee* on the Fuji TV network, in which computer graphics are used to explain things, would be, I believe, 100 times easier to understand than a teacher standing in front of the class, trying to explain things using the blackboard and chalk method. The worst imaginable means of passing information to students continue to be used in Japanese schools. As for the English which is taught to students for examination purposes, the authorities seem determined to pile in sentence structures which are archaic. Nor is the quality of the material up to date. No matter how easy to understand, how interesting or well delivered a class in mathematics presented according to the enlightened *Suidō Hōshiki*[2] pedagogical philosophy might be, or indeed how interestingly presented a science class which employs the 'hypothesis experimentation'[3] teaching methodology might be, the system by which students are forced to sit in a classroom for as much as 5 and 6 hours a day can be tortuous. What's more, in every facet of their lives, including their movements after school, they are tied down by the rules the school sets. It is perfectly natural that children wouldn't want to go to a place such as school when they feel that their very lives could be threatened if they were to break these rules. Consequently, during my time working at a private high school, my blood would boil at the actions of teachers who would punch students without thinking twice.

I can't stand teachers who call students 'stupid', judging them only by the academic grades they obtain. Likewise, I feel no affinity whatsoever with teachers who do not have a good word for students behind their backs or who do not make any attempt to understand the attractions of the teenage years. I get angry at teachers who rip up love letters because they think that falling in love only gets in the way of academic pursuits. I produced a book entitled *Sir! Being Slapped is Offensive*, (published by San'ichi Shobō) in which these attitudes were questioned and lost my job as a result! I also get angry at instructors who, even at preparatory schools, explain to students that achieving admission to an exclusive university is the be all and end all, something which has supreme value and which is more important than any other interests students might have.

I crossed swords innumerable times with teachers, instructors and superiors at schools. I joined students in their enjoyment of life, even though we were breaking school rules. I was involved with all manner of educational movements in the region and although the people I was dealing with were uncompromising in their stance, I believe that I managed to open up a ventilation shaft, as it were, simply by being an unusual adult who could relate to pupils and share their curiosity about life and the world. I was, however, always dogged by a sense of isolation, a feeling that I was alone in this battle. This was because, in the final analysis, I was censured even by the teachers and parents who, like me, resented the violence meted out by teachers and the over-emphasis placed on examination results and school rules. These were people who, like me, hoped to have something done about the situation – precisely those who should have been my natural allies and from whom one would normally expect a measure of support. However, the moment I mentioned that I had dinner parties and played mahjongg at home with high school students or that I went into the city with them simply to enjoy life, their faces would fog over. Sometimes I would be given a lecture along the lines of 'Why don't you just organize them and start a student demonstration? It is a waste of time simply hanging out with them'.

What is wrong with simply socializing with teenagers? It is not as though I was doing it to curry favour with anyone. It just turned out that way naturally – simply and solely because I enjoy learning as much as I can through contact with different perspectives on life, different understandings and different senses of values – and the younger generations provide these. When occasionally I became close to them I would venture to talk about myself, possibly sending up a shower of sparks in the process.

Could we not just let these kids develop their own lives in accordance with their individual interests and without imposing too many restrictions upon them? In my opinion, employing legal restrictions to control things such as cigarettes and alcohol, things that appeal to different individuals depending on personal preferences, is ludicrous. (For the record the laws which attempted this were, for the most part, made before the war to improve the quality of soldiers in the military!) Whilst it appears that in their own way everyone feels strongly that he or she would like to make teenagers into 'good kids', my approach of accepting them just as they are – and admitting as much – didn't go down too well. In fact, it ended up with my being branded a 'deviant teacher'.

Anger directed towards schools which discriminate against minorities. Daring to publicly declare my homosexuality.

Whilst I was attempting to promote the idea of accepting approaches to education which challenged the existing educational set-up, I found myself in an environment where the question of engaging with students on their own level was apparently taboo. As a result of this, my socializing with students was seen as nothing more than my enjoyment of coarse and improper banter with teenagers. The school authorities didn't understand that I was just trying to casually and innocently inform students that sex is something to be enjoyed with mutual respect and to provide them with information about contraception. The fact that I am a homosexual was something I simply couldn't broach. Could you expect otherwise when the level of prejudice against homosexuals was such that it was thought they would sexually harass male students at the drop of a hat? What a joke! The fact is that the rate of sexual harassment by male teachers directed towards female students is far higher than anything that ever existed involving homosexuals.

I am now in a position where I can nonchalantly write 'I am a homosexual' at the beginning of this book. However, to get to the stage where I could actually put this down on paper, an uncommon and extraordinary level of resolution was needed. I have never disclosed this in writing before, except to a limited audience via a gay magazine[4]. I worried about writing this admission for a whole week. Some people will be wondering why this is so, and for their benefit I offer the following remarks which may serve to throw some light on the cause of my trepidation.

Even amongst those who raise objections about the Japanese school system, it is widely accepted that those who derive their livelihood from schools should be held in high esteem. This is so for the entire teaching profession, including those at preparatory schools. Moreover, the esteemed position of teachers is unquestioningly accepted at an unconscious level. Even if we overlook the high-handed and overbearing approach many teachers employ when asserting their authority, even if the use of violence to force obedience and discipline could be considered as a separate issue, teachers simply should not be accorded 'sainthood' and be treated as if they exist on a superhuman plane. Teachers are, after all, merely human beings.

Surely it should be that we permit some room for loosening up and accept a degree of individuality amongst teachers and their approaches to teaching. A teacher should only need to apologize openly to his pupils if he or she put a foot wrong as a result of embracing this philosophy. Under such a philosophy, students might develop a far greater level of perception and insight than they currently prove capable of. They would come to see simpleton teachers for what they are – examples of the sort of adult not to become. I would suggest that, with the exception of those who do nothing but worry about their examination results, students would have a certain curiosity sparked within them in relation to off-beat teachers and develop an appreciation of the concept of individuality as a result.

Be that as it may, it was the teaching business I found myself in and I knew I would run the risk of being hit by the protests of parents and thus stand to lose my job if my employer, Kashiwa Preparatory School, were to find out I was homosexual. The situation in Japan at the present time is that you simply cannot openly declare your homosexuality unless you have a mighty level of resolution. You would need to be prepared to dig your heels in and, perhaps, be prepared to take legal action and fight in the courts if you lost your job as a result of your homosexuality.

One reason for writing this book and detailing the facts of my life is that I have simply had more than enough of getting through life day by day with the constant fear and uncertainty of having someone find out about me. Another reason is because the same rage I experience towards schools that don't tolerate minorities (eg pupils who question school rules, instructors who refuse to wear ties, people with disabilities, etc.), also arises in reaction to a society that displays a deeply entrenched discrimination against homosexuals – treating them as though they were from another planet.

How would teenagers react to my homosexuality?

Since gaining confidence in myself and accepting my homo-sexuality, I have taken to talking with people more openly, in a way in which I don't feel gripped by a preconceived need to ensure that an important part of me is always concealed. I sometimes adopt an attitude which approximates that which is natural for me as a homosexual. I do this when I reach a certain level of familiarity and feel comfortable with them and judge that they are not homophobic. (The term 'homophobia' is used amongst homo-sexuals in America. It refers to a vehement aversion to and extreme fear of homosexuals and homosexuality.) I do it as a means of revealing one facet of my make-up which I wish the other party to know about. It was a very, very difficult path – indeed a tortuous path – that I had to tread in order to reach the point where this was possible, but I will elaborate on that later. What I mean when I refer to talking in a way that is 'natural for me' can be seen in my relationship with the preparatory school students with whom I become friendly each year. Inevitably they show great interest in what has happened with women in my life, given that I'm a single man in my late thirties. I broach the subject with a touch of humour, saying 'I'm on the unique side. I don't mind you being surprised at this but I would ask you not to try to change the way I view things'. At this juncture it often seems that the idea of my having illicit love affairs with other men's wives flashes through their minds! But there are also some very perceptive ones who show an inkling of understanding my situation.

Although you might say I have already spilled the beans, I continue to speak in a guarded way. When the other party comes to realize what I'm hinting at, I find that the response is almost always 'Is that all?' spoken in a very unruffled way. This can sometimes lead to my feeling a little let down! Some have responded by saying 'I was glad to be able to come into contact with a world I knew nothing of'. There are many others who provide light relief and ask 'Am I your type?' and when I reply 'No', come out with little pearlers like 'What's wrong? Don't I have any appeal as a male?' It's quite a difficult job, as you can imagine, to eclipse responses such as these!

Having said this, I was very saddened and depressed to be told by a student several years ago that 'I had never met a teacher as good as you, talking to me as an equal and giving lessons which were easy to follow and I admired you for it. But now you're telling me you're *gay*?' In the end, as a result of friends of mine following through on this one, the student in question came to terms with the fact that my work and how I conducted myself professionally were quite separate things to the issue of my sexuality. It was, nevertheless, a shock for both parties on that occasion. Teenagers are, however, capable of demonstrating an element of flexibility in terms of accommodating foreign concepts and, with time, this studuent got over the shock he had received. On that occasion, however, I felt a sense of foreboding in relation to my finding acceptance with older people. I felt that the more senior the generation, the greater would be the reassessment of my reputation when they found out about my sexuality. That one's reputation can be reassessed based upon a factor such as the revelation of one's sexuality represents the very essence of prejudice.

Ask whatever you will about gays; prejudice falls away through dialogue.

After declaring that I am a homosexual I encourage people to ask whatever questions they have, indicating that I am not worried about whether the questions are based on prejudice or not. I invite people to go ahead and ask about anything they want to know or anything they don't quite understand. Teenagers, whose natural curiosity hasn't yet lost its vigour, get right into popping all sorts of questions, including some quite extraordinary ones – some real 'bobby dazzlers'! They listen to my responses with open minds, and consequently, such exchanges are pleasant experiences. The aim of my engaging them in this way is to nip homophobia in the bud. Here is an example of a couple of typical questions to which frank answers were given:

'Do gays have anal sex?'

'That's up to the individual. Mutually satisfying sex can be had without insertion'.

'Are all gays on the feminine side?'

'Like heterosexuals, there are all sorts of homosexuals. Personally, I don't go around acting like a woman. My partner and I love each other for the men we are. Those who only see themselves as women who want to love men can perhaps, in a sense, be thought of as displaying heterosexual tendencies'.

'What do gays do about falling in love? Do they date each other?'

In response I explain such things as the fact that for gays, getting to meet one another poses enormous difficulties. I explain that gays can't hold hands when out on a date, for this attracts unwelcome attention. I also explain that, although we have many obstacles to get over, we are fundamentally the same as heterosexuals, indeed we are exactly the same except for our sexual orientation. The dialogues between us often go into much greater detail than that given in the exchanges quoted above and the conversations can be quite engaging at times. I find that the provision of even a small amount of accurate information can dispel a great deal of prejudice.

Of course, on occasions one is confronted by nasty, disconcerting questions. The least comforting of these is 'Why did you become gay?' My response is always 'We don't even know why heterosexuals are attracted to the opposite sex. Why is it that you like the opposite sex? Homosexuals should not be expected to explain the corollary of that in relation to their own orientation'. Some take this argument in and are won over by it while others have, to the bitter end, a most difficult job in following this reasoning. On one occasion, justifiably I think, I took umbrage when questioned by an unduly inquisitive lady in her mid to late 20s. She pried just a little too far, asking 'What sort of relationship do you have with your mother?', 'What sorts of incidents occurred when you were little?' and 'Is this sort of thing a reflection of an aspect of your personality, perhaps?'

The fact of the matter is that as *homo sapiens* we are a rather special species. We have been made capable of diverse sexual activity in order to ensure the continuation of the species. Accordingly, it is only a matter of course that a certain proportion of the population will always be homosexual and that homosexuals will always exist, everywhere. This is perfectly natural and only a matter of course.

2 The anguish involved in not being able to admit that you like what you like

My junior high school days, when a strong interest was aroused in me by an article entitled *'The Adolescent Male'*.

Notwithstanding the fact that I reached sexual maturity quite early – I was in grade 4 at primary school when I realized that playing with my penis was a very pleasurable experience – it was quite a long time before I knew without a doubt that I was homosexual.

Due to frequent changes of school and my never properly settling down or developing an affinity with the school system itself, I hardly ever spent any time with friends outside of school hours.

At that time, the accommodation my family rented was not large. I didn't have my own room so I could indulge in playing with myself only when no-one was home. Around the end of my fifth year in primary school I experienced ejaculation for the first time. I remember that I thought I had done a wee-wee and ran to the toilet. I knew intuitively that this was not something I could ask my parents about. As luck would have it, my mother subscribed to the magazine *Shufunotomo*[5] which about that time produced a supplement entitled '*The Adolescent Male*'. Upon reading this, I accepted, in a strangely simple way, that I had produced semen. I was much more shocked to learn, about a year later from an erotic magazine, that intercourse was the act of supplying this semen into a woman's vagina by ejaculation. It had never occurred to me that, other than kissing, there was physical contact between men and women. It is probably not surprising that I was, in my own unhurried way, confused and concerned about how kids came into being – it seemed that men must put something or other into women. At school boys were sent to a self-directed (or 'riddle') study period while a separate class was conducted to instruct girls about their first menstruation. As it didn't bother me in the least that I had been told that I would make ladies angry if I were to broach the subject with them, I asked my mother what a 'first menstruation' was. Mom explained this to me happily and with pride, but actually what she was saying was little more than Double Dutch to me. So for me there was no real means of gaining knowledge about sexual matters.

Thus it was that my interest concentrated on the games referred to as 'Anatomy' and 'M-ken'[6] in the article I had read. I longed to play these games, described as being transient games of puberty, where a group of boys gang up on another boy, take his underpants down and play with his penis until he ejaculates. I wanted to play such games, taking both the active and passive roles. This was in my primary school years, but it was not to be. All that ever happened was that, on occasions, I would look from afar with envy at a pair of boys playing with each other's penises. I also remember very clearly the pair who always knocked around with each other as good mates and who very innocently asked whether or not two men could get married. So it is that the single solitary occasion, in year 6, on which I rubbed the penis of a friend while playing rough and tumble with him and pretending to be a professional wrestler, is etched forever in my memory. All in all I didn't have many opportunities to play with friends and I wasn't terribly good at it.

At school I was especially poor at Physical Education. I was given an E (on a scale of A-E) for this subject in term 3 of year 4 of primary school. I had a terrible inferiority complex in regard to my poor sporting prowess and was not able to bring myself to ask others to let me join in their games, even if I felt inclined to.

I saw the change of school in the second term of primary year 6 as a chance to make friends and I was raring to meet this challenge. As it happened, the top marks in the class I was moving into were always obtained by the girls in the class. However, quite unexpectedly, I topped the whole class in my first test in the new school. Ironically, this resulted in my becoming popular with the girls although this situation came about as a result of something totally unrelated to my sexual orientation. I didn't think of this as a particularly bad situation, however, and I spent my playtime mostly in the company of girls. All the while I considered myself to be heterosexual.

It wasn't long at all before the teacher in charge of the class announced that it would be a waste for me to go to a local school and recommended that I sit for the entrance examinations of Kaisei Junior High School[7] to see if I could gain a place there. This was a private school in Tokyo which led onto an affiliated senior high school which, in turn, prepared students for university entrance examinations. Thus it was that I started attending a cram school in order to improve my chances of obtaining a place at Kaisei. Although I started late, in second term, I just managed to cover all that was required and scraped through the examination, resulting in my being offered a place at that school.

Plunging myself into my studies to suppress my sexual appetite during my junior and senior high school years.

I thought to myself that here at last I had the chance I had been looking for. Kaisei was a boys' school and I easily fitted into the smutty conversations that went on there. In addition I was able to find a classmate who played with his penis. At this school I heard from a guy in the Sports Club that he had been 'given Anatomy' by one of his senior schoolmates, and just hearing this sent a thrill right through me. Because, however, I had no confidence in my level of stamina nor my ability to keep up a rigorous sports routine, I resigned myself to the fact that I would never be able to join that club. I went, instead, to the Social Sciences Research Club, the activities of which centred on going out into society and conducting surveys.

Yet very soon a new element was to appear on the scene, one which would dampen my eagerness to participate fully in the club's activities. The teachers at school told us something we had not bargained for – the fact that we should now set our sights on gaining admission to Tokyo University. They told us of students who had graduated from Kaisei before us who had gone on to make their mark in powerful business houses and government departments. In fact I was able to meet such old boys through athletics meetings and club activities and, partly because of this, I felt I wanted to graduate and be part of the vertically oriented Kaisei network of old boys – to join the elite in other words.

Again at this school one thing I was particularly good at was being the teacher's pet. I found it easy to get into the teacher's good books and I felt that there was really no choice but for me to continue to put in the effort required to get good grades. This was a continuation of my approach to the latter years of primary education, adopted simply to make me feel comfortable at school. This course of action was not driven by the desire to realize a dream as such, so much as something which stemmed from a feeling that this was the only course of action available to me. This being the case, I immediately plunged myself into my studies, nose to the grindstone!

There was, however, no denying the intensity of my sexual appetite. I was dead keen to take part in the game of 'Anatomy' which, from time to time, enjoyed periods of great popularity in every class. In my case, however, I would spend an entire week without masturbating during which I would refrain from self stimulation before and during tests, using the exhilaration of sexual release on the day of the last test as a lever in my pursuit of academic goals. This is a sad thing to have to report. What unfulfilling teenage years I spent!

In the third grade of junior high school I fell in love for the first time, with a classmate whom I shall refer to as 'E'. He was a boy who used hair creme, something which was unusual amongst junior high school students at the time. It was apparent also that he smoked. He was very tanned from snow-skiing and swimming and I lost my heart to him. Just by smelling his hair creme or as a result of the smell he carried as a smoker, my heart would skip a beat. Eventually, in the first year of senior high school, I wangled my way to joining him on a ski trip. I fully believed at the time, however, that I was just seeking a friend as I had never had one. It didn't register with me that, in fact, my interest in him went beyond the bounds of mere friendship.

As a prelude to getting down to study in high school I would masturbate virtually every day, fantasizing about things like being the subject of the game 'Anatomy'. In my life at school 'K', 'M' and 'O' appeared on the scene, one after the other. These were classmates and juniors at school with whom I wanted to become 'friends' and whom I admired. I did manage to strike up friendships of sorts with them but the brakes were always put on by the need to revise and to preview lessons that were coming up. This prevented any deepening of what could have been called a friendship. One night when I was away on a trip with 'O' at the end of my second year at high school, not only didn't I make advances to him but I pulled out some practice examination questions and started to work on them instead, conscious of the fact that our exams were closing in. By doing so I apparently astounded him. What a fool I was!

If I am to be perfectly frank in this book I should say that, until recently, I deeply regretted my days at Kaisei. If I had tried to get to know the heterosexuals there better and perhaps managed to get a little closer to them than I did, I should have been able to make a reasonably pleasant experience out of the time I spent there, especially given that it was a period of strong sexual desires for me. Be that as it may, the fact is that when almost all around you are heterosexual it is exceptionally easy to end up believing that you are heterosexual too.

So it was that in my third year at high school I went on a date with a girl I had met at a school festival. I am ashamed to admit that, to some extent, I used my association with this girl to try to prove that I was a normal human being. I must confess, however, that I was not sexually aroused by her at all. I had absolutely no desire to kiss her or hold her. I didn't even find her attractive. And yet I still did not question my sexuality in any way, and this despite the fact that I was so aroused by the three young men I referred to as 'E', 'M' and 'O'. Incidentally that was the only date I had with that girl. I was somewhat intimidated when she told me that she had participated in a student demonstration and had been punched by the riot police. Yet, as it happened, that wasn't the last time we were to see each other. There was a subsequent chance meeting which provided a sequel to our association. I ran into her again about three years later at another student demonstration after I had 'awoken' to myself.

University days when I lost my heart to many a man while believing that I had to become heterosexual.

Immediately before sitting the entrance examinations for Tokyo University I found myself in a bookshop where a gay magazine called *Barazoku*[8] happened to catch my eye. I picked it up, flicked through it and then wasted no time in taking it to the counter where I immediately made the purchase. I took it home and thoroughly digested everything in it, reading it from cover to cover. It turned out to be the very first gay magazine in Japan and, what's more, the foundation issue. This was towards the end of 1971. This magazine offered tangible proof that homosexuality existed. Up until that time I had only known of it as a word in dictionaries, in sex education books I had bought myself and in a book called *'Basic Knowledge of Modern Terminology'*. Homosexuals really existed! The magazine *Barazoku* was, however, a darkish sort of publication lacking social respectability and one which acted as a shadowy forum for communication amongst members of a sort of secret audience. It very much brought to the fore the fact that homosexuals had no rights as citizens and that there was no place for them in mainstream society. It represented a world for a very limited minority forced to stealthily gain a taste of that which interested them.

This discovery occurred at a time when teenagers were showing an interest in politics and joining various political groups. By contrast, I turned my back on all of that, refusing to sanction such behaviour. I chose instead, the snug and comfortable course within the framework of the fully socially sanctioned academic world at Kaisei. Clever though I was seen to be, it was only then that I started to get an inkling of my sexuality. Perhaps I should say, rather, that it was *because* I had already become aware of my sexuality that I was suppressing it using theory and logic as best I could to convince myself that I wasn't truly homosexual. At this point I took the opposite tack and convinced myself that I would have to do whatever was necessary to ensure I was a heterosexual.

On the academic side of things I passed the entrance exam for the Science Faculty of Tokyo University and immediately commenced the course. I soon found myself in a crisis, however, when I realized that I couldn't keep up with the lectures. I realized that I had only chosen the science course because of its prestige. I knew, however, that I would be able to keep up with the course if I were in the Liberal Arts Faculty, so I re-sat the entrance examinations, gaining admission for the following year. I guess it would be fair to say that I was deliberately choosing a course in life which would deny me the time to look hard at my own sexuality. Although I was re-enrolling at university, in the Liberal Arts Faculty this time, I could not see where I wanted to head nor what it was that I wanted to accomplish. The teachers at Kaisei (who had shown me more than just a touch of favouritism!) and my test results (Kaisei gave me a prize for excellence) were no longer there as background supports.

During this period, while trying to adjust to my new situation and find my feet, as it were, I fell in love with a lad who was 5 years my junior at Kaisei. But I was in no position to even hope that my feelings of affection and attraction would be returned. It was a one-way love affair. 'M' and his friends, whom I met at a school cultural festival, criticized the school system at Kaisei which could only see things in academic terms of reference and straight-out examination results. This quite knocked me off my feet and I joined (should I say 'shadowed'?) 'M' and his friends in all the activities they pursued. I got myself involved in the different issues which kept coming up in their lives – things such as their leaving home and an incident relating to the rejection of a manuscript they had written for a student club's magazine which was critical of the school. During my involvement in these things I pretty much totally neglected my university commitments for six months.

Through my association with 'M' and his friends it occurred to me that I was going through a process of self-denial. I was seeking simply to follow an elite academic course, concerning myself only with academic results while knowing nothing of the contradictions which existed in the society around me. I am, in a sense, still in self-denial even now. 'M' and friends argued that, with all the study I was putting in and the excellent grades I was receiving, I wouldn't be able to understand how deeply they were concerned about the various social and political issues of the day. Eventually I found myself forced to start out on the road to what might be termed 'regaining a place for myself' at university. I guess I would have to admit that it was because 'M' meant so much to me that I changed from being someone whose nose was never out of the books to someone who could take it upon himself to start up a variety of new clubs and circles at university. Falling in love does change people. I developed contacts with friends and fellow club enthusiasts. Imagine this of me, someone who had been hopeless at both getting to know people and socializing in the 6 years I had spent in junior and senior high school! One of the clubs I started up was the Badminton Club. The motto of this club, 'Aim to enjoy learning about the game together', remains unchanged to the present day. I established this club in order to meet the needs of those who were not good at sport but who were interested in having a go at something anyway.

I chose to not simply rely on books alone to acquire information and broaden my horizons. To this end I formed another circle, known as 'That's Another College'[9] or 'TAC' for short, comprised of activists with interests in a variety of different areas. I felt there was a need for me to do this, given that I was in Tokyo University and yet knew nothing whatsoever about the struggles that the university was involved in. This circle was something of an oddity amongst university circles in that we would debate and discuss anything and everything from politics and religion through to the nuclear question, the question of the *buraku*[10] and the situation the disabled were in, reflecting on and questioning our individual personal histories into the bargain. Later came the 'Circle to Improve Education'. Whenever I had free time I would head off here, there and everywhere meeting people who had different interests and coming into contact with a wide variety of issues. It was through one such meeting that I learned about the history and politics of Okinawa and about Ashio[11], the place in Japan where concerns about environmental pollution first surfaced. This new knowledge made a deep impression on me. In a sense I was footloose and fancy-free which was great, but it also meant repeating academic years on more than one occasion.

However, while at Tokyo University, I never faced my central concern, the one closest to my heart and at the very core of my being. I put a great deal of effort into becoming heterosexual, absolutely determined that I should approach girls in the usual way. Deep down in my soul, though, I knew that my heart simply wasn't in it. I remained unable to get an erection when associating with the opposite sex. It was possible that my inner feelings and lack of genuine enthusiasm were picked up by the girls in question. Either way I was jilted time and time again. My lack of enthusiasm meant that any relationships I had with women were effectively doomed from the start.

In one particular instance, I know that I did the wrong thing by a girl, whom I shall refer to only as 'K', in the latter half of my time at Tokyo University. 'K' had clearly taken a liking to me. Even now, looking back at the relationship I had with 'K' and the time we spent together, I feel very bad about the nuisance I must have been in her life and the time she wasted with me. To this very day I feel a need to apologize for allowing her to believe that our relationship might have gone somewhere. Although we dated several times I never put my arm around her shoulder and I am sure she must have been terribly frustrated by this. I was very cowardly in dragging out the relationship, such as it was, hoping to somehow extricate myself from my homosexuality and to throw off the feelings of attraction I felt towards my own sex. In the end, when she was unable to stand it any longer and she left me, I felt a sense of relief. Forgive me 'K', for the wasted investment you made in me. I might add that as a result of my experience with 'K' I no longer support the magazine *Barazoku* which advocates sham marriages for gays.

Unrequited love for Mr 'T'. Coming to the realization that it would not be possible for me to be anything other than homosexual.

No matter how much I might work on trying to create a heterosexual self-image which I could project to the world, I simply couldn't stop myself from buying gay magazines and getting hard as a result of these. And there I was, falling in love with straight guys at university – surely love is blind! Unlike in my junior and senior high school days, however, reason could not win in the battle with love and passion. Whenever I fell for someone at university I would take advantage of the free time I had and do my best to arrange things so that I could spend as much time as possible with him. I even used to make my interests match his. First, there was 'H'. But, it wasn't long at all before he found a girlfriend. One night after a group of us had had a few drinks in someone's apartment, he and his girl started petting. I couldn't stand the sight of this but, being unable to express my jealousy as such, I spent the entire night, right through until morning, wandering the streets of Kichijōji[12] in terrible frustration. Out of sheer desperation I confessed my feelings to 'H', only to have him virtually cut me off as a social contact. Despite this experience, though, I stubbornly continued hoping to become a heterosexual.

As time passed I felt myself being attracted to others in the various university circles I was involved in, yet I remained defiant in my determination not to succumb to the feelings of same sex attraction which possessed me. Of particular note in this regard was 'T', a young man who was a first year student when I was in my 7th year of university studies. For me it was love at first sight. He resembled Shinji Harada[13] in looks and I stuck to him like a limpet. I was by no means backward in coming forward in the approach I took to forming an association with him. After badminton I would join him in whatever he chose to do. If he chose to go drinking, that's where I'd be. If it was a game of mahjongg, sure enough you'd find me there in the mahjongg hall with him, or in someone's flat if that was where the mahjongg game was being played. We became close friends and would knock around together, staying overnight at each other's places.

When the summer vacation came I went with him to his home in the country and wormed my way into staying almost a week, escaping the heat of the city and enjoying the coolness of the countryside. Together we arranged trips and travelled around the countryside visiting and staying at the homes of other members of our university circle. There was, of course, a limit to how far I could go with him. The furthest I could go was to pretend to be mucking around and to hug him while calling out the name of a girl in our circle whom I claimed I felt affections for. The frustration I felt at not being able to go beyond being 'close friends' made me all the more determined in my course of action. Whenever there was a get together I would at some stage of the game force myself in so that I was sitting beside him. Whenever there was something on my mind I would go to his place and stay overnight to discuss it, paying scant attention to whether it was convenient for him to have me stay or not.

Both because I wanted to be with 'T' and join him in whatever he did and because I hadn't the strength of character to come out and admit to those in my life just what I was feeling, it looked as though the road forward for me was post-graduate school at Tokyo University. I was not successful at getting in on my first attempt at this, so my academic pursuits were held back a year. The following year I was accepted into the post-graduate program of Hitotsubashi University[14]. I used this as an opportunity to move into an apartment which was just a 10 minute walk from where 'T' was living.

When it got to this stage all around, including 'T', realized that there was more to my behaviour than what you would normally expect from a friendship, no matter how close. The thing that was funny here was the fact that all those around me at university just thought of me as being something of a 'pesky uncle' and they didn't accuse me of being homosexual. They thought that one day I would 'awaken', as it were, and get married. I don't think that this was because they didn't feel prejudiced against gays, but rather because they were quite unable to actually conceptualize what homosexuality was or visualize the existence of homo-sexuals. Had this not been the case I would have no doubt been ostracized and every year I could have looked forward to being introduced to new students as the founder of the circle, with the added quip 'Croc here likes boys, so watch out lads!' ('Croc' was my nickname amongst circle members, short for 'Crocodile'!) I can well imagine that I would have been asked what sort of boys I was interested in and then, in jest, the new students would have been told 'Oi you, you're his type. It's your job to look after him!' Gradually 'T' also started to feel I was leaning a bit heavily. I responded by trying all the harder, going so far as to practically force him to come and join me in the other activities I was involved in. On one occasion at such an activity I found myself really wanting to speak out against the pronouncement of a certain Mr

'N' who was dabbling with socialism and who stated that 'When the revolution comes we'll kill all the poofters because they're disgusting. Lesbians can be spared'. I was unable to, however, because I had a crush on this Mr N. On another occasion I dragged 'T' along to a study meeting about 'capitalist theory'. I really do feel grateful to 'T' for spending so much of his precious youth with me. I will never forget the time, only once ever, when, after he'd had a few drinks, he said to me 'every now and again I must do something for Croc!' and he danced with me cheek to cheek. Such was our relationship. When, however, the one-sided love affair which had stretched over four very, very long years bade farewell to me with 'T' getting a job and leaving Tokyo, I looked at myself and at how much energy, how much of myself, I had invested in my relationship with him and finally realized, if I hadn't realized before, that I could be nothing other than a homosexual. After that I did meet 'T' again on a few occasions but he moved and didn't notify me of his new address and didn't keep in touch.

Making the decision never again to fall in love with a heterosexual.

Together with this realization I made the decision that I would never again fall in love with a heterosexual. I knew that no matter how much of a struggle it might be, rather than placing hope on a love which could never bear fruit, I should get to know other homosexuals, become friends with them and hope to fall in love. The fact of the matter is that this is a realization that all homosexuals must come to terms with at some stage in their lives. It's a gate through which all must pass. Yet although all must acknowledge this, there are some homosexuals who will choose the path of continuing to pursue the man of their dreams even though it might be a one-way love affair. I was convinced that in my case, however, my partner would have to be a homosexual if I was ever to experience fulfilment and find happiness in a relationship. This was because ultimately the qualitative gap between homosexuals and heterosexuals was simply too great to be bridged.

I now have put the idea completely behind me that a heterosexual, no matter how close he might be to the ideal image I have of an attractive man, could ever be someone I would fall for, even though I might be sexually aroused by him. I had already resigned myself to this before I came to know my present partner. Unfortunately, it appears to be the case that it is very difficult to reach this point in one's understanding of oneself without first being repeatedly torn apart emotionally as a result of experiencing love directed towards heterosexuals.

For heterosexuals it is a simple matter to find potential partners in love. Virtually everywhere they look they can find members of the opposite sex whom they can consider. For homosexuals, on the other hand, finding potential partners represents an almost impossibly difficult feat. Just getting to know other homosexuals is an extraordinarily difficult task. Homosexual colleagues working together in the same office for many years will never get to know of each other whilst they both keep hiding their sexual preference. The various means available to us today for making contact with others who share the minority sexual persuasion, such as gay circles, message dialling systems and the personal computer networks, etc., simply did not exist when I was growing up. Back in the 1980s all we had were gay bars and the personal columns of gay magazines. I did manage to pluck up the courage to visit the former but I just couldn't get used to the drag queen type language which conventionally flies about such places nor getting the once-over by all the patrons the moment you enter the premises. Consequently I ended up solely utilizing the advertisement columns of gay magazines. Strangely enough, in doing so I felt a peculiarly uplifting sensation which made me feel as though I had at long last crossed the line and entered the unknown, the underground homosexual sub-culture. It was as though I had become something of an outlaw in terms of conventional social behaviour.

The initial contact I made through the personal columns of a gay magazine was a university student I chose to contact after doing my very best to get an idea of the sort of person he was from the few lines he wrote in his ad. It did look promising. He was a 4th year student and hoped to become a teacher. For my part I had already written about the terrible time I had had with schools in a book entitled *Fourteen Years in Kaisei and Tokyo University* (I had been in Tokyo University for 8 years!!) and it seemed very much as though dealing with the question of education was set to be my life's work. It looked, relatively speaking, as though we had a considerable amount in common. Our weekly dates were enjoyable except for the fact that, being quite inexperienced, I was not able to please him sexually.

Our association lasted only a brief three months. When I dropped by his apartment one day, after contact from him had suddenly ceased, he told me that a former lover of his had contacted him and told him that he was being forced into marriage and that he wanted to get back together again without his wife knowing. That spelled the end of our association.

Coming to realize the difficulties involved in meeting other homosexuals.

Perhaps I should have introduced the abovementioned incident as the beginning of a run of terrible luck. After that incident I placed my own ad in the personal columns of a gay magazine but I received no responses. When I replied to ads, the men I met were on different wavelengths to me. There was no basis on which a proper friendship could develop. On one occasion I took a copy of the magazine to the appointed coffee shop and placed it on the table as arranged, in order to rendezvous with the other party, but no-one turned up to meet me. Looking back at that episode, however, I recall that there was a patron in the coffee shop who left the moment I brought out the magazine. It would appear that he was the person I was to have made contact with, but it seems I wasn't his type so he left without saying a word. Following that incident I had two bitter experiences involving guys who did not communicate well at all.

Didn't I have what it took to attract a partner? Being over-eager just made it harder for me to form a relationship. On the rare occasions when it looked like all was going well I would be consumed with the thought that this might be the one and only chance in my life to find a partner and that I mustn't blow it. I would then pressure the other party through my attempts to go from being friends to being lovers in just one step. Whenever the chance arose for sex I would have to take it or my sex drive would go wild. In this situation, there was no way we could get to become close friends. Before the other party was able to get to know me – my personality and perhaps a degree of personal appeal – I would lose him to another with whom I couldn't compete in terms of looks, style and age. This was especially so when I was trying to impress boys in their teens.

For the record, my first sexual encounter occurred at the end of 1980 just as I was starting to accept that things would not work out with 'T'. It was with a boy from a circle made up of high school students who had read my book '*Fourteen Years in Kaisei and Tokyo University*' and who questioned the system of examinations as well as their own way of living as students who were getting excellent grades under this system. After a drinking party at his friend's house it ended up that we two were to share a room to ourselves for the night[15]. While we were larking around with each other, neither quite knowing what was going to happen, we ended up stroking each other, hugging and ejaculating. It would probably be true to say that the sense of reassurance that I experienced as a result of at least knowing that I had 'accomplished it' was stronger than any passion that I felt on that occasion. I was not, at that stage, able to fully enjoy the experience as I still carried with me a sense of guilt and impropriety as a result of the norms, conventions and negative imagery associated with homosexuality in the wider Japanese society. I took it upon myself to try to avoid sexual activity from then on. My partner, however, was heterosexual so there was nothing left but for me to experience a one-way Platonic love relationship for nearly a year after that. Thus it was that I would make the two-and-a-half-hour one-way journey to his place to act as his school tutor! This was during the time when I was still unable to extricate myself from the world of one-way love affairs of the sort I had experienced with 'T'.

Human beings, I believe, are capable of doing just about anything when they become desperate. In my case I completely immersed myself in the gay scene in the Ni-chōme area[16] of Shinjuku[17], paying to have young guys and visiting what were called colloquially the 'mixed rooms' of salacious *ryokans*[18], or accommodation facilities where the sleeping arrangements are the same as those on school trips where all bed down together on the floor. Here, with nothing more than eye contact, one could 'make it' with another visitor. Here again though, I was not sought after as 'hot property'. Though I might 'make it' with somebody there was an emptiness in my soul after the event as I made my way home. On the occasions when I didn't 'make it' the emptiness felt was all the keener. Nonetheless, I would find myself going down this path again several weeks later choosing what some would see as the easy way out. I should have been thankful for the times I couldn't afford it as I probably would have virtually drowned in that scene had I had plenty of money.

I have to acknowledge that I must have been a pretty hard nut to crack. I wouldn't accept that what money could buy me was just a business transaction and I would try desperately hard to make conversation on any topic with the guy I had spent money to be with, in the hope that we might be friends, even if just for that one time we were together. I would ask such things as 'What brought you to this business' and 'Are there any clients who give you a difficult time?' in attempts to strike up a conversation. Would you believe that it was at these times and these times alone that I seemed to be able to show some flourish in terms of being successful as a social conversationalist? As a result, often the guy I was with would tell me all about himself. I particularly remember the guy who told me, so vacantly, that his girlfriend worked in a bath house brothel and thanks to this part-time job his problem of premature ejaculation had been solved. It seems that almost all those working in his position are heterosexuals. It would appear that homosexuals are not suited to that line of work because it is more difficult for them, given that they have their own tastes in terms of clients.

Even though it was a strictly forbidden practice I did arrange to have dates outside the business with two of those working there for whom I often asked and with whom I had become quite close.

Blackmail – being threatened with exposure on account of my homosexuality. Hoisting the white flag.

1982 was the year in which I finally realized that post-graduate school and the study involved therein were not for me. As it happened it was also the year in which my father passed away. After withdrawing from my studies and taking up a part-time position as an instructor at a private high school I came, slowly but surely, to an appreciation of the situation I was in. I formally withdrew from post-graduate school the following year and set about having a great time at parties with ordinary high school students, playing mahjongg and attending meetings where we would discuss a huge variety of topics and make deep and meaningful admissions in relation to our lives. We used to go on ski trips and watch censored movies and videos. These social sessions would include such things as playing 'Anatomy'. In the process of being involved in all of this I came to realize just how far removed it all was from school, teachers and the world in which they existed. Thanks to such socializing I was able to regain a pseudo 'bloom of youth', something which I had already lost in real life. For the first time ever I was able to act as myself.

All of these things reflected on my love life. In 1983 I started going out with a high school student whom I netted in a bookshop where he was reading a gay magazine. There was still a rocky road ahead, however. This young man took advantage of my fixation for him and started asking me for all sorts of things. He would let me pay for the food whenever we ate out together. He would let me pay all expenses incurred on dates and he even got me to buy some wool for him saying that he would knit me a jumper. Despite the fact that I had paid for the wool, however, the jumper ended up going to another fellow! In other words I ended up being his 'sugar daddy', as it were. I was heartbroken by this. Yet these incidents, sad as they were, were to be followed by a series of other events which would prove more difficult to cope with. It was almost as though they were being sent to punish me.

I received a reply to a letter which I had sent to the personal columns of a gay magazine, from a boy in his early twenties. Originally a member of a motor-bike gang, he had made the transformation from being a bikie to being a respectable business-man. I must admit that I liked the look of him from the photo he enclosed with his reply. It happened, however, that a few days before we were due to meet he dropped a note into my letter box late one night. It was delivered on the night before he set off somewhere touring. It was just to inform me that he was heading off on this tour and would be in touch when he got back. Then there was no news from him for many days. Thinking this strange, I put a call through to his home only to be told there had been a traffic accident and he had been killed. It seems that he had been driving carefully enough but had had to swerve to avoid a speeding car and this had caused the accident. This news sent me into tremendous shock. Although we had never met I felt, from the couple of letters we had sent each other, that there might have been some sort of future for us.

Then, a month later, when I was finally beginning to put this nightmare behind me, an envelope containing nothing but a gay magazine arrived for me at the private school where I was teaching. When I checked out the name and address on the back of the envelope they proved to be bogus. A week passed and another came, this time with a letter threatening to inform the school principal that I was a homosexual. 'I enclose a love letter you sent to a young man' and 'You have no right to be a teacher' were some of the comments included in the correspondence. This shook me to my very foundations. I thought long and hard about what I could do and decided that, under the circumstances, there was nothing for it but for me to make the first move. That very same day I approached the school principal and informed him of the circumstances I was in. He was good enough to keep it to himself and assured me that my job would be safe at least until the end of the following year. It just so happened that there was an event coming up in a few days to do with a forum magazine I was involved in producing. It was an event that I was supposed to host but I was so very depressed that I had to get a friend to stand in for me and I didn't show up for it at all. As for the blackmail I knew that something had to be done as I couldn't allow my mother or students to find out about my homosexuality. I was desperate and ready to clutch at any straw I could find. Realizing this, I went to the proprietor of a small eatery that my deceased friend had said he had worked at while he was getting himself back on track after being a bikie. I told him anything and everything, holding nothing back. When I had done this he announced that a possible explanation to the puzzle concerning the identity of the blackmailer had come to mind. Amongst the friends of the deceased there had been one punk kid who had given him a hard time. It seems that this punk had been involved in settling the estate of the deceased and it was thus quite conceivable that he had come across the gay magazine and my letter and hit upon the idea of extortion. The proprietor told me that if I paid him some money and left the matter in his hands he could resolve my problem and the punk would not trouble me again. This was the very time when I should have been able to go straight to the police but, being a homosexual, I couldn't. I had no confidence whatsoever in my position in society as a homosexual. I handed over a wad of money containing some tens of thousands of yen[19] and left the matter in his hands. That was the end of the threats. The proprietor of the shop added that if they were to start up again he would deal with the matter free of charge.

As if that wasn't traumatic enough, the next year, just after New Year, I was confronted by the fury of the father of a high school student I had befriended and supported. The father, out of the blue, lashed out with accusations, letting fly with comments like 'Don't you lay a finger on my boy'. It later transpired that there had been some confusion with names and that his outburst had been because he had believed that Bungaku Ito (the name of the editor-in-chief of the *Barazoku* magazine) was a pen name of mine.

And then in June there was reaction from local schools to the publication of my book '*Sir! Being Slapped is Offensive*'. This is a collection of student testimonies (available from San'ichi Shobō publishers) in which high school students described the absurdity of some school rules as well as the violence and abuse meted out to them by their teachers at the different junior high schools they had attended. The teachers had even gone as far as burning students' love letters, claiming they got in the way of studies. In the uproar that followed the publication of this book some junior high schools declared that they would not send their students to a senior high school where there were teachers who spoke badly about them. That was it, I lost my job. Under other circumstances I might have been able to mount a defence, but the principal's knowledge of my homosexuality represented an unbeatable trump card. I hoisted the white flag.

Social action as a homosexual – encouragement received for my new way of living.

With a home tutoring job obtained through the good offices of some kind students, I was able to make ends meet while I was out of work for six months. The following year I worked as both a relief teacher at a Tokyo municipal high school and an instructor at a cram school.

Here I was, a university graduate, flitting from job to job without a proper full-time position. At this point I learned a tremendous amount from being able to somehow manage without a proper job. I also learned a lot through meeting a certain homosexual, 'N'. He was a founding member of a group called 'Occur', the Gay and Lesbian Action Association, and is currently involved with their legal struggle relating to the right of homosexuals to use the Fuchū Youth House. This is a youth accommodation facility located in the municipality of Fuchū and run by the City of Tokyo. Occur has brought a law suit against the City of Tokyo for its decision to deny the use of this public facility to homosexuals. 'N' is a man who, since his first year in high school, burned with enthusiasm for the idea of creating a gay student circle for teenagers. He explored all sorts of avenues in his search for a new way of living in which there would be no prejudice or discrimination levelled against homosexuals. This amazing guy was doing absolutely tremendous things and I tried desperately to control the emotions I felt in relation to him, in order to prevent them from slipping into taking the form of a love directed towards him. My involvement with him as a friend took many forms, including assisting with the organization of a small publication designed to be a communication forum for homosexuals and assisting in the organization of a series of youth events. In addition I was able to offer personal advice to him on a range of issues.

When I began to feel attracted to a particular member of the group we were involved with, I was called to task by 'N' who told me in no uncertain terms: 'That would mean we would be no different from your regular 'dirty old man', wouldn't it? Think of how we'd look and of how old we are. We have to go beyond forming relationships in the way adults have done to date, that is falling in love easily and having sex at the drop of a hat'. I took heart at the clarity and strength of his convictions and at the vigour he displayed in the pursuits he undertook. He said to me 'I'm telling you Croc, there is no need to rush things. All you need to do is stand at the ready and maintain your composure when you are going out with someone. That way, as sure as night follows day, someone will come along who will appreciate what you have to offer'.

It turned out just as he said it would. In the summer of 1985 I met a 3rd year high school student whom I had got to know through the personal columns of a gay magazine. We went out for six months without having sex. I found I was able to develop an unhurried relationship this way, while studying together for exams. Yet that same boy, after successfully gaining entrance into university, said that no matter what he would like to go back to being straight. Receiving an offer of a place at university meant that he now felt a degree of confidence in himself, and with his pronouncement we went our separate ways. As for me, however, I still remained uncertain that a homosexual could find happiness in a relationship and occasionally I would seek partners simply for sex. You see I was completely bereft of confidence in myself as a human being who was homosexual. It goes without saying that I was not able to whisper a word to anyone about the fact that I was homosexual. I was somehow one step behind 'N' in what he was doing.

In 1986 all this was, at long last, about to change.

3 The joy of being able to admit that I like what I like

Good looking Ryuta, a fan of Western music, accepts me for what I am.

In March 1986, with high hopes and this time not lying about my age (was it really me who, a couple of years earlier, had been bold enough to claim I was 29 when really I had just clicked over into being 30?), I forwarded an advertisement to the personal column of the gay magazine *Adon*[20]. The abridged wording ran something like this:

'Is there some guy out there, perhaps younger than me, who would treat me as an equal and who would be happy about going out on equal terms with me? I'd love your company both on a social level and on a very much more intimate and personal level. I'm 32 but my way of thinking is like that of someone in his 20s. I live my life according to my convictions and I'm very young at heart...Let's build a new life together!'

Up until that time I had never received more than two replies to the personal ads I placed in gay magazines. On this occasion, however, there were responses from six people. Amongst these there was one from a certain 24 year old, a Ryuta Yanase, which particularly took my fancy. He wrote that he liked Western music and it took no time at all for me to select his response from amongst those received. Some of the other replies I received were from guys in their teens, but I felt it would be rather difficult to form a meaningful relationship with them, even though achieving sexual satisfaction should be no problem.

Anyway I replied to this Mr Ryuta Yanase, giving my telephone number. Having done this I didn't have to wait long for a phone call to come, and when it did an hour flew by before we knew it as we discussed what artists we each liked and talked about what songs evoked particular memories for us. We wasted no time in arranging a meeting a few days later at the Shimousa Nakayama station on the Japan Rail's Sōbu Line[21]. The rendezvous at the station went according to plan and we went to a coffee shop where we could talk. He was certainly good-looking, very attractive in fact, and I did my utmost to make myself appeal to him. Now what happens in my case is that as I get excited about something I tend to raise my voice and it was only later that Ryuta made reference to this. He told me that he got the impression of someone to be admired for not trying to hide his shortcomings when talking about himself. He mentioned that he was delighted with this but he added that he had felt quite uncomfortable at having me mention words like 'homosexual' and '*Adon*' so loudly that they could be heard throughout the small coffee shop. He also reported that he didn't like being told 'It looks as though we could get on well with each other' as we were about to say goodnight, because he felt that this was a bit unilateral. It was apparently something he didn't feel comfortable with, interpreting it as being a touch presumptuous. He said that he had been to England when in high school and that his dream was to go there again to study. Looking back at it now, I suppose that I probably came across as being somewhat overbearing as far as Ryuta was concerned, wondering to myself, as I was, if I would be able to wait for him while he was away. At that stage Ryuta had already quit university and had had several changes of job. He reported that he was currently employed by his uncle as an apprentice mould carpenter working on the sub-structures of concrete buildings. Two days after we met we went on a date in his car and he stayed the night at the Ito residence. On that occasion I was keen to have sex but he was resolutely opposed to this idea and talked me out of it. On the following Sunday we went off to Yokohama for a drive. As things progressed, going for weekly drives together – as friends at that stage – became a fixed item on our social calendar and I found my feelings leaning more and more towards him. It was good that when topics of conversation dried up we were able to talk about music, mostly Western music, as this would prove to be an inexhaustible topic of discussion which would bring great life back to any conversation we had.

During January and February he started to think of me in even fonder terms than those in which I considered him and from then on it was only natural that we should progress to a sexual relationship. We started seeing each other more than just on the Sunday dates. On Thursdays, for example, he'd come over to my place and we'd watch '*The Best Ten*' on the TBS network[22] together. An additional factor which had the effect of moving our relationship a big step forward was the daily use of the telephone. We never missed a single day talking with each other on the telephone. I had an extension phone in my own room so privacy wasn't a problem for me, but the only phone Ryuta had access to in the family home was in the living room, so he was ever conscious of the presence of his parents and was unable to speak freely. Consequently, half the time he would go to the trouble of getting into his car and going out to a public telephone in order to call me. This arrangement didn't always work either, because I would sometimes suddenly find myself arriving home late, thereby missing Ryuta's call, even though he had gone to the trouble to turn out in the cold. The situation he was in meant that he wasn't able to say 'I love you' or express intimacy or endearment in any way when calling from his home. Although I understood this, I couldn't help feeling frustration as a result of our inability to speak to each other freely. We seemed to face interminable difficulties in this regard. The situation was eventually rectified, however, in February 1989, when I bought him a cordless phone for his birthday. In those days this was quite an expensive item. With this type of telephone it is possible to go up to 100 meters away from the telephone base and still continue talking. The cordless phone proved a huge boon in terms of our relationship in that it allowed us to speak freely with each other every day.

Respecting each others opinions, notwithstanding arguments. For me Ryuta is a partner from whom I have much to learn.

At this point I would like to backtrack a little to explain how our relationship was developing in 1986. Thanks to our being able to meet often we were able to gain an understanding of each others' thinking and how we each looked at the world.

Our first clash was at the end of the summer of that year. We were on our way home after a trip to the coast and we started talking about the people of Korean ancestry living in Japan. Suddenly Ryuta let fly with a comment to the effect that if Koreans didn't like it in Japan they should go back to Korea. I replied that I couldn't accept that comment, not even from him. I got worked up and started shouting, making reference to forced repatriation as I developed my argument. 'Why must I cop such an earful over the Koreans?' was his retort.

In those days he would get really moody and when this happened he would start to head home, refusing to speak to me for quite a long time. On that occasion when he did this I felt a sense of panic come over me and I immediately started wondering to myself what I would ever do if we were to split up on account of this clash. It was as though I was suffering a persecution complex. In my panic I chased after him, apologizing. We got to the car and got in and, after driving for a while, he pulled over in a quiet spot and the two of us cooled our heels. Then, once again, we started talking to each other. Ryuta told me about the very bad image he had of Koreans, thanks to some troublemaking Korean high school students he had known and I, in turn, told him about the discrimination levelled against Koreans that my Korean friends had told me about.

What was so admirable about Ryuta was that after that, whenever we had a difference of opinion about any social or political issue, he would listen intently to what I had to say, even more closely than I listened to him, and when something came up that he couldn't go along with he would be quite thorough in asking questions concerning it. He would not compromise, but he would whole-heartedly agree with me on the occasions when he was convinced of the validity of my argument. At other times I would stand amazed when the limits of my knowledge and the shallowness of my thinking were brought home to me. There were of course times when I would be unable to convince Ryuta of my point of view, though he would listen attentively to what I was saying. When this happened my stubbornness would lead to anger and I would try to force my opinion on him. What had I been doing all my life? Ryuta had already by this stage come to be a great influence in my life and he would accept only arguments which were backed up with facts based on experience, not those which were based on a knowledge gained from books alone. As a result of our locking heads Ryuta learned from me to see things from a different perspective and I, in turn, learned to be more flexible in my way of thinking. I learned to broaden my view of the world. The mutual respect we achieved provided the very best conditions for a partnership to develop.

In the first year of our association I taught Ryuta English to help him prepare to study overseas. I would intentionally speak English in conversation, with the expectation that he would learn from this exercise. Later, however, he told me that after his study sessions with me he had felt a proper fool and had gone home very depressed as a result. I was to carry the benefit of the lesson I learned from that experience with me to Kashiwa Preparatory School where I had been working since April of that year, 1986 – the year in which I met Ryuta.

Having found a partner I feel my life is replete, brimming with self-confidence.

At long last I started to feel a measure of confidence in myself as a person. There was someone – a partner – out there for me. I can hardly find words to describe how fulfilling the sex experience with Ryuta was in comparison to my previous sexual experiences. The sex I found wandering the streets of the gay quarter of Shinjuku had been based simply on physical need. By contrast, Ryuta was comfortable learning what pleased me. The communion with Ryuta satisfied my soul. Moreover, it was a new and refreshing experience for me to achieve exactly this same feeling from our deep and meaningful discussions. A new zest for life welled up within me.

For the first six months of our association, whenever he was even just a little late for our date or if I were to perhaps state my opinion on some matter a little too forthrightly, I would be terror-stricken by the thought that perhaps I had already seen him for the last time – that he might not appear again. The possibility that he wouldn't want to meet me again and that that would be the end of our relationship was never far from my mind. With time, those fears were allayed and gradually put to rest. To use Ryuta's own words, 'Croc used to be unnecessarily aggressive and quick to resent things but when he settled down and started to take things a little easy it turned out that he was better placed to get angry at the times when he truly should get angry'.

Around this time I discovered that when I was more relaxed interesting work would come my way. For example, from September 1986 to March 1990 I was an assistant director in charge of a late night radio program produced by TBS. I also had some script writing duties which provided the opportunity to exchange ideas with the mostly teenage audience. I was also employed as an instructor by the Yoyogi Seminar, a cram school chain[23], where I was in charge of the English and geography classes, subjects which were not my specialty, at two preparatory schools. Through these jobs I learned some valuable things. In fact, particularly for the first few years, I felt I was studying more there than I had for my university entrance exams! The difference was that now I was not simply studying to get good grades. Now I was trying to learn the best way to explain things in order for students to understand and noting the places where students might trip up. This type of study proved to be novel and interesting.

I was able to cleverly incorporate into my lessons the differences between the English taught for university entrance examinations and the English which is used in the real world. I also incorporated into my lessons surprising and interesting facts relating to various countries around the world. In particular, I was a stickler for the 'why' questions. For example: Why is an 's' attached to the end of verbs in English in the third person singular? Why is it that words ending in '-ing' could mean any of three different things? Why are the Arabs and Israelis fighting? These are simple enough queries and ones which, although I had thought about them myself in junior and senior high school, I had never actually pursued. They were the same questions which were asked by students at the preparatory schools I was teaching at, especially those students in the basic classes. I had requested these elementary level classes and was teaching rudimentary English. The handouts I prepared (and there were many of them, including charts and diagrams which were directly useful in terms of examination preparation) and the way I spoke improved each year. One thing to come out of this teaching experience was a publication entitled *Everyone is Capable of Reading English – the Essential English Grammar* (Asahi Shuppansha, March 1993). This book incorporated passages which, when studied in depth, revealed the 'thread', as it were, with which you could unravel English sentences to reveal a systematic pattern. This was a fundamentally different concept to that underlying the reference books which existed at the time, books that followed the 'authoritative rote learning of example sentences and grammar points' school of thought. I continued to enjoy life and pursue the good times as I had before, this time with students from the preparatory schools at which I taught. Ryuta noted that it had initially seemed as though my desire to put the students' interests first was an uphill battle. I was doing my best to provide what I considered to be a service to the students in the classroom, though they sometimes proved to be an unappreciative clientele. Certainly, in many instances, I would be given a hard time by some of the guys who were on different wavelengths to me. Ryuta observed that later on things seemed to iron themselves out a little and when they did I was quite able to get across what it was that I wanted to teach. He concluded that I had developed an ability to associate with the students on truly equal terms, at a pace which was both comfortable and reasonable.

Ryuta loses his job. Facing an impasse. Ryuta's mood swings.

It could never be said that the relationship Ryuta and I have has been characterized by plain sailing. In the second year of our relationship Ryuta started to feel that he had reached the end of his tether at work. His uncle was picking on him because he was his nephew. He also failed to pass on to Ryuta a knowledge of certain skills and techniques which were necessary to work satisfactorily. In addition, he could be inconsistent and unpredictable. This became too much for Ryuta and he finally quit his job as a mould carpenter. He found another job, but this lasted only six months after which he was reduced to unemployment. He felt as though he was useless. I tried to make him feel better by continuously telling him that he shouldn't take all the blame on himself, explaining that his uncle should have handled the apprenticeship better and that he should, if anything, direct his anger towards the company and the way that the society that supports the company is structured. In an interesting reversal of roles, Ryuta has recently presented these very same arguments back to me!

While he was feeling down and worrying about being un-employed, Ryuta, who had never been an outgoing sort of person, experienced a terrible level of self-consciousness. He was bereft of confidence in himself and troubled by the thought that people were looking at him in restaurants, trains and other such crowded places. In addition he experienced a strengthening of the tendency he had to feel nervous when meeting new people. I, on the other hand, tended to come out with expressions like 'I love you' and 'gays are...' irrespective of whether people were within earshot or not. I tended to use such terms without thinking twice about it. In fact I was partial to displays of physical affection – and more. His response would be that he wasn't yet ready for such things. This resulted in our dates being limited to drives into the country where we could be alone. We were unable to visit picture theatres or such places and dinner time meant stopping the car on a quiet, dark road and eating take-away meals together. Ryuta stopped meeting my friends and this frustrated me because I had always hoped to enjoy meals with my partner and introduce him to my friends with great pride. On one occasion, in a fit of anger, I ripped up some free movie tickets I had received from TBS because we couldn't go.

Ryuta was even more emotional. He took to frequent bouts of moody silence. Whenever there was anything which didn't quite please him an anger would seethe within him and he would fall silent. When this happened and we were in the car it was hard to bear. I simply had to sit in the passenger seat and wait patiently for the storm to pass. These storms were not caused by anything I said, but by things beyond my control, like traffic jams and issues in his home life. This made it very difficult for me. Indeed I found that period in our relationship very trying. There were times when he wouldn't come out of it until the date was over and times when there were great scenes at home when I couldn't contain myself and would let fly with a pillow. I thought of leaving him on more than one occasion but his gentleness and the willingness and ability to listen and understand which he would display (when he wasn't suffering his mood swings) managed to hold the fabric of our relationship together.

The desperate need I faced to get my driver's licence. Ryuta's independent life in his own apartment.

In 1989 I came to an important decision. As there was no point in simply getting mad at Ryuta for his mood swings, I decided to lighten the burden of driving which always fell on his shoulders when we went on dates. Being behind the wheel the whole day was a cause of considerable stress for him. Although I acknowledge that he is one for blowing hot and cold at the best of times (the idea of studying overseas, for example, had lost its appeal for him a long time ago), I do remember his mentioning that he had always hoped that one day he might be the passenger and that his partner would drive him here, there or wherever. In order to make this possible I took no less than thirty-five practical driving lessons, in addition to the theory classes, through a commercial driving school. In doing so I learned how to present really boring lessons although I had no time to revel in that discovery. I took fifty hours, twice as long as most people, but I did manage, albeit with difficulty, to scrape through the course. It took me one and a half months. Even after getting my licence my driving skills were by no means polished for the first year or so and until they came up to a certain level Ryuta would turn on the silent treatment at my mistakes. Time and time again I would find myself sulking as a result of his high-handed methods of instruction.

Financially, also, we went through a pretty tough two to three month period. I had zero income during the school holidays. Being an instructor at a preparatory school was exactly the same as having a part-time job insofar as there was no bonus, no insurance and no retirement pay provided. In addition, amongst the TBS employees involved in late night broadcasting there were ongoing problems which came to a head at that same time, causing my stress levels to build. In my second year at the cram school chain their money-making mentality exceeded the limits that I could withstand. The fact that we had to conduct classes with a textbook which was long on bulk but totally lacking in terms of being student friendly for those who were not particularly good at understanding the system underpinning the English language, or indeed systems in general, will serve to illustrate that the ethos of the school was such that it placed financial profit ahead of the needs of students. I have written about this in some detail in a book entitled *The Teacher's Ears are Donkey's Ears* (published by Jiji Tsūshin). Meanwhile Ryuta returned to his trade as a carpenter, but having done this he found the situation he was in was far from being an enviable one.

As for me personally, I was clearly in a situation which was both physically and mentally exhausting. The result of this was that one autumn night I was suddenly overtaken by a severe heart palpitation and had to call an ambulance. Although it turned out that all was normal with my heart, the medical authorities determined that I was suffering from anxiety neurosis. The stress I was under was too much for me and the autonomic nerve had overreacted. In the spring of the following year, 1990, when the symptoms of this were at their very worst, there was a report on TV about a man who had died from acute heart failure. Simply hearing this made me feel very nervous. The fear of suddenly dropping dead enveloped me. I found myself running short of breath and I experienced a fit which I was powerless to do anything about.

Fortunately, the care of the doctor where I was taken by ambulance, the excellent counselling given by the neurologist whom I went to see in 1990 and the gentle medication I was taking combined to allow things to start looking up for me after that. Even now, however, I can't get by without medication and I experience something that could be described as 'mild fits' whenever I am overworked, have a cold or when troubled by something. I am almost certain that the many years I spent fearing that someone would find out that I was a homosexual, together with the fact that, behind the happy external appearance I showed to the world I had harboured a lack of anything that could be thought of as being a reliable and authoritative foundation for having faith in myself, were factors in bringing this situation about.

In 1990 Ryuta made an important decision in relation to where he was going to live. He was to move to a flat, one close to his parents' home as it happened, and start a life of his own where he would stand on his own two feet. By doing so he would cease to be dependent on his parents for his needs in life. This decision was, for us, very significant because it meant that there would now be a place where we two could spend time by ourselves. With Ryuta's moving we were able to telephone and have a sexual relationship without becoming neurotic worrying about those around us. When we argued on the phone it was possible for me to jump into the car and be there in fifteen minutes to continue the argument at our leisure! It was always me who would get very emotional and take to this course of action, trying to clear up the matter at all costs. Meanwhile Ryuta, it seemed, had somehow started to form an idea of how he could create a distance between himself and his uncle. In fact he was also getting the hang of his work and gaining confidence in his ability to do his job competently. As for me, my work was now centring on Kashiwa Preparatory School and I steadily measured myself up against the challenge it presented and moved back into a pace of life I felt comfortable with.

As fate would have it another significant development was about to take place in my life at this time. At the end of 1990 I was the recipient of a telephone call which came from a Mr Yuki who was a director of NHK[24], and this was to spell the start of what can be described as a period of fever-pitched excitement in relation to the remaking of a particular television program which had enjoyed great popularity many years earlier. The notebook which I had compiled on the puppet theatre program 'Hyokkori Hyōtan Island'[25] between primary school year 5 and junior high school year 3, was to play a central role here. In this notebook I had recorded the spoken lines and pictures of the sets used on the program in question. I also had copies of the scenarios presented in this famous program of yesteryear and all of these were to be pressed into service for the production of a remake of that same show. In terms of content, the new version was to be an exact copy of the original, but technically it was very much more advanced. I was interviewed more than twenty times in relation to this enterprise. The momentum from it helped me publish two books, 'A Notebook on Hyokkori Hyōtan Island Mania' (published by

Jitsugyō no Nihonsha) and '*A Volume of Jottings on Hyōtan Island*' (published by Asuka Shinsha). I dedicated the latter to R.Y. who, thanks to the contribution he could make in terms of his recollections of the original show and what I was able to fill him in on, became a huge fan of the new '*Hyokkori Hyōtan Island*' program.

Searching for a way in which a homosexual couple could make their way through life together. Reading and discussing books on religion together.

In the building industry they say that 'it is necessary to have rain in order for the ground to compact'. This proved to be the case in the unfolding saga of my relationship with Ryuta. In 1991, at the behest of an acquaintance of his parents, Ryuta put a simple Buddhist altar into his flat so he could pay his respects to the family ancestors, and he took to chanting sutras. There was nothing particularly strange about this in itself, but I knew things were getting a bit out of hand when he would revert to giving me the old silent treatment just because I had telephoned him when he was in the middle of a chant. He also started saying that he wanted to undertake some Buddhist training in order to learn to discipline himself and find enlightenment through this. Now I have nothing against religion, recognising as I do that it plays a role in helping people sometimes, but it simply isn't good to become narrow-minded and to close your mind off to things as a result of blind faith. What's more, 'enlightenment' is something you attain in the trial and error processes experienced in everyday living. Setting yourself apart from the rest of the world only results in your becoming an intolerable prig of an elitist Buddhist monk. Wake up to yourself, Ryuta! The tone of the rapport flowing between us was something along the following lines:

Ryuta: 'Are you denying the value of religion, then?'
Me: 'No I'm not. I'm simply saying that there are many other things you could be doing and experiencing'.

We hadn't had a cross word for quite a while up until then. Anyway the situation eventually settled down into religious discussions which resulted in our buying books on Buddhism and studying and discussing them together. We talked together about how we two, and how a homosexual couple, might face life together. We also discussed what our plans would be for our old age. After passing through the period when he would simply absorb himself in sutras, we adopted the good concepts of Buddhism, enquiring of a priest at the temple about any points we found to be contradictory. We were then able to objectively reject those which we couldn't go along with. In our everyday lives we were able to get angry where it was right that we should get angry and we made the decision to channel our energies away from negative things and into building up our relationship. I started to l realize that the two of us should be able, together, to establish a common perspective which would allow us to discover a road forward in terms of how we might lead our lives together. The idea was that, by not confining ourselves to the question of a knowledge of Buddhism or a reliance on Buddhist philosophy, we would accept that it would not always be necessary for one party to change positions and agree with the opinion of the other. This was when the feeling that we should actively involve ourselves in 'Occur', the Gay and Lesbian Action Association, and 'Taurus', a gay circle in Chiba Prefecture, was born within us. This we hoped to do without losing sight of who we ourselves were. It was in this context that, in 1992, I attended a court hearing where Occur was the plaintiff in a case against the City of Tokyo. Occur was instigating a civil lawsuit against the City of Tokyo for discrimination. They claimed that they had been denied the use of the Fuchū Youth House accommodation facilities on the grounds that they were a homosexual organization. A certain Mr 'A', a homosexual who happened to be a friend of Ryuta's, was there. Far from supporting the court case, he claimed that it was a meaningless charade and that the gays involved were simply grandstanding! Unable to do otherwise I took him on, and something of a scene developed as a result.

Immediately after this incident I made a beeline for Ryuta's place. I couldn't hold back the tears and complained to Ryuta about the injustice of it all. The two of us confirmed there and then that homosexuals should be given the right to live their lives happily and with confidence and without suffering discrimination or encountering prejudice. We talked, although half in jest, about becoming a model gay couple who would go down in the annals of the history of homosexuality in Japan. After this Ryuta's mood swings ceased, in much the same way as waves subside when the wind drops.

The greatest sense of relief I have ever experienced was obtained as a result of my 'coming out' to my mother.

When we reached this point it was clear that the way forward was for us to live together. But for this to happen it was imperative that we tell our parents about ourselves and our plans. I had been living with my mother ever since my father passed away at the end of 1981. My mother was 78 and relied on a hearing aid and a complete set of false teeth. Although she was doing my washing, preparing my meals and generally looking after me, I would get exasperated and react whenever she indicated any sort of reliance on me. I would even shout angrily when I came home tired and she didn't catch what I was saying. It got so bad that she once said 'If you hate me that much I might just as well die and be done with it!' It was clear that one factor contributing to my short temper was the impatience I felt from not knowing when I would be able to take up residence with Ryuta. Many, many times I had been on the point of coming out to my mother by uttering the words 'I'm homosexual' but I feared that she might just collapse with shock. Then what would I do? It would be better, for her sake, if I were to hide my homosexuality until she passed on. The fact of the matter was that my mother had probably already got wind of my homosexuality ages ago, considering my age and that I was still unmarried. At times I would lie awake at night unable to sleep, churning all these sorts of things through my mind. I lacked backbone and resolve.

September 6th, 1992. The previous day I had got depressed over a trifling matter and I persuaded Ryuta to come over and stay the night. At that stage it was Ryuta who was the one giving positive and useful advice and I was the recipient of it! With a vigour born of the impasse I faced, and after consulting Ryuta, I asked him to wait in my room. I went to my mother and took her into my confidence, unburdening myself of my long-held secret. I told her that I was capable only of loving men and that because of this it would not be possible for me to marry a girl. I told her that Ryuta Yanase was my partner. I was extremely tense about doing this because I was opening up and speaking face to face with the person it was most difficult for me to discuss this with. I also told her that a certain percentage of people in the world would always be homosexual and that homosexuality was not a mental sickness or anything of that sort. I stressed that this only meant that my sexual orientation was different to that of the majority. In addition, I explained to her that I wanted to live a life where I could be both honest and comfortable with myself.

With the confidence I had gained through my long association with Ryuta, I was, from about 1987, able to broach the question of my personal circumstances when speaking with close friends and students at the preparatory school whenever the opportunity arose. This was usually more or less by way of self introduction. But things that I was able to mention to them were very much more difficult for me to bring myself to announce to my mother. When I did, however, her response was, 'Yes, homosexuals are to be found everywhere. It can't be helped if you can't change. If that's how you are then that's the only way for you to live, I suppose. It won't be easy by any means but live your life as best you can and don't let things get you down'. Hearing these words from my mother gave me the greatest sense of relief I have ever experienced in my life. Just hearing these words transported me to another world. I felt as though I was living in the clouds! Mom went on, 'I knew because I had seen the books and things you have in your room but I didn't say anything because I thought even if I did there would be no changing you. But it does mean an end to the Ito family line'.

The fact that I wouldn't be able to have kids was something that had been preying on my mind for a very long time. Yet the notion that I should pass on to my children the fruits of any accomplishments or achievements I had chalked up in life represented insolence as far as I was concerned. The precious materials which I had relating to *Hyōtan Island*, I could donate to NHK and as for the growing collection of records and CDs, if I set my mind to it now I could think of a way for that to be well used, too. I came around to thinking that the things that I would leave when my time came were things that I wouldn't need to leave to children. I decided that it wouldn't really matter who made use of them, and I left it at that. At the end of that encounter with my mother she added, as though she could see right through my feelings, 'You've probably got a load off your mind, now that you've told me' and indeed that was exactly the case. My mother's response to my coming out filled me to overflowing with a sense of being empowered to do anything at all. I recalled the time when I had lost my job as a part-time instructor at the private high school and she had said to me 'Cheer up, you did the right thing. If worst comes to worst I can still get a job'.

Why hadn't I believed in my mother and released myself a lot earlier? After that day the shouting we had experienced in the house all but ceased.

The courage to admit that I like what I like. Groping with the struggle to carve out a new lifestyle.

Momentum is a terrific thing. A month after 'coming out' to my mother, Ryuta also came out to his mother ('coming out' is a term used by the American Gay Liberation Movement. It refers to announcing one's homosexuality to parents and friends and, in turn, to society in general. It derives from the idea of leaving a closet, that is, somewhere where you have been hiding). Although at first she had some trouble with the situation she was confronted with, Ryuta's mother finally accepted it in the same way that my mother had, indicating that she would support him in his future life. As for broaching the subject with Ryuta's father, whom we knew would be a harder nut to crack, it was decided that this was something that would be better attempted a later stage.

The question of clarifying the relationship you have with your parents is a thorny one for homosexuals. Mr 'N', a gentleman who was the founder of the Taurus group to which I have already made reference (not to be confused with the Mr 'N' from the Gay and Lesbian Action Association), was at one stage thrown out of the house by his parents who were quite enraged by his announcing that he was homosexual. As for the parents of the Occur members who came out to them in order to be able to act as plaintiffs in the court case against the City of Tokyo, it appears that they were initially so shocked by their sons' revelations that they were virtually unable to get out of bed in the mornings. Despite this they ended up making sure that they were present in court to lend emotional support to their sons. When I witnessed this I was extremely moved and found tears welling up in my eyes.

I am extremely heartened by the fact that an increasing number of young homosexuals are recognizing that the question of their sexuality is something which cannot be avoided forever and are deciding that it is better to tell their parents sooner rather than later. Some do this while still in their teens. These are young homosexuals who are quite sure of themselves. Compared to my teenage years, when even finding fragments of information about homosexuality and getting to meet others both verged on the impossible, the homosexuals of the present day are fortunate in that they have organizations such as Occur and many other respectable meeting groups to turn to. I believe that it is possible, and I would very much like to see, homosexuals having pride in themselves as homosexuals from an early age and having the confidence to fall in love without being forced to take the very long and circuitous route that I had to take before reaching that point[26].

Ryuta has become an irreplaceable part of my life. He is someone who understands my inner feelings completely. He knows thoroughly, and almost intuitively, not only what it is that I am thinking, but beyond this, all the implications surrounding it – regardless of whether or not I have said anything. Recalling the journey Ryuta and I have made together so far – fraught with difficulties as it was – renders me unable to imagine that I would ever, at any time in the future, be able to again form with another person the same mental bonding that I have with him. In other words, we love each other so much that we could never consider having an affair outside our relationship. Our feelings are so deep for each other that even if I were to experience infatuation with a younger guy (this would be conceivable only for me) Ryuta tells me that his faith in our relationship is such that he would wait with confidence for me to return to him, as he knows I would. This is not to say that there are no little ripples appearing in our relationship from time to time. These might, for example, relate to our dates or our sexual mannerisms. Yet, although one might thoroughly trust another person in every regard, it is only human, on occasions, to seek to be given confirmation of a partner's love through words and actions. Incidentally, we are sometimes told that we have come to resemble each other in the way we speak and even the way we look at things, but this is not to presume that we don't still have differences of opinion on various matters. In this regard improvisation and talking things through thoroughly are both important aspects of our lives. We are fortunate in that, as good luck would have it, we both are fond of talking.

We find fulfilment in arranging our lives so that there are fixed events on our social calendar. For instance, at the end of each year we tally up the personal music hit charts which we have individually compiled each week, making tapes of what we consider to be the best 30 songs for the year and then listening to them together. We have great fun guessing what the other will include in his list (our personal tastes are quite different) and we feel a sense of inspiration when it happens that both parties give the same ranking to a particular song. We also make it a point to accent the various happy occurrences in each other's lives with presents or good food.

We are able to talk through the most difficult things with each other. Because there is common ground in terms of the knowledge we have and beliefs we hold (for example that homosexuals should be able to lead their lives with an attitude which embraces confidence), there is no fear of our separating even when we get into a heated discussion on a particular issue. It is possible for us to unreservedly savour the differences of opinion we may have on a wide range of matters including those relating to difficulties at work, politics and social questions. I find it invigorating to have Ryuta's astute observations pointed out to me. In other words I just wouldn't feel right if I were not to hear his voice every day. Just by being together with him I feel a sense of tension being relieved, an ability to relax. Not only does our partnership allow us to feel this sense of togetherness, which is perhaps stronger than in many families (this emotion has partly taken the place of the thrill and nerves which characterised the early stages of our relationship), but we also respect each other and encourage each other to develop individually within the partnership. The support and security we offer each other are wonderful things.

Having said this, and notwithstanding the fact that we often talk together, there are still many, many things that we don't as yet know about each other. We have never actually seen each other working, for example. We have not, by any means, exhausted that which lies in the innermost part of our beings. That is the great appeal of our partnership. Of course, we recognize the possibility that difficult times might await us in the future because of this. One wonders how the life which we are planning together might change, or might not change, this aspect of the relationship we have.

It is my intention to remodel the house and have two households living together under the one roof· that is to say Ryuta and I living together in the same house as my mother. It is necessary for us both to take our time and to tread carefully as we proceed, taking things one at a time as we clear the way towards our discovering for ourselves a new way for us to live – together as a homosexual couple. I take this opportunity to make a clean breast of it and declare publicly, here and now, and in no uncertain terms, that at last I feel that I have the confidence to state that I like what I like.

2 Self-Analysis Notebook

The Path Leading to My Acknowledgment and Acceptance of Myself as the Person I Am.

1 The know-how involved in becoming an ideal partner

Might it be possible for a homosexual couple to maintain a relationship in the midst of discrimination from mainstream society?

It is often said that homosexual couples don't stay together as long as heterosexual couples. Most homosexuals seem surprised by the fact that Ryuta and I have been going out together now for seven years. Sometimes they even tell us that we have 'done well' to stay together for so long. It is a fact that it is indeed difficult to find examples of couples who have been together for 10 or 20 years amongst homosexuals over the age of 35. It would be entirely wrong to deduce from this, however, that homosexuals are prone to be fickle and have a tendency to flit from partner to partner or that they will never know true love. Those heterosexuals who are homophobic often draw such conclusions and feel happy labelling homosexuals 'abnormal' when they find any small difference between such people and themselves. The fact that gentle homosexuals who use feminine speech are able to find a niche in the TV entertainment industry is because viewers treat them as oddities and as such see them as occupying a position lower than that of the heterosexual majority in society. In doing so they elevate themselves to a position of special status!

One thing I would like to point out is that for partners in a homosexual relationship there are all manner of obstacles to be overcome in order to have the partnership work and the couple stay together. The general public does not accept us showing affection for each other in public. Finding housing where two people of the same sex can live together is by no means an easy task. Homosexuals have been known to be turned away from rental properties. The biggest hurdle of all to get over is the unquestioned and deep-rooted notion, which passes off as 'common sense', that a person only truly becomes a fully fledged and responsible member of society as a result of entering into marriage. The fact that there are only very few homosexual couples over the age of 35 can be thought of as being directly related to the fact that many homosexuals succumb to the various pressures exerted by the heterosexual majority in mainstream society.

It is a sad fact that there are quite a number of middle-aged and older married men with children, who have affairs with other men on the side. There is even the rare case where a man divorces his wife and finds happiness in a new male partner. Most married homosexuals hide their sexuality and are forced into leading double lives, being unwilling to lose the mantle of trust and respectability society accords them as a result of their marital status. I can't place blame at their feet. It is just that in my case I choose not to lead that sort of life. On a slightly different note, though, it seems that the level of 'gay awareness' amongst teenagers is undergoing a big change.

If we go one step beneath the surface when contemplating the durability of homosexual relationships and consider how long heterosexual relationships last, and look at these in the true sense – in other words whether the partners involved actually continue to love each other or not – you will find that there are many question marks and very grey areas coming into the picture. There are many instances where the husband and wife just keep living under the same roof for the sake of the children or where they keep together for appearances' sake or because they fear that if they were to separate neither party would be able to survive alone. It is sometimes said that the man wouldn't be able to run the house and that the woman wouldn't want to go out to work. To me it seems that people have a fixation with, and are shackled to, the notion of the conventional division of duties between partners in marriage. The social set-up which is in place plays a big role in tying people down in this way.

Homosexual partners who lead their lives without the require-ments of fitting the system and without the duty of raising children, rely purely on love and affection for each other to support their relationship. Because of this, succeeding in having relationships that last should be seen as a task involving the utmost difficulty. The durability of homosexual relationships is an issue which is distinct from that of providing love and support for each other in a relationship. It should be considered quite separately from questions about the rights of homosexuals to win the same conditions as heterosexuals in terms of the treatment they receive from the government in relation to the provision of the services and benefits that are acceded to heterosexuals by way of marriage. If homosexual couples were to receive all the social encouragement lavished on heterosexual couples it would be infinitely easier for them to maintain their relationships than is the case at present. Thus, there are no foundations for arguing that homosexuals should make no demands on society with regards to things like public housing, for example.

It is timely here to digress slightly and discuss the stereotyping that paints a picture of homosexuals as promiscuous, 'wanting sex at the drop of a hat' and being ever ready to get into bed with whomever is willing. It has been argued that the spread of AIDS was on account of a lifestyle which allowed many and indis-criminate sexual contacts. The fact that AIDS is believed to have initially spread from the homosexual community (even this is not strictly accurate) lends credence to this argument. Whilst it is a known fact that at 'hattemba'[1], or gay beats, there are instances of men simply seeking sexual release, we should not ignore the equivalent situations for heterosexuals. I openly acknowledge here that there were times when I found some comfort at 'hattemba' myself. For some others it is easy to slip into sex at such places as there is no need to be concerned with matters of contraception.

But what is the heterosexual equivalent of 'hattemba'? For heterosexuals there are any number of spots they can go to pick up girls, starting with the so-called 'pick-up bridge' in Chiba. This bridge gained notoriety after a TV program highlighted the social role it plays. It is no overstatement to say that heterosexuals can come into contact with potential partners simply anywhere. In fact it is the case that there are any number of examples of men and women meeting and ending up in a hotel together that very same night. These days it is unheard of for the brakes to be applied to sexual activity out of a fear of conception. Without arguing the pros and cons of this situation, homosexuals certainly do not have a monopoly on lustful sexual behaviour. In Japan, although certain places might be known as '*hattemba*', or pick-up spots, the great majority of homosexuals are placed in the situation where it is very difficult indeed for them to even get to meet other homosexuals. This is especially the case for homosexuals living in country areas. What we have is a situation where the majority in society, fearing that their value system will be undermined, purposely blow up the slight differences which exist between themselves and the minorities in society 1000 times...no, 10,000 times...and in doing so rationalize that their own lifestyle represents the only proper path for others to follow. That is it in a nutshell.

Aiming to maintain our love for each other as a minority couple and working towards becoming ideal partners.

It is an irrefutable fact that, even though there are essentially no differences between homosexuals and heterosexuals in terms of the roles love and sexual gratification play in their lives, in Japan maintaining love for each other requires greater energy and determination for homosexual couples than for heterosexuals. This has to do with the fact that the Japanese society stubbornly refuses to accept minorities. I would like to pen a few words about how Ryuta Yanase and I have worked to overcome this.

About three years after Ryuta and I started seeing each other, there was a turning point in our relationship. We were talking to each other about what we thought constituted the ideal partner. During this discussion I realized that neither of us was seeking a ready-made perfect partner as such, but rather we were each prepared to work towards becoming the perfect partner for the other. Without putting too fine a point on it, neither of us looked like the entertainers we had admitted an attraction to when we first met: Ryuta had said he went for the looks of Hiroyuki Watanabe and I fancied Morohoshi of the pop group *Hikaru Genji*. We each did fall, however, within the realm of acceptable compromise

(Ryuta went well beyond my idea of an acceptable compromise – he was more on the 'wow' side!) and so we started going out together, though at that stage I always worried about how long our relationship would last. During the period of our going out together the differences that existed between the ways of thinking and the value systems that we each held became clear and as a result I became all the more apprehensive about our future together. To illustrate the sort of differences I am talking about, I might mention that at that time Ryuta supported the Liberal Democratic Party and I the Japan Socialist Party. As it turned out, however, the fact that we were able to not only bring our differences out into the open and air them, but go beyond that and take in the other's viewpoint became, interestingly enough, a source of mutual attraction for us. Life has these interesting turns.

Homosexuals have always been and always will be a social minority and as such I believe that they will never be able to find a partner in life if they have terrifically high expectations and make lasting evaluations of those they have just met, solely on the basis of the situation that party happened to be in at the particular time they met. It is better to start your relationship from a point where, to a certain extent, you share some common ground in terms of attitudes and interests (in the case of Ryuta and I, we had a trump card in that neither of us would ever get sick of talking about Western music) and from there influence each other and move towards changing so you more closely fit the other's idea of what constitutes the ideal partner. This can impart a sense of creative (am I overstating the situation?!) joy and is also something which is very practical. When you reach this stage, aspects of discontent you might feel in relation to your partner come to be seen in a positive light and change into subjects for consideration in terms of how you yourself might approach the situation at hand. Of course the other party must be worth all the energy you need to expend in this regard. That is not to say that he has to be your idea of an ideal partner. Just having a portion of his personality approximating this is quite sufficient as a basis for seeking to develop a partnership.

The actual process of becoming the perfect partner isn't such a simple matter. First and foremost, you must become aware of his sensitivities and how you should conduct yourself in your dealings with him. Quite small things play an important role in strengthening a relationship.

Cultivating 'natural' expressions of affection together. Their misinterpretation.

One of the things I wanted from Ryuta was to be seen to my car when I was leaving his place.Whenever Ryuta came to my place I would always see him to his car when it came time for him to go home. I would always stand and wave until his car disappeared from sight. This is a practice I maintain even today, as for me it is a natural expression of my affection for him. Ryuta didn't do this for me, however. He would stand at his door and give me a quick 'see you' and I would be left to walk to my car by myself. I let it go for a while without saying anything but one day I came right out and let him know how sad this made me feel. His reply was 'I thought it would be easier and better all round to just not make a big deal of the parting'. The fact of the matter was that he feared the thought that those who caught sight of us might suspect what sort of relationship we had. He feared this to the point of being absolutely terror-stricken.

We had a few rows about this. On one occasion, very early in our relationship, Ryuta got terribly angry and refused to speak for several hours when, in a *sushi* shop[2], I said to him 'Good food is all the more delicious when we eat together'. The same thing happened on another occasion when I spoke to him in fond terms in a parking area off a freeway. On yet another occasion, when he ran out of my house one day after we'd had words, I clung onto him and, tearfully, stopped him in front of our gate and begged him not to go. This exchange was surely audible to the neighbours. Such emotion-charged behaviour on my behalf allowed, in degrees, the message to get through to Ryuta that my love for him was far more important to me than any concerns I may have had about what the neighbours might think. Nowadays, as a result of his appreciating this, he always comes to where my car is parked to send me off whenever I leave his place. The first day that he came out of his flat with me when I was leaving, I felt incredibly happy, right down in my soul, for the entire journey home.

Amongst the things Ryuta expected of me was to navigate when he was driving. Early on in our relationship I was delighted to be taken here, there and everywhere by car. I did not realize that, although he claimed to enjoy driving, being the driver was really a very tough job. Not being a driver myself, I was unaware of the level of fatigue Ryuta would experience behind the wheel and I would get carried away suggesting we should drop into this place and that, even though the places I would suggest were often out of our way and visiting them would have involved extra driving. My insensitivity about this would lead to my having cross words with Ryuta, whose driving fatigue would catch up with him and put him in a bad mood. The fact of the matter was that I never realized how mentally tiring driving can be until I got my own driver's licence. Anyway, eventually I realized how much energy he had to expend driving every time we went out on dates together and ever since I have been a devoted navigator when he's driving. My job is to read maps accurately and decide what route we should take when we head off to unknown parts. My skills in this department took off like a rocket.

But even before I came to understand the pressures of driving, as the navigator I was in control of the car stereo. I would always play songs from the Japanese Idols Pop chart, but Ryuta didn't like these much. When we were first getting to know each other, the all-female singing group *Onyanko* was at the height of its popularity and my perhaps persistent playing of their hit songs got on his nerves. As I came to better appreciate the pressures of driving I learned to, for the most part, play music that Ryuta liked and then, occasionally, when he had heard enough, slip in a tape I had made myself. It was quite pleasurable to say nothing and listen to the music he enjoys. A side-effect of this was a growing appreciation of Rhythm and Blues and black contemporary music, two kinds of music for which I had never had much of an appreciation. I also did my best to be in charge of opening and closing the car windows, lighting cigarettes and buying soft drinks. I did whatever I could to reduce the burden of driving. Apparently I became overly keen on being the driver's assistant. I must have got a bit carried away, because at one stage Ryuta asked me why I was so concerned about how he felt! I remember feeling somewhat miffed when he asked me that and I wondered to myself why it was that I was under the impression that I was doing all the things I was for his sake. It was then that I made a major decision

– to obtain my driver's licence[3]. I put so much effort into this endeavour that Ryuta now looks back at that episode, acknowledging the amount of work involved, and says, 'You really did put your heart and soul into getting your licence, didn't you!' Through getting my licence I came to fully understand just how demanding driving in Japan is. After that we were able to enjoy something much more akin to carefree driving.

One thing that Ryuta and I both agree on is that there are many things which need to be said in order to be understood. We try to say such things to each other whenever the need arises. In doing so we recognize that human beings are apt to sometimes erroneously presume certain things about what other people might want or like to know. Although we might be convinced that something or other would suit our partner, or that he would be pleased with it, often it turns out that the opposite is the case and we have misread things. The arrogance of thinking that 'we have come this far together so there's no need for me to mention such-and-such, he'll understand' is something we don't allow in our relationship. No matter how long you have been together it is not possible to communicate by mental telepathy, knowing just how the other party is feeling and thus not needing to confirm this in words. Rather, it is necessary for you to express the love and affection you feel for your partner in actions and words. This allows you to avoid unexpected misunderstandings and pitfalls.

Expressing 'I love you' and 'I want to be with you' in actions and words.

I don't wait for Ryuta's birthday to give him presents. If I see something I think he would like I go ahead and buy it for him. Occasionally, when we go to each other's house or flat we'll buy cakes or sweets when the mood takes us and eat them together. Likewise, if we come across an advertisement, a pamphlet or a newspaper article we think the other will be interested in we cut it out for him. In other words 'he' always occupies a central place in our minds. Initially we were very conscious of ensuring this but I'm delighted to say that nowadays it is just something that comes naturally and requires no effort from us. It has become second nature to us.

In this regard I would like to record here one symbolic incident which happened about two years ago, when Ryuta was still living at his parents' home. On the Sunday, which was our regular dating day, I had an appointment, so Ryuta went off to the coast with a homosexual friend, a Mr 'A'. In fact if I may digress a little, this Mr 'A' was something of a central character here. He was a member of a gay circle that Ryuta used to belong to before he met me and moreover, a friend with whom Ryuta had had intimate relations in the past. Ryuta introduced 'A' to me soon after we met (this is the same 'A' I had the argument with during the court case against the City of Tokyo) and I remember being quite taken aback by the fact that Ryuta apparently thought nothing of our going on a double date with him and the boyfriend he had at that time. I felt a real sense of jealousy when, referring to Ryuta's holding an opened can of coffee between his legs while driving, 'A' said 'Ryuta you don't change – still got the same old habit, eh?' I did not mention the jealousy I felt to Ryuta until quite a bit later. Anyway, the fact was that I just didn't hit it off with 'A'. As far as I was concerned he displayed a touch of haughtiness and always acted as though he was trying to test the level of knowledge that other people had. For example, knowing that I was an English instructor, he would, out of the blue, use that language to ask me the time as though he was checking my level of proficiency. I put up with him, though, as he was one of the few friends Ryuta had.

I had come to the point where I felt I could trust Ryuta and I believed that he wouldn't have sex with 'A'. Nonetheless, I felt some resistance to the idea of them going to the coast together. I wanted reassurance from Ryuta to the effect that I shouldn't worry as he loved me. Alternatively, he could have suggested that I follow on later and join them. Ryuta didn't say either of these things though, when we spoke on the phone the night before the planned excursion. One reason may be that he was calling from his parents' house. Perhaps another factor was an element of rebellion against the persistence I showed in my hoping to get him to reassure me that all would be well. Anyway, I somehow just didn't feel quite comfortable with the arrangements that had been made and the next day I promptly finished the business I had to do earlier than planned, and headed off to where Ryuta and 'A' had gone. I was thinking to myself that if I couldn't locate them I might wait at A's flat for them to return, as I presumed they would drop in there on their way back. I feared, however, that this might incur Ryuta's wrath and thus I felt quite tense and nervous as I walked down the hot road the considerable distance from the railway station to the coast. As it turned out, I found Ryuta much easier than I had expected. He was extremely surprised to see me but on our way home, when we were alone after saying goodbye to 'A', he thanked me for taking the trouble to come to meet him and told me how delighted he was to learn how deep my feelings were for him. After that incident Ryuta and 'A' gradually saw less and less of each other.

Several months after the coast incident I attended a talk held in the Kunitachi City Community Centre in Tokyo. At that time such sessions, where guest speakers were invited to address young audiences, were held once a month. After the talk I went off with the others for a social drink. When that was over and I stepped out into the street what should I see but Ryuta's car! He explained that he had made the trip all the way from his home in Funabashi to collect me in order to reciprocate my having gone to the coast to meet him! Such actions really help to reinforce the love that exists between us. It would be fair to say that this one incident acted to perfectly cement the first stage of our love for each other.

In the same way that these incidents express love, I really wanted to be told that our relationship was important and that I mattered. I wanted to hear expressions like 'You mean a lot to me' or 'I love you' expressed early in our relationship. For my part, I would try very hard to find ways of expressing my love, including sending love letters even though the message contained therein could easily have been spoken on the telephone. Ryuta's response to such things was 'Surely it is not necessary to say it all the time. For one thing it can be quite embarrassing'. Yet this same Ryuta came to frequently voice expressions of endearment for me as he came to appreciate the joy I felt in hearing such things being said. Finally, after seven years, we reached the point where we had no doubts about the shared bond in our relationship. I will illustrate this point by way of a sort of symbolic conversation Ryuta and I once had. It was not all that long after we had started going together seriously that I asked him what he would do if I were to say that I wanted to break our relationship off. His reply was, 'If you really disliked me that much there would be nothing for it but for me to accept that, and because I have my pride I probably wouldn't cry or make a scene, nor would I try to stop you going'. To me this reply was very much less than I had hoped for. I responded glumly by saying, 'If it were me I'd desperately beg you to stay…'

Just recently I recalled this incident and asked Ryuta another question. The question was, 'If I were to have an affair and come to you and say that I wanted to finish our relationship, what would you do? ' His answer was unchanged, 'I wouldn't try to stop you'. As I began feeling disappointed at the thought that his attitude hadn't changed, he added, 'I would wait for you because I believe that you would definitely, in the end, come back to me'. This response struck close to my heart as I am sure you can imagine.

Sundays were our days for dating. On other days we would make contact by telephone at the appointed time of 9 o'clock.

During the initial stages of our love we were both very, very keen to meet and so, naturally we did everything possible to ensure that planned dates went ahead. We made exceptions for only the most important work or appointments. After about 3–5 years, however, we would both (especially me) get into a bad mood when a scheduled date had to be cancelled. Sometimes we would find ourselves quarrelling as a result. Eventually, during one of these quarrels, Ryuta said he didn't want to be tied down to regular – and inflexible – Sunday dates. Before I knew it I found myself drawn in by his provocation and made ridiculous retorts like 'Does that mean you don't want to see me? I'm always happy to see you, anytime at all!' This would then be followed by a series of wearing exchanges along the following lines:

Ryuta: 'That's right. There are times when I want to be alone'.
Me: 'How cold can you get!'

…and on it would go. Eventually things would settle down when we agreed that dates shouldn't take precedence over any and everything and that we should both give time to other business in our lives and also treat other friendships as important. As it turned out, when there were no pressing appointments we went on meeting in the way we always had and gradually our dating arrangements settled down. Our dates became a regular and natural part of our lives, just like eating. With this our feelings of trust grew immensely and the odd occasion on which we were not able to keep a date made no dent whatsoever in the bond that existed between us. It became hassle free to cancel a date. Thinking back now it seems quite unbelievable that we should ever have felt tied down to our dating arrangements!

I have already explained how the telephone played a very important role in the early stages of our relationship. Every evening at 9 o'clock one of us would ring the other, and we would talk on average for about 50 minutes. It didn't particularly bother us that there were some friends who got a bit annoyed and complained that they could never get through after 9 pm as the phone was always engaged. We would always arrange beforehand to adjust the time of the call whenever there was a TV program we wanted to watch or when we knew we would be late home. We would report in detail to each other on the events of the day – from such trivial things as our having seen a cute cat through to mundane grumbles about work – everything, sometimes including our feelings about the social events of the day. Of course there were many silly things that we talked about too. Music was a topic we liked and something we always had plenty to comment on. This was especially the case on Mondays and Tuesdays when the music industry's magazine *Orikon*[4] and the American music world magazine which contained a section called *Billboard* would be delivered to my house. Informing Ryuta about what was on the charts and analyzing this information together was a very pleasurable experience indeed. Just hearing Ryuta's voice would make me feel comfortable. When I was talking to him my physical fatigue and a good measure of my mental despondency would just disappear.

Whilst I would like to be able to report that because this routine had become a completely natural part of our everyday lives, in much the same way as cleaning our teeth was, and that there was never anything trying encountered, the fact of the matter was that the quite complex things which we call human biorhythms came into the picture. It is indeed strange how fate can take a hand in determining how things develop. There are in fact days when one's mental state is such that it is just very hard to talk to people (even with one's lover) and days when one is just too exhausted to be able to enjoy a conversation. When both parties have had such a day it is a simple matter to make the call short, but it is very often the case that one party has something he particularly wants to talk about when the other hasn't the energy to hold a conversation. On this point I must admit that I was quite unable to shake off a certain selfishness which took control of my actions. When Ryuta didn't have the energy to listen to what I wanted to tell him I refused to accept that we shouldn't converse. I would sulk and fret and expect the impossible. It didn't help matters that I believed I would always be sure to listen to whatever Ryuta had to say, even if I was exhausted. Sometimes the determination I demonstrated by calling him back after he said that he was too tired and had hung up would lead to our having words. I felt that this was a problem which ultimately we wouldn't solve unless we were to live together.

Just recently we again had words after going through a similar development to the one outlined above. This was despite the fact that we hadn't had an argument for a very long time. On this occasion, however, thirty minutes after the incident there was a phone call from him and he said, 'I was only thinking that I have to get an early night tonight as I have an early start at work in the morning. I had forgotten to consider the most important person...'. This was the first time he had expressed this sentiment in the seven years we had been going out together and I felt that this display of his love for me was very powerful. Later, when it came to the publication of this book and I felt uneasy about the possible repercussions involved therein, his emphatic words to me were 'If you are in two minds about using your real name, go ahead and use my name as well. If you do that we'll be able to do the worrying together'. This was really something else! It used to be that his sole concern was to hide the fact that he was a homosexual! Was this really the man who used to be panicky and so very lacking in confidence in himself? Uncontrollable joy welled up within me at that moment as a result of this sentiment being expressed by Ryuta.

The derivation of the pet names we use for each other, 'Nyāgo' and 'Nuta'.

Another thing that we found awkward in relation to the use of the telephone had to do with the days when neither of us had anything in particular to say about ourselves and when there wasn't anything of particular note happening around us – days marked by their unremarkability. On such days, if we were to meet in person, the fact that we hadn't much to say to each other wouldn't really matter as it wasn't an issue of any particular consequence if our conversation were to dry up somewhat, but when this happens on the telephone things fall very flat. What do you do at such times? I'm sure that if I were simply to explain that in the early stages of our relationship the answer to that question was '*Tanuuu!*' and now it is '*Nyaaa!*' you wouldn't be any the wiser. I've got to take the story back five years to fill you in on this one!

Ryuta and I loved the comic strip '*Suit Yourself Polar Bear!*'[5] by Kōji Aihara. At one stage I took to imitating the sounds of the animals which appeared in this comic strip and my doing so proved to be a source of great amusement for the two of us. Ryuta would always egg me on whenever I imitated the cry of the badger, the character which was always the butt of jokes and pranks played by the polar bears in this comic strip. The badger would often end up in a real fix as a result of these polar bears and when this happened his pathetic cry of distress was '*tanu*' or '*danu*'[6]. Every time I imitated the badger's cry, Ryuta would say to me 'You weren't really a 'croc' after all, you were a '*tanu*' were you not?!' and from that time on the name '*Tanu*' stuck.

About this time Ryuta was drawing lots of cartoon badgers. He kept telling me that I looked cute, a bit like a badger, when my tummy stuck out. (I must admit that Ryuta is the only person to ever have called me cute!) Incidentally one of the badgers Ryuta drew adorns the front cover of an edition of the magazine *Match* which I produce. It is a magazine which incorporates contributions from readers and provides a forum for communication for those in their teens and twenties. With all this influence the badgers were having in our lives I started, in spite of myself, to feel a bit like a badger! I felt a bit silly doing it but I started playing around with the word '*tanu*' putting all sorts of emotions into it, then, thinking that there was nothing particularly clever about just saying '*tanu*'. I reversed the syllables and gave the name *Nuta* to Ryuta as the names rhymed and were thus quite similar to each other. Now at last I can refer to Ryuta as *Nuta* – the name I'm used to using! In the progression of things, and for no particular reason, the name *Nuta* started to take on a personality of its own and this character became a sort of 'spook' for us! Now there might be some people wondering why they must endure me rattling on about the sweet nothings of my love life. There is, in fact, quite a significant point to this, so please bear with me.

In 1991, about two years after we started using the expression *tanu* with each other when talking intimately on the telephone, as lovers do, we happened upon a fat and very comfortably relaxed white cat whilst we were walking in the grounds of a temple in Kamakura. That cat, strange though it may seem, made quite an impression on us. When we first laid eyes on the said feline we were in the throes of a debate about whether it was possible to achieve an understanding of truth through the study of Buddhism. The cat was stretched out fast asleep, as though she had transcended all matters of this world and had supreme knowledge of all things. We decided to name this cat the 'Honourable *Nyāgo*'[7]. About this same time two cats started making appearances at Nuta's apartment, most likely because he is a soft touch and couldn't resist giving them food. Nuta named the tortoiseshell one 'Tubby *Nyāgo*' and the white one 'Baby *Nyāgo*'. From that day on Nuta grew very fond of cats. Indeed, this whole-hearted launching into something is typical of Ryuta's behaviour. Whenever he gives himself over to anything he tends to absorb himself in it completely. The reverse situation is true, too, in that he is able to snap out of these things quite easily! Anyway one day Nuta came out with '*Tanu, Tanu* you are every bit as cute as a chubby cat!' and with this I was given the nickname '*Nyāgo*', the name we had given the cat we had seen in the temple grounds. That led to many variations of '*Nya*' peppering our telephone conversations. What's more, to pass time we started giving, 'the Honourable *Nyāgo*', a character of his own…He was 3000 years old, and his eating and sexual appetites were above and beyond anything of this world. However, he hadn't managed to rise above the desire to expose his tummy and demand that we tickle his throat. We established the world's most exalted religion '*Nyāgoism*'! The imaginary tales the two of us came up with escalated. We explored the difficulties to be overcome on the path to spiritual enlightenment and joked about how to propagate our new religion and recruit teenagers into the flock! And all the while there were more and more cats appearing on the stage! We had a lot of fun playing with totally nonsensical conversations like:

'Ah, I'm tired today'

'OK I'll send over 10 *nyāgo* cats to give you a massage!'

'Ah – here they are but you'll have to wait, they've found something nice to eat first', or

'I've got some good news today'

'I guess you mean such-and-such'

'Well how did you know?'

'Cause I love you – also it was revealed by the hand-mirror *nyāgo*! '

'I didn't even know there *were* such *nyāgos*!'

Such light-hearted exchanges of banter proved to be a source of great amusement for us.

Setting off on the path to being a model couple, partners in life.

It is time I got back to matters of a more serious nature!

One aspect of 'love' is the creation of a 'world for two to share'. I am of the opinion that the richer and more enjoyable that world is, the more zest for life the partners have. (Of course I acknowledge that there are two sides to this coin; the flip side being the danger of cutting yourselves off from society, shutting out the world and creating an exclusive 'world of your own').

Perhaps this can best be illustrated by looking at a celebrity couple, the husband and wife team, Kenya Ōsumi and Rumiko Koyanagi.[8] From about 1992 all their work, including their television appearances and dancing, seemed to veritably shine. By contrast, at one stage – before becoming involved with her partner – Rumiko Koyanagi seemed washed up and unable to produce a hit song. She had completely lost her lustre and watching her perform was a painful experience. She only started to return to her work with vigour and life after the relationship with her partner blossomed, and this despite the fact that she had no particularly big projects in hand. This surely illustrates the most positive sort of power that love can bring to a person. The other day (February 28th, 1993), for example, she and her husband appeared together in a television interview. It was a pleasure to witness just what a happy and fulfilling relationship they had developed in the five years since they first met. Watching them really being open with each other conveyed a very warm feeling to the television viewer. They displayed none of the falseness nor concealment associated with show business personalities and there was none of the Japanese reticence to discuss private matters – like love – in public. They spoke frankly about their feelings for each other. They shared with the TV audience how they coped when Rumiko went to Vienna by herself to work and how she wrote to Kenya every day because she loved him so much. It is rare in Japan for couples to show just how light and happy love can make you and how love can provide the strength needed to cope with life. As I watched this interview I keenly felt that the underlying reason for the Japanese hesitancy and inability to speak openly about love is to be found in an acceptance of the notion of there being an unavoidable complexity surrounding human relationships. This is graphically and frequently portrayed in traditional songs about tragic and unrequited love. I will return to this later.

It is in this vein that Nyāgo and Nuta are also now coming out and making public our own 'world for two to share'. This world provides the energy base for each of us to pursue our work and the various other activities in which we are involved. My own participation in 'Occur', 'Taurus' and in setting up the publication *Match* are only possible due to the confidence thus found.

We consider that we are part of a movement which proclaims that the very fact that we continue to be a happy couple together proves that it is possible for homosexuals to find happiness in this world. Further, the 'world for two' we share isn't confined to the creation of a fantasy world on the telephone. It goes far beyond that. For example, every week we make our own 'Nyāgo chart' and 'Nuta chart' based on hit Western songs and exchange our opinions on these. From time to time we draw on all the experiences we have had and all the knowledge we are able to command and together debate such questions as life, war and the way human beings should live. In this way the things we do together take on a greater breadth and depth of significance. We can't conceive of a situation where we would confine ourselves to just one area of interest and allow ourselves to get bogged down in it; this would be a very, very restricting experience.

Having come this far, I feel I should state that the notion of 'becoming the ideal type of partner' for each other, referred to earlier, is somewhat imprecise. Perhaps I should say that we are decidedly moving in the direction of becoming the 'ideal couple'. The sense is that we are approaching the point where we should be considered partners in life, or even members of the same family, rather than just lovers or boyfriends.

2 The sexual pilgrimage I made before meeting my partner

From being an only child who changed schools four times during primary school.

The fact that I am now able to admit such a bold and intrepid thing as the fact that I am a homosexual, and yet was terrified ten years ago by a blackmail attempt which threatened to expose my homosexuality, makes me feel that I am a completely different person now to the person I was then. Having reached this juncture I would like to spend some time reflecting on the Satoru Ito that I used to be before meeting Nuta. One clue to help fill in the picture would have to do with my level of personal forbearance at that time, in other words how much I was able to put up with. I would like to trace this aspect of my character back to my early childhood and the influence my parents had on me.

My father was a person who had no desire to go off to war and kill people nor any desire to join the army and be treated like a nobody as a second class soldier. Realizing that he was soon to be conscripted, he made the first move and chose the path which led from his forensic medical rooms to his becoming an army dental officer. When he returned to Japan after the war he knew he had had enough of being a researcher and he opened up his own medical practice in the town. He often spoke with pride of how he had refused a 'Medical Doctorate' which he had been told he was entitled to. He was offered this by dint of the confused state of affairs which resulted from the post-war revamping of the medical system and because he had never participated in 'testing his sword', as it were, on prisoners of war.

During my primary school years he worked as a dentist but we moved as a result of run-ins he had with his employers on a whole range of issues. Personally I didn't want to change schools but I did feel an affinity with the anti-authoritarian spirit displayed by my father and accepted the changes of school as something unavoidable. After his death I learned of the high regard the local people had for him. Dad would not think twice about telling patients off. I remember how exasperated and impatient a particular Olympic athlete had become when he came to the surgery for attention and was not treated any differently to dad's other patients. These reflections brought home to me that I agreed with the way my dad did things and his rationality for doing them.

My mom was also a strong person and a forward thinker. Indeed, of her first marriage she said, 'He ran out on me because I tended to go ahead and do what I wanted to do'. Mom raised my elder half-sister (who is 18 years my senior so we never lived in the same house together) and me in a proper and happy home environment. She got the former medical practitioner to act as a home tutor to my sister who was facing university entrance examinations and that was how she and the 'former doctor' fell in love and eventually got married. I was born after mom thought she was past child-bearing age.

My sister told me that, after obtaining entry to university, she took part in the 1960 political demonstrations against the US-Japan Security Pact. She was terribly frowned upon by our relatives for doing so. Yet despite this, mom stuck up for her. She used to tell my sister 'You can't go past doing what you want to do in life, that's the way to go'. She said the same thing to me to encourage me when I lost my job and when I opened up to her about my homosexuality. Such were my parents. I have inherited my full share of irrepressible energy and non-conformist spirit from them. These, naturally enough, surface in my refusing to go along with things that I cannot agree with. Perhaps I am considered a bit on the wayward or unconventional side as a result. Despite this, however, I was forced to entertain a value system which went against that which was intrinsically me; initially by social expectations themselves and later by constraints I applied to myself as a result of social expectations.

I first made friends with people other than my parents, with kids my own age, between the ages of three and six. I went through the phase of relating to, and wrangling with, people outside the family – in other words those viewed as 'outsiders'. At that time dad's first practice failed and he set up rooms in a village in Chiba which had only a few dozen households. There were no kids at all my age near where we lived and I relied on my parents to be my playmates. In terms of knowledge, I became a very precocious little know-it-all, but after going to primary school I found that my lack of experience in making friends compounded the difficulty I had in that regard. So it was that I hated school initially. For the most part I hung around by myself. This was because I couldn't bring myself to ask other kids to let me join in their games and, what's more, I saw their games as being quite puerile. I couldn't stand the classes either; not because I didn't understand what the teacher was on about nor because I understood it too well, but because I was always selected by the teacher and ordered to do things which I didn't want to do. Moreover, I failed to endear myself to the teacher because I would blatantly point out how unfair I thought he was. Nor could I stand the way the school tied us down for such long periods of time. I never really became part of the group, but rather was a bit of a loner. During six years of primary school I attended five different schools. Gradually, I got used to travelling between home and the various schools I attended. I would distract myself by doing things such as making up imaginary bus routes and collecting maps, tickets and stamps, etc.

This situation continued until I was in year 5 when the teacher in charge put up a poster on the classroom wall that indicated the ranking of the average results of our class tests. Suddenly he launched into an explanation of the value of getting good marks in tests. The year was 1964 when public awareness of academic competition and the need to do well in exams was not as high as it is today. It so happened that this was also the year that the TV program '*Hyokkori Hyōtan Island*' started and it took centre stage as far as my interests were concerned. The results of my efforts became evident the following year (1965) when, in the 1st term of year 6, I topped the class. We also had a new teacher in charge of the class, who took an exceptional liking to me and started lending me books and all sorts of different things. More than a touch of favouritism was evident. This was the first time the place called 'school' became enjoyable for me. I found a friend in the teacher. Very soon, though, the summer holidays came and I, yet again, changed schools. The teacher in charge of my new class recommended that I try sitting the entrance examinations for Kaisei Junior High School in order to try to gain a place there. Although I exceeded my year 6 peers in the knowledge needed for school tests, the gap closed when it came to knowledge about things outside school study, particularly in relation to sexual matters. Those guys who were 'full bottles' really were quite amazing in terms of what they knew. They really were miles ahead of me. I knew nothing at all about things such as electric guitars, for example, which had just broken into the Japanese market. Guys who knew all about such things seemed to me to be nothing short of incredible in terms of their specialist knowledge.

Anyway, after a long dormancy, the desire to get out there, enjoy myself and have a damn good time returned. This desire was thwarted, however, by the need to study to gain a place at Kaisei Junior High School. No-one could expect that anything spectacular would happen in terms of forging friendships in just the second and short third terms remaining in that year. Knuckling down to study with a view to gaining a place at Kaisei represented the beginning of what might be described as a period of self-denial and stoic endurance. In other words it marked the beginning of a period in which I put my personal desires and needs last, a time when I decided to put off making friends until after getting into Kaisei.

I got through that first stage and thought for a fleeting moment that it was now time for friends but, as previously stated, in junior high school my thoughts turned to what occupation I might pursue in order to support myself in life. I had no hobbies and no special interests or areas of expertise. I had no desire to follow in my father's footsteps and take over his dentistry practice and, fortunately, he didn't expect me to. Moreover, there wasn't any particular line of business I wanted to follow. This being the case I couldn't see an attractive alternative to the path my teachers had recommended and, for the time being at least, I set my sights on trying to get into Tokyo University[9]. My teachers told me that if I followed their directions and kept my nose to the grindstone I would be able to win a place there.

At this point I was prepared to put having friends and having a good time on the back burner. Indeed, I began to feel that the self-analysis I had conducted in the early period of my primary school life, which led me to conclude my isolation and loneliness were because I was a strong-willed person who didn't try to adapt to the school system, wasn't a good thing. I fully believed that amongst only-children (my sister was a university student and had already left home when I was born) it was common to find those who always wanted their own way and for whom it was difficult to make friends. I didn't analyze personalities beyond those stereotypical ones portrayed in magazines. Hence, I concluded that a definite attempt to suppress my assertiveness would help me along the road to making friends and this in turn would be a positive thing for my study which was geared towards getting into Tokyo University.

Thus it was that for six and a half years plus one year of break (as explained earlier I had to resit some exams due to my changing from the Science to the Arts Faculty) I stoically denied my personal and social interests in favour of academic pursuits. The frustrations experienced as a result of doing this were just tremendous. The strength of will I had inherited from my parents proved, in many respects, to be nothing short of a curse. This is why I am greatly concerned that so few people question what the ultimate goal is, or what the overall objective is, when they spur others on in academic or sporting pursuits with cries such as 'Hang in there!' and 'Stick with it!' I don't believe that schools and sporting events should require the same level of determination to succeed and achieve goals as that needed to be victorious in war!

To escape from the restrictions of the value system of the majority in mainstream society, a value system at odds with my own demand for freedom, I felt I needed about the same amount of time that I had already lived, all over again. That was how deeply the said value system was inscribed in my being. Teachers must always be respected! A good university! A position in a good company! Advancing your career! These were the unquestioned, absolute goals in life! Getting ahead was deemed to be the most important thing in life, indeed nothing less than the ultimate goal! You must not involve yourself in actions that depart from the norm, like skipping school, or actions that are contrary to the interests of society, like public protests and demonstrations! Merely starting to query these precepts is often interpreted by society as trouble-making. However, as certain things can be dealt with by simply altering the way you conceive them in your mind, I would audaciously take it upon myself to perceive the way society interpreted my querying various aspects of the societal set-up as being nothing more than a response to my conducting a fight to regain control of the right to see myself as being respectable, in other words a fight to regain control of myself. I believed that if I were to widen the scope of the contacts I had with people and broaden my view of the world, though it would take time, I would somehow manage to be able to change the way I lived. What's more, if I were to search I would be able to find any number of precedents in terms of people whose lives had taken similar courses – role models who had turned their backs on elite courses in life and who had steadily fought against the system. There would even be people who listened to them, although societal constraints would mean that there were limits to this. An example of a man who had bucked the system was Mr Jun Ui, leader of the anti-pollution movement, whom I had met and spoken to many times. Likewise, there was Mr Kōichi Murata, a man who carried out very perceptive educational practices. I surrounded myself with people who shared the trait of having the confidence to stand up to the contradictions of society which stared them in the face.

Though I dabbled with the history of my struggles at school, I didn't touch the 'sacred area' of my own sexuality.

Although I was able to question many aspects of the set-up of society, some matters were firmly rooted in my mind and stubbornly established in my psyche. These were matters about sex, and were treated differently. Falling for a member of the opposite sex, getting married and having children are actions which are a matter of course for the majority of Japanese people. Yet while I could visualize leaving the elite academic course I was in, and was in fact convinced that life would be more interesting were I to do so, I was totally unable to picture myself achieving something which was a matter of course for the majority of people. It was of a completely different order to the uncertainty and fear arising from trying to make friends at university which, it would be no exaggeration to say, was as daunting a challenge as I had ever faced in my life. My inability to even conceive of doing what is normal for the majority in society was only to be expected as neither my body nor my mind sought anything more from girls than pleasant conversation. In my case there was no reason, though, why I should have even considered homosexuality as the explanation, despite being as troubled and unhappy as I was. In the first place, I had never in my life even met a homosexual, although I had heard rumours in high school that in such-and-such a club the more senior members would 'do' the cute looking junior members and that certain individuals would go travelling together and 'get up to all sorts of things'. There was no information coming through about the American gay liberation movement and there were no homosexuals living openly. There were gay magazines, but these were viewed as being something akin to the organs of a secret society that was totally rejected by mainstream society. These magazines consisted largely of correspondence columns and very soft pornographic pictures. They didn't ever carry any message along the lines that homosexuality wasn't abnormal or that homosexuals should be able to live their lives with dignity and confidence. They merely served the valuable purpose of confirming that homosexuality existed as a phenomenon in Japanese society.

I once discussed the issue of homosexuality with two classmates and a student who was our junior from my Kaisei days, drawing on a vigour that came to me as a result of having my mind freed from the pressure of university entrance examinations. The former two flippantly dismissed my appeal to discuss what was on my mind. They claimed that it was a groundless fear, that I was overly anxious and was spending too much time thinking about something I didn't need to worry about. It might have been because I hadn't been able to go so far as to say that fantasizing about women did nothing for me when masturbating, but they both put my concerns down to a reaction to not having had close male friends and reckoned I would get over it in time. To digress for a moment, I find it amazing that even now in the 'Agony Aunt' columns, homosexuality is referred to as a transitory phenomenon occuring at puberty or in situations where members of the same sex live together in a group situation for an extended period of time. While it is certainly true that the phenomenon occurs under such circumstances, we are told that 90% of a person's sexual orientation has already been determined by the time he or she is born. Exactly when one becomes aware of this orientation varies depending on one's environment. But it is not something you have any hand in choosing or something easily changed!

The student referred to above who was present when I broached the subject of homosexuality, told me of a homosexual liaison he had had with a junior involved in club activities at his university. I must admit to having been so excited by this subject that I was unable to pay attention to precisely what he was telling me and as a consequence I now can't remember what he said, but I think he said he didn't know if he himself was homosexual or not. I remember that he made no comment about me at all. All I can remember is that I asked him what he would do if I were to ask him to go out with me and he replied that he couldn't be sure but that he would probably say 'no'. I also remember that after he said that I couldn't ask anything else!

In the final analysis my time at university, the 1970s, was spent immersing myself in club activities, dabbling in campus struggles, trying to deny my past self and regain a sense of being a normal human being. Yet, though I groped for a way to live my life outside the constraints that society expected me to mould myself to, and the constraints of the elite academic course I was in, my sexuality stood alone as a 'sacred area', one that I was not able to encroach upon. Far from having the courage to be seen to be different on this score, I simply kept my nose to the proverbial academic grindstone and continued on with life as I had always done.

It even occurred to me at one stage that I should seek psychiatric help. At that time, however, I had a number of reservations relating to the treatment psychiatric patients received. My main concern centred on the quality of the medical service as it really was, compared to what it should have been. I was aware that patients with mental problems were treated as less than human and I stubbornly dug my heels in and told myself that the strength of my own will alone would allow me to overcome the difficulties I faced in relation to the situation concerning my sexuality. Can you imagine that?

My one-way love affair with 'T'. He taught me about relationships between people and about mutual understanding.

When I experienced love at first sight with 'H' and 'T', I kept thinking that if I could extricate myself from the feelings I was experiencing, I would. This was despite the fact that the emotions

I felt could only ever have been interpreted as love, especially towards 'T', to whom I was extremely attracted. We were on the same wavelength in terms of what we liked to talk about and what we liked to do in our spare time. Both his facial features and his personality were very appealing to me. The reason I wanted to extricate myself from the feelings I had towards these guys was because my love was being directed towards heterosexuals. I fully believed that in order not to have to taste the bitterness of a fruitless love I should become heterosexual myself. I further believed that I should not associate with homosexuals.

Having said this, I cannot deny that in the latter half of the 1970s my long one-way love affair with 'T' gradually started to inch towards its next stage. The audacity I displayed in moving close to where he lived, a move which could have surely been seen through by anyone, was no doubt because the wraps binding my prohibited desires had to a large extent loosened up and allowed the painful, indeed heart-rending feelings I had for 'T' to come to the point where I was unable to suppress them by will. It was the first time I had ever experienced such terribly strong emotions. I was in love with 'T' so very much that I simply had to follow my heart and act accordingly. Even looking at this situation in a slightly more detached way, and as objectively as possible, I can state that while 'T' had no way to confirm the actual truth in relation to my feelings for him, I am definitely able to look back at the four years that I was in love with him as a very rewarding period in my life. For me, 'T' was irreplaceable during those four years. He is very close to being the first real friend I ever had. There is no doubt that 'T' was the closest anyone has ever come to Nuta in terms of the various steps we have taken to mould each other into 'perfect partners' and in terms of the level of communication we attained. I threw everything at him in a far less refined, and what's more far pushier, way than I did in my later approach to Nuta. 'T', for his part, was not to be outdone. He pushed it back at me in a way that was far more gentle than the approach I had taken. In doing so he taught me many things. I learned a considerable amount about the temper and disposition, the diplomacy and tact and also the poise needed in order to be able to come face to face with another human being and build a relationship in which the two parties could develop a deep and proper understanding of each other.

Our relationship might actually have developed into a close friendship if my jealousy and the feeling that I wanted to have him all to myself, things which were borne out of the one-way love experience, hadn't come into the picture and turned everything terribly maudlin. I tried to grasp hold of his every movement every day, just like a lover would. I hung around him everywhere he went, even when it meant I had to change my plans to do so. I would tell him more details of my life than he ever wanted to know. I was audacious enough to get into a bad mood whenever he got on well with another guy. I even pushed in sometimes when he started getting fresh with a girl, although this course of action had to be restricted to times when I could call upon the assistance that liquor affords because such behaviour was definitely beyond the scope of even the best mateship. Had I not pushed so hard, we might have actually become close friends. Now I find myself hoping that he might retain a trace of some positive contribution that I made in his life. But, I shouldn't kid myself so cruelly! Rather, I should feel gratitude. I feel grateful to 'T' from the bottom of my heart for the huge role he played in maturing me as a person. The years I spent with 'T' were a very meaningful period in my life, a period I simply had to go through in order to become a person capable of falling in love.

My first homosexual experience and my fear of ending up a homosexual.

Of course my first sexual experience was a significant event in my personal development. This was something that came along without great fanfare. 'M' – whom I briefly introduced in Chapter 1 – was one of a number of high school students who, after reading my book *Fourteen Years in Kaisei and Tokyo University*, came together to form a discussion group concerned with a range of questions surrounding education. I felt attracted to 'M', who appreciated his own simple and humble experiences and whose bright eyes were just lovely. He displayed keen insight and was very perceptive in his questioning of the school and examination systems. He opened my eyes to a new approach, that is, to questioning the merit of certain aspects of formal education. He would look at various facets of things being studied at school and query them, one by one, to see just what sense or level of merit there was in each of them. Through my contact with him as a private tutor my own narrow view, which accepted unquestioningly the idea that having certain facts knocked into you at school was for your benefit, was demolished.

What occasioned our getting together was the fact that neither of us had any trace of artificiality or design about us. One evening, after a large group of us had spent our time talking and having a merry old time together, it turned out that the room allocation for our sleeping arrangements was such that 'M' and I were to share a bed together in a room to ourselves[10]. We sported with each other, touching each other's penises through our trousers, and in doing so we both became excited. There was tacit agreement that, having come this far, we would have to find sexual release with each other. We stripped from the waist down and hugged each other. At this point 'M' asked me what we were to do next, but I was not in a position to enlighten him as I didn't know what the next step was myself. I couldn't admit that I had never done it before so we just hugged, touched and stroked each other. Even so the pleasure derived simply from being touched by another person was mightily powerful. The two of us readily discharged and the 'formalities' were over without any effort at all. This was when I was approaching the end of my 27th year. 'M' never did come out to me but he did hint that he had had something along the lines of a homosexual experience in the past. It seems, however, that his basic orientation was towards the opposite sex and eventually he was to elope with a girl. Subsequent to our first sexual encounter 'M' often said things like 'Croc, you've got to fix up your 'bad habit' as soon as you can' and 'I'm glad that you've managed to get on top of things since that incident'. Despite this, however, it was not very long before we once again found ourselves having sex together, this time assisted by alcohol. On this occasion our experience included fellatio, increasing our knowledge about sex. When I think back to these shared experiences I wonder what might have eventuated had I openly expressed my feelings for him. In fact I was on the verge of losing my heart to 'M'.

There were two things that kept me from expressing the love I felt for 'M'. One was that 'T' was still the great love of my life. The other, strange though it may sound, was because although I knew for a fact that 'T' was heterosexual, it might just have been possible that 'M' was homosexual. This being the case, I feared that if we got on too well with each other I might just end up turning into a homosexual myself and I certainly did not want that. So, even though I went and stayed at 'M's house several times after that, I suppressed my physical desires to the extent that I would go to bed and sleep without even touching him.

To be perfectly honest, before my encounter with 'M' I had, on two previous occasions, experienced mutual masturbation with heterosexuals. One of these experiences took place at my house and the other at the other's flat. On the occasions in question we talked about arousing things, touched each other and arranged the timing of our getting excited. Then I suggested we should stroke ourselves together. I am sure you will realize from this paucity of encounters in the sixteen years between my discovering what masturbation was and my experience with 'M', in other words from the fact that there were only these two occasions on which it happened, that these were exceptionally rare incidents and ones which came about through a considerable injection of courage for one reason or another. As love did not accompany these experiences they were carried out in quite a heterosexual frame of mind. We just happened to find sexual release together, nothing more.

3 The agonies homosexuals experience as members of a minority group

Getting over the major hurdle of seeking other homosexuals…but how to go about it?

Although I had had an experience with 'M', I found that refraining from sex didn't change the person I was. Both of the times I had sex with 'M' I experienced extremely powerful feelings; good feelings which erupted from the depths of my being and remained with me as something very substantial and lasting. I was able to continue denying myself the pleasures of the flesh, I think, because of a fantasy that sustained me. I believed I was forming a psychological bond with 'T', although I acknowledged that I wouldn't have physical contact with him and we would thus never become true and permanent lovers. I was intoxicated with the satisfaction derived from the belief that 'T' knew everything about me and protectively enveloped my being. I now see that this was all my own fabrication.

In 1981 with graduation and job hunting in front of us, 'T' found himself in a position where he was no longer able to be just 'Croc's partner'. As slow as I was at catching on to things, I perceived our relationship was in its autumn years, much as I hated the idea. The following year 'T' received offers for positions at two different companies. One would have allowed him to stay in Tokyo; the other involved moving. When he had difficulty in choosing between the two I encouraged him, out of a purely selfish desire for him to stay in Tokyo, to take the former, even though no matter how you looked at it the latter company was the better option for all sorts of reasons. He commented quizzically that it was not like me to make the recommendation I did, and chose the latter. He left Tokyo to live by himself. At this point I felt a decisive gap had developed between us. After this my sexual appetite, which I had done everything in my power to suppress up until that time, grew in direct proportion to the size of the loss of the psychological bond between 'T' and me, and it took control of me like a raging storm.

The realization that one-way, unrequited love affairs with heterosexuals, though they might offer a temporary fantasy-like sense of fulfilment, could ultimately only ever prove to be fleeting and would inevitably end up shattering me to smithereens, meant that at long last I faced the reality of having to turn my attention towards a homosexual relationship. Yet having reached that point (in 1981), I knew hardly anything about homosexual groups or circles. I had to negotiate a tremendous learning curve trying to get over an absolutely huge crevasse in order to be able to meet homosexuals in a social setting. I would have to take myself to places where homosexuals were if I was going to meet them. Just waiting and hoping that I might meet some homosexuals in my life simply wasn't going to work. It wasn't a viable option as no homosexuals were ever going to come up and introduce themselves to me as such. You just can't tell who is homosexual amongst those you come across in your everyday life. In terms of meeting homosexuals, I thought that initially the safest way might be to place an advertisement introducing myself in the personal columns of a gay magazine. Alternatively, I could read other people's ads and reply to those which looked like they were written by people

I might get on with. This could be done via the magazine's editorial department, which would forward items of correspondence on for me, thus ensuring any secrets would be kept safe.

However, as mentioned in the previous chapter, I was jilted by the first man I made contact with this way, even before we spoke. More often, though, I simply got no response whatsoever when I replied to an ad. And virtually the same thing happened when I placed my own ad, I would get no replies at all. It was just not working for me. My sexual appetite, ignited by my experiences with 'M', started making me impatient. I set myself to wondering if perhaps there was another, quicker way of meeting homosexuals. And there was: it involved going to the Ni-chōme section of Shinjuku, an area known as 'the gay quarters' of Tokyo. The history of homosexuality in Japan is inseparable from the history of this Ni-chōme area.

While it would be stretching it to say that in the past homosexuality was properly accepted as such in Japan, it did occupy its own place as a recognized non-mainstream sub-culture up until the Edo period[11]. This can be seen in the equivalent status accorded to the terms 'male allure' and 'female allure'[12] in popular culture. I could also cite the attraction that boys held for samurai warriors and the practice of stationing pageboys in Buddhist temples and Shinto shrines. In addition the male erotic literature of Saikaku Ihara[13] and others at least proves the existence of homosexuality at that time, if not its acceptance. Since the Meiji period[14] the status of homosexuality has plummeted. This co-incided with the rapidly growing influence of Christianity, a phenomenon which is directly related to Japan's modernization. After the Second World War the place of homosexuality in Japanese society dropped to the point where its existence could only be verified through a genre of soft pornographic magazines. The homosexuals were tough, though. They would stealthily pass information by word of mouth about places where it was possible to meet. When the police chased them away from a particular place they would immediately make another meeting place. Gay bars eventually gravitated to the Ni-chōme area, a former red light district, from other parts of Shinjuku and in the 1960s this Ni-chōme area took on a unique character. It was a mixture of gay hotels, adult literature shops and gay saunas (formerly, discos too) centred around hundreds of gay bars.

Mustering the courage to cross the threshold of the gay district in Shinjuku.

Working up the determination needed simply to enter the gay quarter and explore it was no easy matter. Indeed a considerable amount of resolution was required in order just to set foot there. How many times did I attempt to venture into Nakadori Avenue, the heart of the area, only to abandon the plan at the last minute? Just crossing the threshold of the area was hard enough, but having accomplished that, the next step – approaching one of the establishments – was equally daunting. It is by no means an easy task to get yourself inside one of those bars the first time. What would I do if someone were to grab me and hug me the moment I stepped in? What would I do when I did get in and was all on my own? Such concerns swirled around in my head, stopping me in my tracks. I was even gripped by the fear that if I were to cross the threshold of a gay bar, that would be it, I would end up becoming 'one of them'. I imagined that entering one of those bars was tantamount to 'passing the point of no return', as it were. I feared running the risk of ceasing to belong to normal society and becoming, instead, a person who belongs to that 'other world'. The closed doors of the bars represented both a physical barrier and a psychological barrier. I imagined and feared the prospect of being unable to return to my 'normal status'. That fear included an element best described as being a mixture of curiosity, excitement and trepidation which was egged on by my sexual drive. But it very soon changed to a very sombre feeling with the realization that I had already fallen as far as I could, that I had hit rock bottom and that there was nowhere else for me to go.

I don't remember the name of the first bar I found the courage to enter but I do remember how I felt when I first opened the door. I remember a strange feeling as I thought to myself 'Should have guessed they would play the songs of male pop stars!' the moment I entered the bar and found the song *Terete Zinzin* by Takayuki Takemoto being played loudly. With this bar as my introduction to the area I went to two or three others. The experience was totally different to my expectations on two counts. For one thing there was nothing at all scary about them. There are exceptions of course, but generally speaking I found the proprietors, the *mama-sans* of the establishments, to be quite easy going. They spoke the 'language' of the Ni-chōme area, using drag queen speech for the most part. And whereas on occasions they have been known to display something of a malice as though they are making fun of newcomers, in my case, when they realized that I was a first timer, they came over and talked to me about a range of things, offering advice and filling me in on all the information relating to the Ni-chōme district. Neither did the customers venturing into the gay bars particularly mind being placed under the *mama-san*'s visual scrutiny, something which enabled her to make an instant evaluation of them. Nor were they hassled by her. As long as they didn't approach her she was prepared to leave them be.

The other thing I discovered contrary to my expectation involved the realization that when you go there you don't automatically come across a potential partner, someone who could become your boyfriend, straight away. It might seem to some that such a thing should be obvious and indeed I can't help now but laugh at the naivete I displayed at that time, feeling both fear and a contradictory but very powerful sense of palpitating expectation as I prepared to enter the gay bars.

Most of these places allow you to stay for a long time once you have bought just the one drink. I enjoyed listening to the chatter that went on between the proprietor and the regular customers and I even felt more at home there than I did in an ordinary bar. Though I had steeled myself for a jolt to the system as a result of visiting these establishments, I found that the fact of the matter was that visiting gay bars wasn't anything to get so worked up about after all.

To my mind, the homosexuals who frequented these bars could be categorized into two different types. There were those who came to enjoy the camaraderie of the bar, talking with the *mama-san* over drinks and enjoying the atmosphere engendered by sharing the *karaoke*[15] experience together, and those who were there simply to find someone to have sex with as soon as possible.

I didn't feel comfortable with the first category of customer. While it was true that on occasions people from some surprising walks of life, representing the whole gamut of trades and professions, would come into the bars and the presence of such people would allow you to hear conversations on a range of topics you would never normally get to hear, for the most part these guys spoke like drag queens. This was something I just couldn't get comfortable with at all. This is a personal thing for me. I realize that social minorities use language that is different from that of the mainstream to confirm their identities and I don't deny anyone the right to do this. All I am saying is that that scene doesn't suit all homosexuals and I happen to be one that it doesn't suit. Also I couldn't stand the posturing of those who were not being straightforward and honest in their lives, those who would come in hiding the fact that they were going to a gay bar from their wives and kids. And yet it was hypocritical for me to take the moral high ground since I myself was by no means being very 'up-front' in terms of my behaviour. My own posturing was nothing to be proud of! For these reasons I very soon grew tired of such places and didn't feel as though I wanted to become a regular at any particular establishment.

I soon considered myself to be different to the latter category of customer, too, inasmuch as I had come to the bars to meet a person with whom I could develop a partnership. But there was a part of me that was ultimately starting to join the ranks of those in that category. Fortunately (or otherwise?) I wasn't considered hot property or much sought after.

Another element involved in my visiting gay bars was the time factor. The Ni-chōme area was a long way from Chiba, where I lived. I was also busy on weekends, spending time with students and organizing the production of our forum magazine, so it was not easy for me to get to the gay bars of Ni-chōme often. With the distance involved and my busy schedule it was physically impossible for me to make long stays in Ni-chōme in the hope of finding a partner, sexual or otherwise. There were many factors involved in the low level of 'efficiency', as it were, associated with my visits to Ni-chōme and they combined to result in my drifting away from the practice of visiting that area.

The sense of feeling guilty of being involved in something underhand which accompanies visiting gay 'rest houses'.

I had better add a comment about the assertion just made that I wasn't considered hot property or sought after. It would be a very dubious line of argument to claim that those people who don't believe themselves to be hot property are in fact not sought after at all. I would imagine that in this regard both heterosexuals and homosexuals would find themselves in the same boat. For homosexual guys, claiming that you aren't hot property simply means that you are not hot property amongst the type of guys that appeal to you. Generally speaking, few people would be in the position where they were not fancied by anyone at all or where they did not have the same interests as anyone at all. It could well have been the case that the sort of guys I am personally interested in – guys who, though perhaps younger than me, would act as my equal and go out with me as such, and as far as looks go be something of a cross between the cute-faced boys of the ilk of those working for the *Johnny's* enterprise[16], the rebel-type bikies and the athletically built guys who work out in sports centres – were in fact there in the bars that I visited. It was just that I had never been so much as looked at by any of the young guys who frequented the Ni-chōme area and who fitted that description. That is not to say I hadn't been looked at by others of my own age or older.

In the Ni-chōme district a special welcome was reserved for young guys and a great fuss was made over them. There were also, however, many older men who proved themselves to be a bit of a pain by throwing their money around trying to impress and pick-up, and consequently rendered it a seller's market. There was no way that someone of my face and form could vie with the competition I was up against. It is hard to make an impression with what you have on the inside. Either way, my personal esteem took a bit of a beating. I genuinely started to believe that I had very little in the appeal department. I started to feel very heavy hearted in comparison to the fantasy-like three or four years I had spent with 'T'. I felt as though I was somehow not connecting with the real world. I experienced a sense of uncertainty and adjustment in my understanding of who I was, what I was and where I was. Though I might go to the Ni-chōme area I never felt quite at home there.

Inside, I eventually felt the urge to relieve the sexual tension that had started up a mighty vortex within me. I had to have sexual release! But now I needed brute courage even greater than that required to go into the bars in Ni-chōme. There was a sense of exclusion from society and a sense of guilt that accompanied my going where I was going. In spite of this, several times I made my way to a certain gay hotel in Ōkubo[17]. The first time I arrived there I walked back and forth in front of the entrance many times before finding the courage to overcome the difficulty and awkwardness of approaching the front door, crossing the threshold and getting myself inside. This hesitation was borne of timidity, shyness, embarrassment, eeriness and lack of experience and knowledge.

Once inside I asked the silliest of questions to hide my embarrassment and to keep my courage up. I would ask things like, 'Is there a time limit for staying here?' The hotel in question was a so-called 'mixed rooms' establishment, a facility providing overnight accommodation with common sleeping areas everywhere. It was a place where you could stay until the following morning or leave at any time you liked. The entrance fee was about ¥1000 [18]. I left my clothes in the locker provided, changed into the bathrobe supplied and went to the main room where I encountered two guys engaged in sex together and others lying down suggestively. Others were fast asleep, presumably having already spent themselves. Yet again, I felt a sense of eeriness but my curiosity and sex drive proved stronger than the urge to pull out and go home. With surprisingly little fuss I found myself being attended to by someone whose face I couldn't clearly see in the semidarkness, and ejaculating as a result. He disappeared soon after our encounter. Suddenly I felt as though I didn't want to hang around there any more but I took my time getting changed as I did not want to appear to be in a rush to get out. This was for all sorts of illogical reasons – for example, that perhaps it would be considered odd if I were to leave the hotel so soon. Visiting such establishments was, in the short term, to become a passion for me. Such infatuation, however, usually is relatively short-lived. The emptiness of the feeling involved in having sex where you can just barely make out the face and form of the person you are with, ultimately proved stronger than my sexual urges. Further, I was aware that if I was to be judged on my face and form alone I would hardly be considered the object of many people's sexual desires. These things were more than enough to make me realize that my continuing to go to these establishments which offered 'mixed rooms' facilities would remain nothing more than a short-term comfort seeking strategy and not lead to anything in the way of a relationship which I could nurture and develop in the future.

Now you might have the impression that these 'mixed rooms' are synonymous with guys indulging in unscrupulous sex, in other words that they are places where guys have sexual relations with any and everyone who happens to be there, but this isn't the case. I believe that they differ from heterosexual sex orgies in that the patrons in the half light are somewhat discerning in terms of selecting a partner whom they find attractive. There is very little evidence of forced relations and the right to refuse is exercised fully. Also with both parties sharing the same frame of mind and interests the situation was different from simply paying for sex. Of course a greater pleasure can be derived from sex between two people who mentally engage with each other and who love each other, because such sex derives from the genuine feeling of wanting to satisfy your partner and this in turn heightens one's own pleasure. This is not to say, however, that seeking pleasure and enjoying sex on a one-off basis is necessarily a bad thing.

This raises a related and important issue. The catch phrase of the AIDS Prevention campaigns we encounter these days always includes the message 'avoid sex with numerous random partners'. Taken in isolation and without regard to other factors which are relevant to the question of the spread of AIDS, this is in fact quite a silly statement containing a misleading message, as it misses the point that you can become infected by HIV as a result of having sex with just one partner, unless it is safe sex that is practised. It also overlooks the fact that you might safely have relations with many people as long as you adhere to the practice of safe sex or, indeed, if none of them carries the virus. Surely the message should be to practise safe sex. It shouldn't centre on the idea of restricting yourself to one partner as such. While I believe it is desirable on an individual basis to have just one fixed partner with whom you have sexual relations, I have misgivings in condemning either the craving felt by some for the sexual pleasure attainable in the 'mixed rooms' of gay rest houses or those who have sex with multiple partners, on the basis of so-called 'rational thinking'. We should bear in mind that these days having sex simply for pleasure is so common that you come across couples in which both parties openly acknowledge infidelity in marriage.

Turning to narcissism in the face of the pathos of my being unable to meet a partner.

When it came to the point in my life where my infatuation with visiting gay rest houses passed, the only simple way left for me to find sex was to pay for it. This narrative so far has depicted my life as I moved from utilizing the personal columns of gay magazines to going to gay bars and then on to patronizing the 'mixed rooms' of gay rest houses, but in fact I made fairly constant use of the personal columns throughout this period. I would turn to them every few months or so from 1981 to 1985, whenever the mood took me. And as for visiting 'mixed room' facilities, even though I would sometimes tell myself 'Okay, that's it. I'm never going to those gay rest houses again', I would find myself back there and the resolve I had earlier displayed would count for nothing. I would be back to the start of a somewhat irregular cycle which would then be repeated. Sometimes I would head out to the coffee shops that had been created as 'beats' where homosexuals could meet one another. These would appear on the scene from time to time, only to close down again quite soon after. I recount my story in this way in the hope of conveying the general flow of my consciousness at that time.

Despite having reached the point where I felt that the only simple way left for me to find sex was through the purchasing power of money, and despite my engorged sexual appetite, I felt a great resistance to paying for sex with someone who wasn't personally interested in having sex with me. Also, as mentioned earlier, I soon discovered that it is usually heterosexual men who engage in part time employment selling their bodies. In order to get over this resistance, an 'intoxicant' of a sort was necessary. I will need to add a word of explanation in this regard.

As I said earlier, when 'T' and I went our separate ways (it would probably be more accurate to use the expression 'when the time came to accept the closing of an era'), I should have set out on the journey of looking for a partner who was homosexual. However, though I might try to meet someone through the personal columns of gay magazines or by going to gay bars, I never managed to meet anyone I felt I could form a long term relationship with. I even had great difficulty having one-off relationships in the 'mixed rooms' of gay rest houses. Things were looking decidedly black for me. Later, I was hit with blackmail and the threat of having my sexuality exposed. With each passing day an awful sense of despair and hopelessness grew in me. It grew relentlessly, finally reaching the point where I was unable to cope alone. I resorted to narcissism, seeing myself as a desperate hero of pathos. Though I sought a partner for a meaningful long term relationship, I was unable to find one. My life entered a realm of unbearable emptiness and, again, I would head off to buy a young man with the little money I had. Such a pathetic character I painted! If my lot in life was going to be this wretched I couldn't be blamed for going out and surfeiting myself with guys I paid to be with, although I knew that this way of thinking was merely a self-justification of my actions. But I don't believe it has anything whatsoever to do with homosexuality; I know of heterosexuals who have used the same rationality to convince themselves they would never find a partner, and thus turned to regularly visiting bathhouses to have girls at their service who would toy with their attempts to strike up a relationship. And, like me, their egos received a battering and they were left in a worse state as a result of visiting such places.

When you have been unlucky in love several times a self-protection mechanism is triggered and you tend to interpret things in such a way as to prevent the total destruction of your ego. Often you blame your wretched situation on others, or society, or even the Creator. You immerse yourself in narcissism, never squarely facing the question of how you approach forming relationships or trying to forge a new path forward. This, I would wager, is a common phenomenon amongst the Japanese people and is not restricted to homosexuals. The more you see yourself as a hero of pathos, the one being wrongly done by, the more egotistical you become and the deeper you become enmeshed in that vicious circle. The frightening part is that if you have gone down this path you cease to be able to do what is necessary to foster a relationship, even if you find somebody with whom you think you might get along nicely. I realized this, at long last, in 1985.

Even at the best of times there are precious few chances for homosexuals to get to meet one another. The level of difficulty encountered in meeting another homosexual is compounded if you hope to meet someone who, in addition to being homosexual, is also a person with whom you are likely to be compatible. With all potential partners, all you can think about is the consequence of missing the chance to get to know each other. You feel that if you miss the chance at hand you might end up never meeting anyone else and never finding a partner in life. You often find yourself pushing yourself forward, even forcing your company onto a person you have met but a few hours earlier, as you start to panic and become very worried about missing a possible opportunity to get to know someone. If all goes well you will seek sex that same day. When it happens that the level of interest displayed by the person you are with is fairly low and he becomes brusque as a result of your wanting to share his company, you become even more panicky. You bombard him with phone calls from the day after you meet him and you can sometimes even catch yourself paying direct visits to his residence, if you're not careful. This is followed by repeated applications of the strategy 'If pushing it doesn't work, try pushing harder!' Little wonder that under such circumstances it is well nigh impossible to actually find a partner. And yet you somehow don't seem to realize the contradictions involved in repeating this pattern again and again whilst convincing yourself that you will end up never finding a partner. I managed to conveniently ignore the fact that humans are only capable of understanding others with time. Unfortunately, the impatience underlying the behaviour described above is by no means unique to me. The percentage of homosexuals who, as a result of a similar impatience, have become snarled in a vicious circle and ended up nihilists who seriously doubt their ability to ever find a lover, is quite considerable.

I only hope that from the description of my personal history in this veritable quagmire of emotional experience you might be able to perceive something of what searching for a partner was like for a person in the position in which I found myself.

The dark side of obtaining sexual gratification – paying to have sex with men.

The fact of the matter is that the image of homosexuals that I held at the time I was desperately seeking companionship and reassurance for myself as a homosexual was, as a result of the circumstances outlined, a terribly dark one. On one occasion, several friends happened to catch sight of a gay magazine in my room and, by way of trying to justify (if this is the appropriate word!) my having this, I went to great pains to emphasize that homosexuals suffer discrimination and prejudice and are simply not in a position to be able to locate partners in the way that heterosexuals can. I tried to win them over by explaining that homosexuals are victims of discrimination. To illustrate, I would mention an incident in Kyushu where a high school student had been caught shoplifting a gay magazine. He had the money to buy it but he simply couldn't bring himself to take the magazine to the cash register. His parents were called and he was given a terrible tongue lashing, after which he suicided by jumping off the roof of the building that housed the bookshop. I would also often allude to the fact that in Nazi Germany it wasn't just Jews, but minority groups generally – including gypsies and homosexuals – who were rounded up and packed off to the concentration camps and liquidated. Incidentally, I always made a point of including this in the high school classes I taught on modern society.

Even now I tremble with rage when I think about such discrimination and prejudice. But when trying to get the message across to heterosexuals I feel that I tended to approach them with accounts of tragic events, trying to evoke their sympathy. That is why nowadays, when talking about myself as a homosexual, I focus on the fact that although I am homosexual I have found a partner in life and am living happily. This is because I have found that rather than seeking their sympathy, which represents nothing more than a metamorphosis of a discriminatory mentality (which is based on the premise that they are in a superior position), it is actually more effective to point out the areas of commonality that homosexuals share with heterosexuals. The reality is that homosexuals don't have to project a terribly dark image.

Be that as it may, on one occasion I found myself standing in front of a premises offering private massages in the Ni-chōme district of Shinjuku. I pushed open the heavy door and entered the building that housed several condominiums. One of these had a room that was divided into smaller rooms and in one of these five or six young men awaited selection by a customer with eager anticipation. I tried to select the best on offer through the one-way mirror provided, without wasting any time. First, he took me to the shower where he washed my body thoroughly, in every nook and cranny. This was followed by a body massage and a massage that invited ejaculation. For the most part, the young man provided a one-way service. I was not accustomed to this arrangement and I went to return the compliment to him, but as he worked with several clients he was not in a position to perform with every client he serviced. Even kissing was not allowed. I tried desperately to strike up a conversation with him to somehow arrange things so that I did not merely represent a business transaction. As a result of this desire, which I have alluded to earlier, I arranged on one occasion for a guy to come on a date with me outside the shop, though he risked losing his job if he were caught. As it turned out, all this proved was that I was trying to justify my behaviour to myself. It was a most unsuccessful venture. But if I hadn't tried my best to engage him in conversation the situation would have been just too wretched for words. I felt that if we could at least get to know each other even a little bit, my buying sex perhaps could have been tempered with the excuse that I was actually seeking a meaningful relationship.

There was another way of buying a man and this involved visiting an *urisen* bar[19]. At these establishments, over a drink, you have the opportunity to select a young man from the other side of the counter. If there is one who takes your fancy you pay a fixed sum per hour to the establishment and so much to the young man himself and leave the shop together. It is also possible to stay there overnight and have him stay with you. You don't have to have sex just because you leave the shop together, but this eventuality was out of the question in my case. In some instances an older man would come into the shop and leave with several of the young men and enjoy nothing more than their company and a drink together with them. There were other cases where, for example, homosexuals who were moving house but had not finished all the preparations that needed to be done in that regard, would hire out the guys to stay overnight and help out. As the facility in question was a hotel incorporating accommodation facilities, once you had spent yourself you had plenty of time to engage in a wide range of topics of conversation. However, while it cost more than twice as much as a private massage, there was essentially no difference in what you were doing. The worst part of utilizing the services of an *urisen* bar was having to choose a sex partner from amongst those lined up waiting. This was something *urisen* bars had in common with private massage parlours. Some of you would probably say that if that's how I felt then I shouldn't have gone through with it at all, but the fact was that I had closed my mind off to the possibility of ever finding anyone who would have sex with me otherwise. I felt that I had no choice but to rely on this means of managing my sex drive.

Despite the fact that most Japanese homosexual men do not engage in anal sex...

I want to make a point about the type of sexual practice that homosexuals engage in. Even those people who have no in-built sense of discrimination or fear of homosexuality tend to believe that homosexuals, without exception, engage in anal sex. When one denies this they are simply amazed. Even some homosexuals themselves have been made to believe that all homosexuals engage in anal sex and find themselves worrying that they too ought to practise anal sex even though they don't feel they want to.

Essentially it comes down to the question of what we consider constitutes the sex act. If we consider sex to occur when the partners sexually stimulate each other in a way that is most pleasurable and where both parties reach the pinnacle of pleasure, then there is no need to insert the penis into the anus. There are many and varied ways of achieving such physical pleasure. By way of illustration I could mention, among other things, stimulating each others erogenous zones and practising fellatio on each other. I have never even once had anal sex yet I am able to experience the pinnacle of physical pleasure when having sex. I would be inclined to say that for Japanese homosexuals in particular, it is probably the case that not even half would have ever experienced anal sex. One is left wondering how the idea ever came about that homosexuality equates with the practice of engaging in anal sex. One explanation could possibly be that this conclusion was drawn as a result of a notion that has its genesis in the belief system of a male-centred world, a notion that suggests that sex has to be the action of inserting the penis into an orifice. Perhaps there are just too many people believing this. Despite the fact that heterosexuals should also be able to enjoy sex without inserting the penis into the vagina, it would seem that many of them are tied to a cut-and-dried 'common sense' mindset and make no attempt to experiment with new, alternative ways of achieving sexual pleasure. Some ignorant men are just such simple-minded fools that they believe that as long as they put their penis into the vagina, their partner will be satisfied. Can you imagine that! Sex is something much, much more complex in nature. It is something where each couple together create their own 'world for two'. This world is different for every couple. For each couple the partners develop their own unique and personal sexual world. There is nothing nicer than for partners to engage in the process of improvising different techniques which they feel comfortable with, noting each other's reactions whilst experimenting with, and from time to time talking to, each other in the process. (It would be strange to feel inhibited at this stage!!) The fixed idea that homosexuals must rely on anal sex because they can't gain sexual pleasure without penetration is borne out of a lack of appreciation of this point. I really feel that those who limit their field of vision to a prescribed and narrow set of possibilities in relation to sexual activities are doing themselves a disservice.

Another likely reason why homosexuality is equated with anal sex would have to do with the portrayal of this idea on a grand scale in TV shows and in comics. Whenever a homosexual appears in *manga* comic strips[20] the males around him invariably are portrayed as panic-stricken and make a big fuss about keeping their 'backs covered'. Alternatively, the story develops with one of its characters being unable to sit down comfortably after staying overnight at the house of a homosexual. This way of thinking must be terribly deeply ingrained in the general psyche as, even thinking back to my own high school days, there were guys who would make fun of other guys who were not very clued up on sexual matters, by saying things like, 'Oi, lend me your arse' and when the other party would respond, 'Okay' they would then make fun of him by coming back with the retort, 'What? Do you mean it?!!' Is there not something we can do about these would-be-humorous stereotypical representations of homosexuality? Homosexuals have all sorts of different ways of seeking pleasure and different interests and the variety to be found therein is by no means inferior to that known to heterosexuals.

Returning to something I touched on a little earlier; I found that after my sex drive had been released from a terribly long period of abstinence, it lost some of its momentum. I also found my own ability to love reaching the point of expiry as I remained unable to find someone who could satisfy my need for love. Furthermore, I had exacerbated the situation by allowing fantasy to build upon fantasy. All of this was happening at the same time when, in 1983, the man I contacted through the personal columns was killed in a traffic accident before we were able to meet in person. This man had represented a potential partner with whom I might have been able to form a bond. If that wasn't enough I was then blackmailed with a threat of exposure by a friend of the deceased. I was working as a part-time instructor at a high school at the time and this man threatened to inform the school about me. In the end, I made a pay-off to settle the matter. At that time I wouldn't have been able to manage if I hadn't released myself from the lingering regrets in relation to my high school life. I sought to make amends as best I could by letting loose in the pseudo-experiences to be had by 'reliving my youth', as it were. By this I mean enjoying the fun and good times I had not experienced during my high school days. My compensation included socializing with the less academically motivated students at the high school, sometimes in a slightly bawdy way, turning my house variously into a party venue, a mahjongg hall and a campsite. However, if it had ever become known that I was a homosexual I might have found myself bereft of the only support I had in my life – my students at the high school. The torment I experienced was extraordinary and exceeded the bounds of that which could be considered to fall within the realm of reason. It bordered on being absolutely intolerable.

4 Towards movements which aim to eliminate discrimination against homosexuals

Two defining moments experienced when I was at my lowest ebb.

When I was at my lowest ebb I experienced two defining moments in my life. The first of these defining moments was when I was fired from my position as an instructor at a private senior high school. I had arrived at that point in my life with relatively few setbacks other than in relation to my sexual orientation, so the shock of losing my job was very great. For days on end I was summoned by the principal and interrogated with questions that seemed designed to wear me down. It seemed that the vice-principal had, from somewhere or other (possibly a parent or a student?), got wind of a rumour that I might be homosexual, although he never directly accused me of this. The principal didn't broach this subject directly, either. I heard a suggestion that an affiliated junior high school was considering legal action against the instigator of the rumour, for defamation of character. There were nights when I couldn't get a wink of sleep. As previously related, when the blackmail incident happened the previous year, I was told by the principal that my employment would continue until I had seen out the current year. So I knew that even if I stuck it out – for the remaining half year, I would still have to leave eventually. In the final analysis, the fear I had of being found out as a homosexual prevented me from putting up any form of resolute resistance. If I was to carry on fighting to the bitter end my enemies would undoubtedly produce their trump card. The word would be out not only to my students but to the whole of society including, most importantly, my mother. I was far from ready to imagine a way to ride out this dreadful predicament. Indeed I was terror-stricken, haunted by the fear that I might find myself quite unable to make a living and tossed out onto the street. It would be a simple enough matter for someone to fabricate an article and give it the title 'Gay Pervert Teacher Harasses Students' because I had put myself on the same level as the students, considering them all as my equal, and put my arms around them in harmless fun. At that boys' school there was a lad who looked like Tsukasa Ito, a heart-throb singer at the time, and to relieve the frustrations which were building up within me I had, on one occasion, hugged him and jokingly told him that I thought he was cute! Having done this, I remember immediately thinking to myself 'That's it – I've ruined my future now altogether'.

Here I was in the midst of battle, knowing full well that I was to be given the sack. Yet it can sometimes be the case that human beings, when they are at the lowest point they can reach, find an inexplicable and amazing strength to draw upon. In this connection the comment made by a clerical officer at the school is indelibly etched on my memory. I called in there one day during the summer holidays to collect some personal belongings when he said to me 'Not to worry. I know full well that the students all support you. Bad times don't go on forever. If there is a god who casts you aside there is another who looks after you'. And sure enough, after I left the school my students did in fact come to visit me at home and continued employing my services as a personal tutor. There was even a group who went to the principal to try to negotiate my employment with him. In the junior high school too, far from having accusations made against me, there were students who, armed with my book, pressured their teachers to support the views I had expressed therein. These were students questioning the physical violence perpetrated at school and the implementation of unnecessarily restrictive school rules. This support meant that I was not to be further hammered by the authorities.

Being out of work gave me plenty of time to take a long, hard look at myself. It was, in every sense of the expression, a learning period. Ironically, I achieved a sense of mental calm in which I made up my mind to take my time and start forming friendships with homosexuals. I gradually mollified my sexual urges, which were still apt to run wild from time to time, and gave priority to the notion of making friends. I frequented the coffee shops in the Ni-chōme area and added my name, personal details and thoughts in the notebooks provided as bulletin boards for customers. I also sent straightforwardly worded letters to a number of people via the personal columns of gay magazines.

It was at about this time that I made contact with a nascent gay circle. Such groups were, at long last, beginning to be formed. I had made contact through the personal columns with another gay circle about two years earlier, but my memory of this is not very clear. The meeting I attended on that occasion was not conducted at all professionally and I was put off when, out of the blue, a guy there asked me in drag queen tones 'Are you experienced?' What was worse, he then ranted on with no reference to, or interest in, me, a newcomer. Accordingly, that was my first and last attendance there. In 1984, when I was out of work, there were many such ill-structured groups and circles which existed simply so that gays could get to meet other gays. Later, various groups, each with its own flavour, gradually started up. Those aimed at teenage membership were prominent. As these developments were taking place I made positive and definite moves towards forging relationships with people in positions similar to mine, though I was ever mindful of ensuring that I wasn't guilty of trying to rush things.

From here the stage was set for me to experience the second defining moment in my life: meeting Mr 'N' and coming into contact with 'Occur' – the Gay and Lesbian Action Association to which I have made reference earlier. This was a group of homosexuals who were committed to a movement which strove to change society into a place where homosexuals could thrust their chests out and live with pride in a way which I hitherto had never dared to seriously consider, dismissing it as nothing more than a pipedream. Thus, the existence of such a group came as a tremendous shock. All of a sudden I could see a possible future opening up for me. Even so, I had to wait until Ryuta came into my life before I found the energy to become involved in this organization in a very serious way.

It is undoubtedly the case that when circumstances take a turn for the better they do so in earnest. At the same time that I became aware of the Occur group I came across another group with members in their twenties and thirties who were going about the business of publishing a handbook for homosexuals. They planned to respond to the difficulties faced by homosexuals by increasing public awareness of the issues involved and explaining that homosexuality was not abnormal. They sought to portray the situation of homosexuals in Japan rather than just produce a book of general interest. I got involved in this and used my connections to find a publisher for the book. Later, 'N' came aboard, saying he wanted the voice of homosexual teenagers themselves to be published. This project took nearly two years before, in the spring of 1986, we produced the first book written in Japan by homosexuals about homosexuals. It was entitled '*Boyfriends for Boys*'[21] and was published by Shōdensha. This book is still available today. When I read it now, though, I feel it doesn't go beyond an analysis of the gay scene of that time. It doesn't address issues such as how homosexuals might live as a minority in society or what is needed for this to be accomplished. I now feel that it lacks something in its failure to address these issues. Nevertheless, in attempting to accurately portray the gay scene in Japan as it was then, working on this book provided the impetus for me to feel a new sense of hope. It provided the first real opportunity for me to look at myself and my situation in a cool, collected and objective way. Furthermore, despite the fact that, with the exception of 'N', my working association with the members of the group which formed the authorship of '*Boyfriends for Boys*' (they remained anonymous) ceased after the book's publication and our lives drifted apart, the very fact that we were friends without any sexual involvement and that we were able to produce a book together were factors that contributed to a considerable stabilizing of my frame of mind. I was delighted with this.

I am not the only homosexual. There is a network of support.

For homosexuals, after you have become aware of what you are, the question of how soon you can meet other homosexuals and forge friendships becomes vitally important. Just being able to gain reassurance, through contact with other homosexuals who are real live people, that you are not the only homosexual in the world proves a tremendous source of relief. Although recently we have seen some increase in the media's interest in news items relating to homosexuals, and more and more features in the press, there are still many homosexuals who, due to their family circumstances, are unable to write any form of letter which relates to this subject and who can't summon the courage to visit gay bars or join any gay groups. This is particularly the case in country areas where the absolute number of homosexuals in the community is small. They simply don't have the opportunity to meet any other homosexuals. For this reason we can sometimes feel like we have gained a million allies just by reading a newspaper article that merely acknowledges the existence of homosexuals. Confidence in oneself is bolstered by the realization that there are many homosexuals, both in historical and geographical terms. Homosexuals have existed at all times and continue to exist in all places and, therefore, considering homosexuals to be queer is something that is queer in itself.

If you can meet a homosexual who doesn't submit to the dictates of mainstream society by getting married, you can speak right out, without embarrassment or shame, against the logic of exclusion that the homophobic mind invariably fosters. This idea of exclusion is embraced by homophobes simply because they are afraid that their own concept of rationality and their understanding of the world will be turned upside down if they do other than reject those of a different sexual persuasion. Such heterosexuals put forward arguments such as 'Not marrying and having children goes against the way set down for man, it's just not natural'. In this connection I might add that if that were the case it would be very difficult to explain the number of single people who always feature in statistics that show the male/female ratio of the adult population. Does the rationality in question mean that married couples who are unable to have children, due to sickness or whatever reason, are eccentric because they deviate from the norm? What about sex for pleasure that doesn't involve procreation? Any number of examples can be cited to counter the arguments of homophobic rationality. Engaging in sexual activity to confirm one's love or to gain pleasure should be the natural path that humans follow. In our species the genes have been programmed such that homosexuals will always exist in our midst. In the company of a homosexual who has resisted the pressure to get married, that part of you which is always misrepresented and concealed in heterosexual company, for the time being at least, ceases to be something you are conscious of the need to be able to satisfactorily explain in accordance with the dictates of mainstream society. It ceases to be something akin to a character stain you feel you must hide or a wound you feel you must be ever ready to explain. I say 'for the time being at least' not only because you are able to relax your guard for the duration of the time you are with the homosexual in question, but also because in the long term homosexuals aim for a society without discrimination and prejudice, one in which they won't be perpetually worn down to the point of mental exhaustion from being guarded about their lives when in the company of heterosexuals. Perhaps this point is obvious and doesn't require stating but when speaking with homosexuals there is none of the stress which accompanies forcing yourself to join in conversations that you don't want to be part of. Here I am referring to the sort of conversations you are subjected to when heterosexuals talk about the opposite sex, a subject which accounts for a considerable proportion of their conversation. You are able to speak freely from the heart, grumble about heterosexuals and speak openly of the popular idols you like in the entertainment world and about your love life and the difficulties you face in life. The mere awareness of the possibility of there being such a person to talk to dramatically decreases the amount of energy you must expend on creating your 'other face'.

The first time you come across a homosexual who asks nothing more than a clear cut 'yes' or 'no' question as to whether or not you two could become friends and possibly partners, and then if the answer is 'no' simply wants to know if you could just have sex together, can be something of a wretchedly sobering experience. I know this well, having been through a period in my own life which involved such an experience. When such encounters come in succession the result can be that some homosexuals start to lose their faith in society as well as feeling naive for not realizing that there are frivolous individuals to be found among homosexuals just as there are among heterosexuals. For them it is not a question of whether there are more or fewer of them, but simply the rude realization that such insincere homosexuals exist. They start to feel that perhaps there aren't any homosexuals who are sincere, genuine and serious about forming long term relationships of mutual support. I was feeling like this when Ryuta came into my life.

Nowadays, however, there are homosexual networks that can be accessed by those in need. It is now possible for homosexuals to obtain a great deal more knowledge and information about the question of homosexuality than ever before. Moreover, it is not necessary to wait until you first meet another homosexual to access this network and obtain information. The availability of this network has resulted in a very welcome decrease in the number of people who are consumed with the fear that if they are not successful in forming a partnership with one particular person they face the prospect of never having the opportunity to meet anyone else. The tragedy and drama that I experienced in trying to get to meet other homosexuals is, thankfully, becoming increasingly less common.

3 Explanation Notebook

From Us, Members of a Social Minority to You, Members of the Social Majority.

1 The homosexual lifestyle

For the first time in a long time, a great altercation with my partner – over my aged mother.

The other day I had a great argument with Ryuta, the first in a long time. It started at the beginning of our date. Whilst out on a drive, I got angry with him and, stopping the car on the roadside, said 'Why don't you get out then?' Ryuta actually did get out, walked away and disappeared. I was left to drive round and round looking for him. What a day that turned out to be! Both he and I can be fairly stubborn individuals at times and on occasions we must pay the price for this. Anyway, we were discussing an alumni meeting of my mother's old high school when this altercation occurred and it resulted in my clamming up and sulking! The alumni had been meeting for more than fifty years but the woman who had assumed responsibility for organizing the meetings had recently passed away and it looked as though this get together would be the last.

Tension had been building up between my mother and me. I was trying to come to terms with the changing circumstances that had precipitated this tension in our lives. My mom, who will turn seventy-nine on her birthday this year (1993), rapidly became hard of hearing two to three years ago. It reached the point where she could hardly hear people talking on the telephone. She often misheard things I said and made totally unrelated responses. When I came home late at night, tired after a long day's work, I would get sullen if I found her hard to communicate with and would reproach her in a ridiculously loud voice, saying things like 'I said so-and-so, didn't you hear?' In the end, when things got too heated, mom would be reduced to tears, and retreat into a stony silence for a while. Then she would come out with comments such as, 'So I should just go off and die, should I? And to think of all I've done for you though my legs used to sometimes nearly kill me! It hasn't been easy for me, by any means!' Of course, I couldn't walk away from that and just leave things as they were, so I would try to settle matters by giving her a hug. Such histrionic dramas were played out in our house from time to time.

You see I could not accept my aging mom as she now was, and was foolish enough to expect her to still be the young and fit mother I used to know. I was terribly saddened by the aging process I was witnessing her go through and I didn't want to accept it. Mom didn't accept it very well either. When she couldn't catch what I was saying, rather than acknowledge that she couldn't hear she would just answer as she thought appropriate. This annoyed me terribly, thus setting up a vicious circle. And yet I was already showing her as much patience and consideration as I was capable of. In anger I would shout unreasonable things such as 'How am I supposed to make myself heard?' even though I guess mom would have liked to have known the answer to this question herself! When things got to this stage mom would, as a token of resistance, mumble something along the lines of, 'You really are persistent. You don't give up, do you?' I could never resist continuing the quarrel by shouting something like, 'Don't talk behind my back'. Unfailingly, her retort would be, 'Never lets up with the shouting'. Every time I shouted in anger she would close off that much more from me. I doubled my efforts to say things clearly, never comprehending that she simply wasn't able to hear. As a result even the way we argued changed. It used to be that whenever I would get angry at her she would be able to hold her own and fire salvos back at me, but now she would be easily moved to tears and the communication which until then had taken the form of verbal arguments, was no longer possible. I found this very exasperating. When Ryuta turned up at our house I would continue to have spasms of temper and, although I would do my best not to let my frustrations get on top of me, when I was alone with him I would cry my heart out on his shoulder. The whole thing was an exercise in stress.

I was always concerned for my mother and when Ryuta and I would go off somewhere on holiday I would get overly worried about her being left on her own. In the past she had forgotten to turn the gas off once or twice, burning things which had been left simmering on the stove, so I used to approach relatives about keeping an eye on her while we were away – only to be taken to task by them! When we did eventually get away from the house it would take me ages to appreciate the fact that mom was actually quite capable of doing things for herself. This was a real dilemma for me. I was at quite a loss to know how on earth I should approach the question of forging a relationship with my mother under such circumstances.

Working with my partner to somehow find a way of forming a good relationship with my aging mother.

I discussed this question in great depth with Ryuta, trying hard to appreciate mom's words to me, 'When you get old yourself you'll see how hard it is'. I came to realize that it didn't really matter if some of the finer details of the things that were said were misheard or indeed if we weren't always talking about quite the same thing. All that was needed was for us to take it easy, to go with the flow and let things we miss slip by. Firstly, I was to refrain from getting angry and shouting. A secondary and less direct cause of the situation that needed to be addressed was my hectic lifestyle and I hoped to work on changing that because, as I was always busy and pressed for time, I tended to act in a self-centred way, always putting my own schedule first. An example of what I am referring to here relates to the fact that my mom, who was living on her own, was always anxious to engage me in conversation the moment I got home. This was a source of frustration for me as I would come home tired and just wanting to have a few moments of peace and quiet before anything else. But there was no chance of this and I had to do my best to lend an ear to mom the minute I walked in the door.

One of Ryuta's suggestions for forging a new sort of relationship with my mother was to get her to teach me a bit of cooking. I must do this one day. I haven't got around to it as yet!

I was still in a quandary about how I should adjust to living with someone who was becoming hard of hearing when a development occurred which would prove to be something of a turning point in my relationship with my mom. In the spring of the previous year Ryuta had passed an advertising leaflet to me and suggested that perhaps the place being advertised would be able to help us out. It was a small hearing-aid centre. The trouble was that mom's pride wouldn't allow her to rely on a hearing aid, so I took the bull by the horns and, in a pretence of taking her shopping, put her into the car, took her to the place in question and pressed her into going inside, suggesting that at least we should hear what they had to say. The shop manager was, as anticipated, a most friendly person. He placated my mother and sympathized with her, nodding to her (there is something for me to learn here, too) as she stuck to her guns and claimed that she could hear well enough but the problem was that the young people spoke so quickly. He tested her hearing and explained that it was a natural enough process to find yourself becoming hard of hearing as you got on in years, but added that, 'If you were to employ the services of a hearing-aid...' He went on, arguing along these lines. He was really most persuasive and selected a hearing-aid for my mother to try. Neither my mother nor I had been aware of it but not only do modern hearing-aids have a greatly improved performance (the old-fashioned ones used to pick up and magnify every sound there was), they are also small and almost undetectable. We were both surprised by all of this. Mom was unreservedly satisfied with what she had been shown and decided to buy one. Mom's walk back to the car was brisk, at more than twice the pace of the heavy steps she had taken on the way into the shop. With this one purchase communication with my mother became comfortable again and I found myself once again able to tell her about what was happening in my life. Our conversations came back to life. That day saw an end to the unpleasantness we had been experiencing due to her hearing problems. Subsequently, arguments between us virtually ceased.

Having said this, there is no getting away from one's age. Since the latter half of last year the pains in mom's legs have been quite severe and after walking she complains that her legs are killing her. She was never really one for running around and with her legs causing so much pain she found herself increasingly disinclined to go out. This was a constant worry for me. I couldn't help thinking that we should try to 'cure' her legs and somehow stop the aging process. I wanted somehow to fully accept my aged mother as she now was and to put the relationship between us on a new plane, one where I could interact with her in a natural way. This wasn't to be, however, as I lacked training in this discipline and still found myself clashing with her from time to time. After finishing drafting this manuscript, however, I located a most genial bonesctting specialist who practises Oriental medicine and massage therapy and mom started going to him for massages. Once she started on his massage program things got a lot better and she started to return to her old self.

It was whilst I was being dogged by such trials and tribulations that Ryuta had summarily and casually said to me, 'You should let her do whatever she wants to' and it was the ignorance of the mental anguish I was going through which he displayed by saying this, that sent me into the moody silence referred to in the previous section. In the end, as a result of her friend's telephone call, mom decided that she would go to her school reunion and I booked a hire car to take her there and back. She thanked me, later reporting that she was very glad she had gone. When this incident had blown over Ryuta said to me (even though I had been at fault), 'I didn't give sufficient thought to the difficult situation you were in, Nyāgo. If we were to live together we would be able to share the burden of your mother from now on and your personal troubles might be halved'. Thank you Ryuta. I love you for caring.

In the homosexual lifestyle there is no division of labour based on gender.

At long last it has come to pass that Ryuta and I will live together at my house with my mother. We fully expect that we will come up against many hurdles which will require skill to negotiate, not the least of which will be our relationship with my mother. However, as can be seen in Ryuta's words above, the two of us even thrill at the prospect of the invigoration to be experienced after over-coming these difficulties.

We care not a toss for the immense restrictions which the rationality of the majority in society represents and which bind the thinking of heterosexuals hand and foot. This is because we are able to map out our own lifestyle on a blank canvass with complete freedom. There is no need for Ryuta or me to refer to each other using the terms 'husband' or 'wife' or 'father' or 'mother', terms which by their very use give rise to all manner of constraints in terms of social roles and expectations. We will decide how to divide up the jobs that need to be done in our life together by discussing them together and we accept that we will be able to change the decisions thus made at anytime, depending on prevailing circumstances. If one party likes cooking it is easy enough to have that person prepare the food and the other do the cleaning up afterwards and likewise it could be that we both prepare the food together and do the cleaning up together. Every day will offer something new and fresh to experience. As there are no fixed roles for us there is no need for us to be untrue to ourselves. We have no preconceived images to live up to and are able to breathe easy as we open up to each other. We are able to open our hearts and bear our souls to each other without worrying about how the other party might feel about what we say. In fact it is because of this that we are able to offer each other exactly the support we require. In addition we are even able to preserve a level of privacy which I imagine is all but lost when heterosexuals get married. I should especially like to mention in this regard that, although we are both partial to availing ourselves of each others' kindness and occasionally being pampered, there are times when both Ryuta and I choose to be alone, times when we each like to listen to our own music and times when we prefer to sleep separately. That is why what we have in mind in this house, which has a kitchen and four other rooms, is for the three of us to have a room each and the fourth room to be a living room for Ryuta and me to share. With this arrangement, we will be able to be together or have personal space to ourselves depending on our mood on any given day. We predict that allowing such distance will, contrary to what people might think, prove to be a factor in preserving stability in our relationship. As for sex, we can have this in either one's room. It will be interesting for each of us to 'visit' the independent space of the other. We will be able to live together while each still has his own world. There will be no need for the troublesome aspects of a relationship that accompany an accepted marriage arrangement. And although it is still very difficult in Japan, if we were to ever feel that we would like to try our hand at child rearing we would probably even be able to adopt a child and take that responsibility on too. We'll get by as long as one of us is working or, alternatively, we can both go out to work. The notion that 'the man must go out to work' and 'the woman must look after the house' simply doesn't come into the picture in our case. There is no way that pursuing this sort of relationship could be anything other than enjoyable.

For the benefit of those heterosexuals who are not familiar with the situation modern, forward-thinking homosexuals are in, I should point out that the traditional notion of dividing work up according to the preconceived categories of the 'man's role' and the 'woman's role' is fast becoming a thing of the past for homosexual couples, although it was once fairly common. In times when homosexuals had to go to extraordinary lengths to hide their sexuality and when trying to meet other homosexuals proved to be a terribly difficult job, they were placed in a position where they simply didn't know, nor could they imagine, what form their love or their relationship might take. The only role models they had were heterosexuals. It can be presumed from this that homosexual couples felt that their relationships had to reflect the gender roles which applied to heterosexual couples. Therein lies the explanation of the genesis of the notion of male/female roles in the lives of homosexual couples. Such poor role models as those who pressed themselves into what might be described as 'the gender-based role model mould' are of course no longer needed these days. We see more and more young couples who are truly equal partners in a way that heterosexual couples are unable to be. Heterosexual couples cannot emulate the parity of esteem that is displayed in homosexual partnerships.

On this point I would like to make mention of the fact that the Japanese terms *tachi*, to refer to the one who takes the active role in relation to sex and *neko*[1], in reference to the passive partner, are all but extinct. This is only to be expected given that even amongst heterosexuals the idea that the man must instigate sex and the woman should remain passive is now outmoded. We have to realize that each party's excitement of the other enhances the experience of mutual pleasure. The idea assigned to the instigator of the sexual activity, namely that he should be able to expect a one-way provision of service, lacks any appreciation of mutual sexual pleasure. Likewise, the suggestion that the passive partner should do nothing but be on the receiving end is nothing more than self-justification of indolence. I accept that some will claim that how they approach sexual activity is a matter of individual taste, but it is certainly a fact that where one partner takes responsibility for all the action and the other participates only passively, it is extremely unlikely that the couple will ever experience the greatest heights of physical pleasure. I do believe that most heterosexuals really miss out on some things in this regard. If only they were able to allow themselves to question, however slightly, the fixed format as laid down by the majority in society, something which they unquestioningly accept and deem to be 'common sense', and by questioning this escape from the restrictions which it imposes, they would discover a quite new, refreshing and enjoyable approach to their relationships. They would no longer need to worry themselves about getting into a rut as a result of doing nothing other than that prescribed in the sex manual produced by the heterosexual majority in society. I believe that people do themselves a disservice by limiting their own potential and narrowing their views of the world if their sexual life is governed by what they believe members of one sex or the other generally should or should not do. This argument extends beyond the realm of sexual activity. Insisting, for example, that 'women should not smoke' or that 'boys should not cry' is the sort of generalized notion that surely acts to limit the potential of individuals. Could we not loosen up on the slavish adherence society demonstrates to such gender-based notions of what constitutes acceptable and unacceptable behaviour?

When people of the mindset described above come across homosexuals they find themselves all at sea. They are quite at a loss to know what to do, as homosexuality falls outside their understanding of the realm of 'common sense'. It would never occur to them, for example, to reassess their own position and perhaps expand the parameters of their interpretation of rationality as it applies to human sexuality. What is an even more disturbing thing is that those who do not wish to have their own little stable, steady, settled, staid and stationary worlds threatened do everything they can to actively reject homosexuality and ostracize homosexuals.

The next section can be read as something like my medical prescription for the treatment of homophobia.

2 From me, the homosexual to you, the heterosexual

Discrimination against homosexuals which is instinctive, based on it being considered a sickness or based on religious grounds.

When it comes to defending discrimination against homosexuals the first argument to be brought up is usually 'human instinct'. Now whilst it is true that humans are generally programmed to produce offspring, and having children is considered to be linked to prosperity, it is also true to say that this programming doesn't apply to all people. The human experience is too rich to be coloured only one hue. Yet often people can't entertain the notion of the existence of humans who have been programmed differently to the majority. Science has, as yet, been unable to shed any light on what it is that causes people to be attracted to the opposite sex. In precisely the same way as this question eludes scientific explanation, it also remains a mystery why homosexuals are attracted to their own gender. Thus it is that we always ask heterosexuals the question 'Have you ever stopped to think why it is that you are attracted to the opposite sex?'

When they find that they can't follow through on the 'instinct' argument they hit upon the safe idea of declaring homosexuality a 'sickness'. They claim that it must come about as a result of some kind of a flaw somewhere, in other words that an 'irregularity' must have somehow occurred. Some elaborate explanations put it down to a confusion of sexual orientation resulting from a male being kept in confined conditions for a long period of time with only other males for company. Alternatively they might argue that homosexuality represents a developmental stage that all people must go through on the journey to heterosexuality. Protagonists of this argument claim that the question of homosexuality is only a matter of some people stopping *en route*, as it were. Others may argue that the family or local environment has warped the formation of the personality of the individual in question. It is not unknown for some parents to try to put their children into mental homes when they realize that they are homosexual. Unfortunately for such heterosexuals, however, medical science in relation to mental illness is far more advanced than it used to be and nowadays there are no doctors who would agree to try to 'cure' homosexuality if approached to do so. Homosexuality was removed from the list of mental illnesses a long time ago in both America and Japan.

There simply is no established theory to explain how homosexuality comes about. We are not able to state anything beyond the fact that somewhere along the line the human race has been programmed to bear a certain proportion of homosexuals in its ranks. It used to be (and in some places still is) the case that a barbaric 'treatment' took place that involved giving electric shocks to someone when he was aroused by a picture of a member of the same sex. This was carried out in order to cancel any feelings of attraction and thus correct the sexual orientation of the individual. Surely this sort of torture represents a splendid example of crime!

If homosexuality is not to do with a flaw somewhere in the person's make-up, the next argument people latch onto is 'religion'. This is something they can depend upon. All sects of Christianity and Islam reject homosexuality on the grounds that it goes against 'Divine Providence'. Between them these two religions account for nearly 40% of the world's population so they are potent forces in terms of shaping public opinion. In very, very general terms we can say that Buddhism does not reject homosexuality as such. It acknowledges various viewpoints in terms of what sex should be and it says that what is aimed at is a transcendence of one's sexual urges. Recent research into the two big religions reveals that their prohibition of homosexuality came about because in the distant past, when they were new, fledgling religions struggling to gain a foothold in the world, they felt it necessary to encourage the birth of many children in order to increase the number of followers they had and thus propagate their beliefs and in turn extend their spheres of influence in the world. That idea has been carried through unchanged right up to the present day. Thus we can state that the argument for the prohibition of homosexuality by religions is built on a very shaky foundation. Ironically, this history serves to prove that there were gays around in times long past, but heterosexuals would hardly be inclined to give countenance to this assertion.

In order for religions to gain solidarity they need an enemy. In the absence of any enemy it is common for 'heretics' to be concocted. Allow me to give an example that is far more disturbing than the practice of holding witch-hunts. In Christian societies, until quite recently, left-handedness was deemed to be the work of the devil and those unfortunate people who were born that way were openly discriminated against. Some were even executed. When left-handed children were born parents would do their utmost to rectify their child's condition. The reason for this was that the churches took it upon themselves to incorporate into their dogmas the idea that 'left' was unclean while 'right' was clean. Get it? Right is right! If you consider discrimination on the basis of left-handedness to be absurd, would you not find it just possible to imagine homosexuals as the left-handers of the world of sexuality?

When the case against homosexuality based on religious teachings is discounted, there is no further argument for people to fall back on. Okay then, the next strategy we find employed is people calling upon the strength of the majority in society to place a legal ban on the offending practice. This is formidable stuff! A well known case in point relates to the remaining sodomy laws in the U.S., mostly in the South. According to the letter of the law, no sexual contact other than heterosexual intercourse in the 'normal' position is legally acknowledged or sanctioned in the states involved. The laws in question are something of a mysterious masterpiece of legislation which shores up the notion that the common belief of the majority constitutes an absolute truth that is not to be questioned. It is pretty frightening to think that those caught engaging in homosexual activities, which are described as representing the last step before the degeneration of civilization, get arrested and are dealt with by the law. Let's not forget Iran, where male homosexuals are subject to corporal punishment but where the punishment for women is comparatively quite light, 'just' a whipping. We look with envy at places like Holland and France where their constitutions declare it illegal to discriminate against people on the basis of sexual orientation.

In 1992 Amnesty International, a body that helps prisoners of conscience – the political prisoners of the world (that is to say the people who have been thrown into prison simply because they have

different ideas to the governments of the countries they live in) –
at long last included homosexuals as a category of people to be
considered for assistance. We can take some heart also in the fact
that the number of countries and states around the world which are
considering giving homosexuals the same rights as heterosexuals
is on the increase. This is something that has, in all places, come
about only as a result of movements where homosexuals have put
their lives and livelihoods on the line. Virtually no heterosexual
has mediated to assist this world trend.

**My response to the argument that Japan is still one of the better
places to be, as homosexuality isn't proscribed by religion or law.**

From time to time, one hears a homosexual express the sentiment
that 'Japan is still one of the better places for homosexuals to live'.
Unlike America, we don't have groups aiming to eradicate
homosexuals nor do we have anything resembling the sodomy laws
they have there. Nor do we have corporal punishment, as in Iran.
In Japan the influence wielded on society by religious beliefs is
relatively small and it is true to say that in this country, just because
you are homosexual doesn't mean that you will automatically find
your life endangered or that you must live in fear of being arrested
by the police. So, while pursuing your everyday life in the
heterosexual world, it is possible to lead another life, one of stealth,
in a dark, sub-culture world, putting up with the duplicity involved
in never explicitly behaving like a homosexual but always giving
an outward appearance of heterosexuality. It is because this
duplicity is possible that I cannot condone marriages where the
man's heart is not in it and where his marriage partner is hurt as a
result of his being incapable of loving her. Conversely, I believe
that nothing could be unhappier than the situation where two
people are in love with each other but where they are unable to
share their lives openly and with dignity.

On this point it is noteworthy that young homosexuals these
days seem very sure-footed. It is often the case that they state
unequivocally that they never feel like going out with a member
of the opposite sex who has marriage in mind. Thus, when they find
themselves involved with a member of the opposite sex who has
ambitions in this regard, they are forced to declare to her that they

are homosexual in order to avoid any misreading of the situation. At times like this, as I have mentioned earlier, heterosexuals are apt to indicate a rejection of homosexuality by displaying all sorts of negative reactions. They do this out of a fear borne of leaving the comfort zone of 'common sense' and the accepted world known to them. It is a reaction based on the mindset of the heterosexual majority that sees conformity as an integral element of social unity and harmony, and is not something which has to do with any legal or religious considerations. Having said this, there are also people who, even though they do not subscribe to any religion, find it suits them to suddenly bring up arguments relating to 'God' and 'the essence of human nature' when confronted with the question of homosexuality, even though they never do so at other times.

I don't believe that it is simply the case that in their minds they seek to deny the existence of homosexuals and come to voice this using religion as a backup argument. The cause of their distrust of homosexuality and unwillingness to consider it with an open mind runs deeper than this. We often observe, especially in the case of men, that when they learn that one of their male friends is homosexual they become seized by a sense of fear, wondering what they should do if attacked. It is by no means unusual to come across this school of over-reactors who jump a mile when you happen to brush past them and who avoid sleeping in the same room as you. Surely such reactions must represent a classic case of exposing an underlying fear based on ignorance and prejudice.

If you think of it another way, what we are actually saying could be interpreted as an acknowledgment of the fact that there are men who are prepared to seduce women at the drop of a hat. In a sense, the situation described depicts a splendid reversal of roles for such men. It is as though the tables have been turned and these men now consider themselves to be in the position of the woman with the homosexuals as the predators. This just demonstrates how, ordinarily, such men would see a woman as simply an object of their sexual desires. With the tables turned they perceive themselves to be in the position of the one likely to be seduced! The way that they normally see the world is exposed and they feel a sense of fear at being placed in what they perceive to be a vulnerable position. Their understanding of the distinction between the role of the male and the role of the female comes to the fore vividly, with the male being perceived as the predator and the female as the one subject to male advances. In fact, there are some male heterosexuals who, having come into contact with homosexuals, demonstrate the degree of ignorance they had held in relation to the question of the roles men and women play in the heterosexual world by saying things like 'I was never before able to understand how a woman must feel' and 'I was able to imagine that it must be frightening for a woman to be alone amongst a crowd of men'.

To give a slant on this from the homosexual viewpoint, I should mention that there is no such thing as a homosexual who feels that he wants to sleep with just anyone as long as he is a man. The great majority of homosexuals disregard heterosexuals as potential partners from the outset and the question of preying on women just doesn't come into the picture. As for forcing sex on someone when sharing the same room to sleep, there are far, far more instances of this amongst heterosexuals. People should not be so arrogantly vain as to take it on themselves to presume that the homosexual who is beside them will have any feeling of desire in relation to them!

I would like to further consider the arguments against those who assert that Japan is still one of the better countries for homosexuals to live in. Let's look at schools and business enterprises. Here, the mindset of the majority in society forms the nucleus of their operating principles. Accordingly, any difference or sign of individuality displayed by a member of the organization will, in all cases, be eliminated unless it represents some particular benefit to the organization. This is because in Japan, in particular, manifesting corporate strength to the maximum level possible in a framework of unified action as an organization takes precedence over concerns relating to individual or personal levels of competence and ability. This manifestation of corporate strength takes many and varied forms. For example, whilst those in the teaching profession are held in high esteem by the community and considered to be reliable sources of authority whose credibility is beyond question, it is this very sector of society which persists in trying to gently persuade homosexuals to change to become heterosexuals. The actions of such educationalists are based on what can best be described as a self-endorsed interpretation of rationality as they understand it. This interpretation is deemed to be an absolute truth that must be passed on from generation to generation.

As far as the school is concerned it is simple enough, you either give homosexual teachers the sack or steer them clear of conducting the important duty of encouraging students to acknowledge heterosexuality as being the accepted, desirable goal of society. Everyone must bend to the idea of homogeneity. Students who have succumbed to this homogenizing process and who no longer question it hound homosexuals into a fear of attending school and subsequently into withdrawing from it completely. They do this by initially making 'fun' of them, with this later leading onto harassment.

Work colleagues who have succumbed in a similar way hound homosexuals into quitting their jobs and leaving the company at which they are employed. Again this is done by initially making them the butt of jokes and jibes, with this later leading onto full-blown harassment. Even if the situation doesn't quite reach that stage the very least that happens is that the value placed on a person and his work and achievements is greatly reduced as a result of his minority sexual persuasion. It becomes impossible for him to have his true level of ability judged accurately simply by virtue of the fact that he is homosexual. It doesn't occur to heterosexuals that this behaviour is discrimination defined. It hangs over my head as I write this book: I stand to lose my job at the preparatory school and face losing opportunities for work as a writer as consequences.

The Education Department's charter states that homosexuality runs counter to the moral code of a healthy society and that it acts to destabilize the sexuality aspect of the public social order.

I would like now to quote some passages from a document entitled '*Basic Data Relating to Student Problem Behaviour, the Junior and Senior High School Edition*'. It is published by the Ministry of Education and remains the guidebook set down for all educational committees to follow, even though it hasn't been revised since 1979. It must be considered to be a source of authority, even today. I would like to draw your attention to a section of Chapter 4, which is entitled 'Sexual Aberrations':

'Part 4. Sexual Perversions.
Section 5. Homosexuality:
   The situation where sexual activity takes place between members of the same sex. As for the cause, there are instances where the principal cause is congenital and examples where normal heterosexual love turns, for whatever reason, to a feeling of loathing and, as is the case of dormitory arrangements, we find that an outlet for sexual urges is sought in a love directed towards the same sex. This is due to the absence of members of the opposite sex. It is often the case that as students get older they return to being normal but it sometimes is the case that homosexuality is carried over into adulthood.
   Whilst in America and other places we witness the appearance of citizens' movements which look at this issue from the angle of the acquisition of citizens' rights, generally speaking we can say that homosexuality brings with it a fear of the obstruction of healthy, heterosexual development. Homosexuality works against the accepted norms of social morality and can be thought of as contributing to a breaking down of the established sexual public order of society. Consequently it should not be sanctioned in modern society'.

At a glance, this might appear to be presented in neutral terms, but these terms can be taken to mean very different things by different people. That is to say, terms such as 'acceptable human behaviour' and 'morals', or expressions such as 'normal', 'healthy' and 'public order', are all subjective and dangerous expressions by dint of their being open to very diverse interpretation. These terms can be used by people in positions of authority to dress up any argument that suits them; to afford it the cloak of respectability and have it accepted as being reasonable. They are typically interpreted by the majority in society in such a way that they deny validity to members of social minorities, representing them as not worthy of being considered on a par with members of the mainstream. Minorities are thus thought of as something less than human. It isn't long before members of minorities come to be seen as immoral, abnormal and unhealthy – a threat to the order of society no less! Terms which are very relative by nature, and which could never have absolute criteria attached to them, tend to be interpreted in many different ways. Often people are sent off on all sorts of tangents as a result of idiosyncratic interpretations that they apply to the sort of relative expressions mentioned. There are many dreadful cases of counsellor education and telephone and television consultations relating to concerns people have about homosexuality, and the sort of document referred to above simply doesn't help at all. It can be thought to be responsible for the dreadful advice some counsellors give. Citing just one example here will suffice to make my point. The following comment, reported in a certain magazine, comes from the so-called sex education specialist, Mr Yoshikazu Kurokawa:

'In their roles as husbands and wives, and in turn in their roles as fathers and mothers, people are able to find fulfilment in life and be happy, although this fulfilment and happiness brings with it a responsibility that must be shouldered. For homosexuals, however, the door to all of this is closed.'

By implanting this idea in the minds of people this 'specialist' encourages people to 'wash their hands of homosexuality'. The strength or persuasiveness of these views does not result from any sort of specialist knowledge, though. Rather, it is based on nothing other than the fact that it is the view held by the majority in society. When dressed up in academic jargon, these views can start to sound plausible. Rest assured that Ryuta and I lack no confidence in the fact that we are happy and find life fulfilling!

How to approach communication between homosexuals and heterosexuals.

Not all heterosexuals are so completely bound by the stipulated, 'common sense' view of the majority as to agree that it should be considered a mortal offence to be late for school[2] or that they label children delinquents for something like smoking behind their parents' backs. There are some heterosexuals who unreservedly acknowledge and accept the existence of homosexuals. Often such people are women, and the reason for this can be easily comprehended. Because they are women they have, for a long time, been prevented from doing that which they might have wanted to do in life. Not only have they not been given the opportunity to demonstrate and prove their capabilities to society they have, in fact, been singularly pressed into a life of carrying out house duties. For any woman who, even in a small way, identifies with the issue of the traditional lot of the Japanese woman and considers it to be one which concerns her personally, it should not be too difficult an exercise to see, or at least imagine, the parallels that exist between it and the lot of homosexuals in society. Even though they might not have a particularly great in-depth level of consciousness in relation to the issue of homosexuality it is, nonetheless, often the case that it is the mother who is the quicker party to accept a child's homosexuality. This is simply because it is her own child that is involved. Even so it may take a considerable time for her to accept the situation. The father[3], on the other hand, is so used to being the boss of the household and acting in a high and mighty manner that he might not be able to accept something which doesn't fit the familiar pattern of social arrangements.

All we would ask is that homosexuals be accepted as ordinary people. This requires that heterosexuals extend the courtesy of not changing their assessment of someone simply as a result of learning that that person is homosexual. This request extends to the issue of having sympathy for us. Sometimes there are heterosexuals who go through mental contortions in an attempt to somehow understand the feelings homosexuals have. These people perplex us more than anything else. Unless such people can somehow or other come to terms with something which is very foreign to their being and foreign to their personal concept-ualization of common sense, they just don't feel comfortable. They worry about whether or not homosexuality might be something that applies to them and they try their best to comprehend the emotions and feelings which are experienced by homosexuals. However, in the same way that homosexuals don't understand the attraction heterosexuals have for the opposite sex (and indeed formerly never attempted to), it is close to impossible for heterosexuals to conceptualize what having a different sexual orientation means. Nor is there any need for them to.

There are also heterosexuals who swing right the other way and, in the most extreme cases, idealize homosexuality. Suggestions are made that homosexuality is both beautiful and the ultimate expression of true love. They go on to say that homosexuals are pure because their genius is given priority over other things. Moreover, they claim that love between beautiful young men epitomizes supreme love. All I can say is that this sort of interpretation isn't helpful either, as the fact of the matter is that there are no differences whatsoever between homosexuals and heterosexuals in regards to being worthy of being placed on a pedestal. For homosexuals, as for heterosexuals, love takes many different forms. There are examples of homosexual love that is mushy and murky and equally there are examples of homosexual love that is fresh and pure. There are guys who are skilled at netting partners and, in just the same way as heterosexuals, there are times when homosexuals get entangled in love triangles.

Let me report here what a visually handicapped friend related to me on one occasion. He said:

'Nowadays, when a disabled person commits a crime, you can be sure it will be reported sympathetically. I figure that this is essentially a discriminatory practice. Of course the fact that disabled people in society are not given a 'fair go' can be a contributory factor in their committing crimes, but ignoring that fact for the moment, we should recognize that there are all sorts of different people who are disabled, both good and bad. It will only be when people don't feel awkward about reporting that those who have committed offences are in fact deserving of blame, irrespective of whether or not they are handicapped, that we will be 'released', as it were, and be seen to be on a par with everyone else'.

The point is that people should evaluate others by their words and deeds alone. They should not look at them through glasses tinted by prejudice. People should not form opinions or judge others simply on the basis of group association. By this I mean that identifying factors such as gender, sexuality and race, for example, should not be issues when evaluating an individual's worth. Likewise the presence or absence of some disability or the part of the country from which an individual hails should not be allowed to give rise to preconceptions about the sort of person someone is.

It is true, however, that just as the groupings with which people are identified vary, so too do the ways in which the people belonging to these groups see things. I believe that widening your view of the world by becoming aware of such differences, in other words, by having a sense of curiosity about things and an interest in finding out about alternatives to the things which you know about from your own world, is desirable and should always be welcomed. As for me, I find it easier to respond to questions people have about homosexuals or homosexuality when I am asked in a simple, straightforward way, as opposed to being questioned in an awkward and analytical way. I feel that prejudice most easily dissipates when I'm asked things in an uncomplicated way.

You will appreciate, however, that certain lines of questioning can invite my anger when there is no willingness on the part of heterosexuals to question their own understanding of the world. In certain cases it is necessary for people to have a somewhat flexible approach to accepting changes to the fixed ideas that they have in relation to the world. Having said this, the other day a heterosexual said to me, 'I'm not able to ask many things because I don't know what will cause offence'. Further, he asked, 'Ought you not refrain from getting angry at ignorant people and instead cultivate patience and try to convince them of your arguments?' I consider the former comment to be a way of avoiding the issue, a cop out. You have to think, do you not, that unless you get embroiled in a discussion of some sort with people who identify with a different social grouping, or in much broader terms, with people who hold views that are different to yours, you'll never be able to properly understand them. With this in mind, my response to the second comment he made would be that unless you get angry when you have been misunderstood or unfairly treated, your position will never be truly appreciated or understood by the other party.

The terms used by the majority in society in reference to homosexuals.

When engaging with heterosexuals in the sort of communication referred to above, one thing that often presents itself as a problem is the question of how to refer to homosexuals. I didn't use a word processor when preparing this manuscript and having to write out the long terms 'homosexual' and 'heterosexual'[4] every single time I wanted to use them was a bit troublesome. Be this as it may, these are the terms I used. When speaking also, as far as possible, these are the expressions I get by with. Only when it is necessary to speed things up somewhat do I use the terms 'gay' and 'lesbian'.

Not surprisingly, often the terms used to refer to minorities are chosen and popularized by the majority. Even though the members of the minority may feel unhappy with the expressions chosen, they find that the pressure of numbers means that these terms get used generally and, inevitably, they take on something of a pejorative nuance. People in positions of authority consciously put labels on minority groups, even on occasions fostering discrimination towards them, in order to divert unwelcome attention from themselves. Consequently, the terms '*okama*'[5] and '*homo*' are used with very negative, disparaging connotations by the majority. The term '*okama*' refers to one's buttocks and the term '*homo*' is short for the respectable term 'homosexual'. It is an abbreviation, like 'Jap', which is used where the original word is deemed not worthy of being stated in full. Often such abbreviations become terms of deprecation. It is for this reason that I don't like using the abbreviated expression 'les'. The expression 'gay' comes from the adjective meaning 'bright' or 'cheery' and is a term homosexuals chose to use for themselves but the nuance it embraces changes when it is used in mainstream society by heterosexuals. Insofar as 'gay' is a term selected by homosexuals to refer to themselves, it can be considered the second best choice as a term of reference. The terms 'homo' and 'gay' initially were used in reference to both male and female homosexuals but things developed in such a way that their usage came to refer only to males. Sadly, this perhaps suggests that the liberation of lesbians lags behind that of male homosexuals.

In a nutshell then, there isn't any term of reference which can be applied to homosexuals which we can feel very comfortable using. Of course, no word in isolation, that is presented without any context, has derogatory connotations *per se*. It all depends on the intention of the person who uses it and the circumstances under which it is used. For many homosexuals, however, being made fun of by being called '*okama*' or '*homo*' or watching other homosexuals being treated with contempt through the use of such terms of reference is a fact of life, one which they cannot fail to be affected by. If human sexuality can be considered to essentially have a dual nature, I would say that having terms to represent both its component parts with equal respect and without discrepancy in the value or merit allotted to each is the way things should be. There is far too much discrepancy implied when the word pair 'homo' and 'hetero' is used. The same imbalance is seen when the terms 'gay' and 'straight' are used. In fact, strictly speaking, these are not even terms that are complements of each other. Until homosexuals come up with a pair of expressions that both provide complementation in terms of representing the duality of human sexuality and at the same time are a bit easier to understand and easier to say than 'homosexual' and 'heterosexual', these will remain the terms I choose to entrust my sentiments to.

The difficulty involved in announcing one's homosexuality to heterosexuals.

There is no reason to presume that heterosexuals have any idea just how stressful it is for homosexuals to continuously try to ensure that their secret doesn't get out. It is probably close to impossible for them to imagine just how much resolution and defiance is necessary for homosexuals to even consider announcing their sexuality to heterosexuals. When I first met Ryuta he spoke to me frequently of his fear, both when he was young and later as an adult, of his friends, one after another, moving away and his ending up alone. He was unable to speak about his sexuality with his friends. He tells how, whenever the conversation turned to the opposite sex, he would feign interest, tailoring what he said accordingly, in order to maintain appearances. He was always aware that he had a secret he was hiding from the person he was talking with. Likewise, when other matters were discussed, he held part of himself back; he was never able to become a really close friend, someone who could open up to anyone. For these reasons he would turn down invitations to socialize with his friends. He was hesitant to be the one to make the calls to friends and suggest meeting. In fact, that is not half of it. Simply meeting with heterosexuals became a stressful experience for him. Things got to the point where he feared meeting people face to face. This was an intensely heart-rending situation. He related to me that although the chance to talk about himself with friends did sometimes present itself, he felt he always missed the moment. He feared that if things were to continue on as they were he would end up having no friends.

I did my level best to encourage him but, as you might imagine, initially it was all I could do to comfort him. I could be of little support otherwise. In my case, however, building an unwavering relationship with Ryuta as a partner enabled me to extricate myself from the pitiful situation my love life was in. The joy and confidence I experienced as a result allowed me to speak out to my main friends and later, whenever the chance presented itself, to students with whom I was on particularly good terms. With these people I could finally broach the subject of my homosexuality and allude to the things which I have penned in this chapter. Thus my life started to undergo a major transformation.

I accept that those friends who couldn't accept me, even though I did my very best to explain my circumstances to them, were never really friends at all. At the end of the day, if all my friends desert me and I am left alone I will be alright as long as Ryuta stays by my side. That will be more than enough for me.

When you find a partner you love it is only natural that you want to arrange things so that you can spend as much time together as possible. I found that the way I related to people changed rapidly as a result of my acquiring a partner. The level of involvement I had with most people was based on an extremely broad yet shallow foundation, but with Ryuta the association I had was very deep. With other people my association always involved concealing the misery of my mental anguish. I always positively pursued contacts with people who were not your average Joe Blow, but rather people who had something special about them – interesting people who, though they were heterosexuals, were not held captive by the conformist mentality. I had so many such contacts that my long university holidays would be filled up just catching up with them all. Ryuta was initially very envious when he saw that I had contacts with so many different people. He came to believe, however, that homosexuals were best placed to understand other homosexuals and thus ceased being afraid of becoming alienated from heterosexual friends. He had a partner now, so he didn't have to worry! He stopped making contact with his heterosexual associates but from time to time would still be invited to *karaoke* by one of them. On one such occasion, when the opportunity presented itself, he seized the moment and stated to his friend that he was homosexual. He reported that the friend seemed really and truly stunned, unable to believe what he was being told. Their friendship, however, continues to this day, as strongly as ever.

There are some homosexuals who, despite the fact that marriage is out of the question for them, lead their whole lives doggedly resolving to hide their sexuality from society. They move far away from where their parents live and lead them to believe that they are just single men, ordinary bachelors. As for social contacts, they are very careful about where they have their dates and they always act in a very discreet way. At their place of work they are obliged to fit the mould of the majority every inch of the way, training their own consciousnesses to that end. And if things get just too hot in terms of suspicions being cast upon them, there is always the strategy of scraping their way out by claiming to be bisexual. As long as they state that they are attracted to members of the opposite sex heterosexuals will usually interpret any suspicions of same sex attraction as something of an aberration, albeit an off-colour one, and generally conclude that the person in question is basically straight but with an inexplicable, and most likely ephemeral, interest in his own sex.

I might mention here that I have never yet met a true bisexual person as such. In the final analysis, people are generally either heterosexual or homosexual. This is something which can be determined quite simply from their masturbation fantasies, that is to say from the sexual thoughts entertained when masturbating. It probably isn't the case that there aren't any bisexuals in the world, but I would think that there would be more homosexuals masquerading as bisexuals in society than actual bisexuals as such. As far as I am concerned, those who opt to follow this path in life will, somewhere along the line, be it sooner or later, find themselves in an untenable situation. I believe that this path will ultimately fail those who choose it and I suspect that the regret felt when this choice of path does prove a failure must be very great indeed. I myself used to respond to questions from students at the preparatory school as to whether or not I had a girlfriend by setting the situation up as though Ryuta were a girl, but it would end up being very difficult to keep it all coherent. As things are at the moment I don't believe we can blame people for concealing their homosexuality from society. I state this for two reasons. Firstly, because the circumstances which prevail in society are such that it is the narrow-minded rationality of heterosexuals that governs at every turn and end and secondly, because this means that the mental and physical inexpediencies encountered through being openly homosexual are still quite formidable to contend with.

Gays in their teens and twenties who are actively working to remove discrimination in relation to homosexuals.

I would like to tell you about the plight of Mr 'N', whom I have already intoduced. Mr 'N' is a representative of Taurus, a homosexual lobby and social interaction association based in Chiba Prefecture. Taurus' members try to live their lives true to themselves and their sexuality. (This is a different person to the Mr 'N' who was a founding member of the Gay and Lesbian Action Association, Occur). When his parents found out that he was homosexual his father drove him out of the house. He found a job at a gay bar and while working there related the following to me:

'All the customers who come into the bar are gentle-hearted, good men. When they hear that I am not living at home they do things like press ¥10,000 notes[6] into my hand, without seeking anything in return. Though they are so kind they are forced to live furtive, secret lives hiding from the mainstream society which does not sanction their existence. No opportunity is provided for them to ever be considered as worthy of belonging to mainstream society. They are rejected by society and forced to lead stealthy lives in a shadowy world. I would ask myself why such good people as these should be forced into such wretched existences. It was when I decided something had to be done to change things that I became aware of a group of people taking action in the courts over the fact that they had been refused the use of the Youth House in Fuchū on the grounds that they were homosexual. The Youth House is a public accommodation facility run by the municipality of Tokyo and supposedly available for the use of all ratepayers. Those instigating legal proceedings were members of the Gay and Lesbian Action Association. I was greatly encouraged by what they were doing and felt that I wanted to be active, as they were, and make a contribution to the struggle they represented. I wasn't so much thinking in terms of having society understand us, but rather making society acknowledge our rights'.

Clearly this man was speaking from the heart about something he very sincerely felt. 'N', who is now 22, initially became active by standing in front of railway stations and handing out leaflets by himself. Subsequently he formed Taurus, aiming to provide a forum through which homosexuals could meet and support one another. The Taurus group is imbued with a determination to fight to create a network through which homosexuals can find a way to live positive lives. Activists like Mr 'N' are growing in number across the country and are making their mark. I have joined the Gay and Lesbian Action Association as a support member and also hold the position of secretary in Taurus.

In stating the above I am acknowledging that Japanese homosexuals are changing. In recent times, there has been a rapid increase in the number who come out and tell their parents and friends that they are homosexual while in their teens. If their friends don't accept them, they resign themselves to the inevitable outcome in the knowledge that they will easily be able to make friends amongst other homosexuals. I am delighted that group networks have developed to the extent that getting to know other homosexuals is now possible. As for the question of informing parents, in my opinion it is better to deliver the shock earlier rather than later. By this I mean that the older parents become, the less they are able to comprehend things beyond their own experience and the lower their degree of tolerance. Accordingly, the longer you wait to break the news, the greater the shock. Here again, there is now a group network in place which can be consulted when encountering difficulties informing parents of your sexual orientation.

It is a great pity that, in response to these sorts of developments, there are examples amongst the senior generation of homosexuals of those who feel envy at the positiveness displayed by homosexual youths but who withdraw from it, saying things like, 'You'd be happier just leading your lives lying low and not drawing attention to yourselves through the courts' or making comments like, 'Nothing you do will change anything'. This attitude can be seen in the comment made by Osugi and Piko[7] who said, 'There are other very different ways of going about it' when criticising Occur's court action against the City of Tokyo.

Certainly for me, coming to terms with both my sexuality and my place in society represented a tremendous struggle, taking twenty-eight years for me to acknowledge myself as a homosexual and thirty-three years for me to find a partner. To be honest, I feel quite envious of those in their teens and twenties who are able to find release from their mental questioning and torment through at least knowing how to handle their feelings from a much earlier age than I was able to. It is because I had such a dreadful time that I believe homosexuals such as I must not let others go through what I went through. Naturally, I support the young homosexuals in their goals in life. I do not feel at all odd about working together with them to improve the lot of the homosexual. At the very least, I would like to see the work and pursuits of all those who are homosexual viewed with a far, far greater degree of tolerance by mainstream society than is currently the case.

Let me now point out something that, for some, only exacerbates an already unenviable situation. Homosexuals are not the only minority in Japanese society. It is clear that disabled people, those of Korean ancestry in Japan and the native *Ainu* people [8], for example, form minorities in our society. But also teachers who, like me, in the rigid framework of the school system seek to become part of the social life of students, constitute a substantial social minority. It follows, therefore, that in certain situations homosexuals, who are a minority group themselves, can form a majority grouping where there are minority groups existing within minorities. Some people can end up belonging to minorities two or three times over. Those who find themselves in this situation certainly have a real cross to bear. It is frequently the case that homosexuals, notwithstanding the fact that they themselves are members of a minority in society, cannot come to terms with other minorities in society. In one sense this is easy enough to understand, given that only the rationality of the majority in society is taught in schools, and in life the majority run the show. Minorities have no place in the accepted social set-up. For example, town planning is carried out in such a way that it allows the approval of designs for public developments which are difficult for disabled people to negotiate. Similarly, the position of a Japanese of Korean ancestry is so disadvantageous that legal restrictions come into play. Japanese born people of Korean descent cannot become government employees, nor can they vote! Minorities are never seen on the surface. This being the case it leads to certain minorities having great difficulty getting to know about other minorities. I would like us to find some way by which we could all expand our minds and join hands together, sharing that which we have in common as minorities in Japanese society.

3 Towards becoming a pioneering homosexual couple

The need to have an almost overconfidence in gay pride.

As I mentioned earlier, heterosexuals who harbour a phobia about homosexuals represent the overwhelming majority of people in society. Homosexuals are persecuted at school and at work. Those in the work force find that ultimately they are given the sack from their jobs. For more information on the persecution of homosexuals I urge you to read the *Gay Report* (published by Asuka Shinsha) edited by the Gay and Lesbian Action Association. In this report numerous examples of the consequences of naked prejudice are poignantly revealed. Homosexuals suffer in their dealings with heterosexuals in many different ways, from actions of direct discrimination to the silent pressure to conform which is applied by the majority. They suffer in both a private capacity and in a social capacity. The pressure to conform emanates from the majority as a blindness to the existence of minorities.

The other day I was speaking to a man who was training to become a Protestant pastor. When I told him I was a homosexual he said 'I don't intend to cut you out of my life but think carefully about your lifestyle and try discussing it with others. I'm not able to sanction homosexuality'. This was a most unpleasant encounter for me. The attitude this man showed is by no means restricted to people with religious affiliations. It is particularly striking in schools where they build up a profile of how people should be in order to comfortably fit the majority mould and all imagery centres on this portrayal of accepted respectability. Within this framework people's actions and people themselves are branded 'good' or 'bad' in a dualistic approach to classifying people and this goes unchallenged. It is probably easier that way for the authorities involved but surely they realize that human beings cannot be categorized so simplistically!

I am fully aware that I may lose my job as a result of this book going to print. This is why I strongly believe that, no matter what, we homosexuals should make heterosexuals (read 'the majority' or 'society in general') accept the reality of the fact that we are not ghosts or ghouls or anything of the sort and that we exist and live together with them as part and parcel of the fabric of society. When doing so we should not adopt the awfully servile attitude that I adopted in the past, an attitude marked by a terrible lack of confidence. I used to be what could be described in a good sense as someone who liked relating to people and in a bad sense as someone who was terribly dependent on others. I couldn't stand being so totally untrue to myself as I was when I remained silent on the question of homosexuality. When I first started admitting that I was homosexual to heterosexual friends it was as though I was prostrating myself, entreating them not to desert me. I did this because if they had walked away from me I would have been left alone and bereft of companionship. I would beg for their acceptance, desperately explaining that homosexuals were not abnormal and that we were the victims of discrimination in society. This subservient attitude only changed after I acquired my wonderful partner, Ryuta, and acknowledged myself, fully accepted myself and acquired confidence in myself as the homosexual I am. This, ironically, was after I had already realized that I had developed into a better, more broad-minded human being as a result of my having been born a homosexual. In other words it is probable that where the rationality of the majority dominates every possible facet of society's thinking, homosexuals can only take their place as equals with heterosexuals by having an almost over-confidence in their convictions. Perhaps this is what is referred to as 'gay pride'.

One hears the argument from both heterosexuals and homosexuals that even if we were not to take a stance, if we were just to let things be, the discriminatory mentality of heterosexuals with regards to homosexuals would, with time, most likely disappear of its own accord. Certainly in the 1990s we have seen what might be described as a veritable 'gay boom' in the mass media's reporting of homosexuality. The mass media is unquestionably starting to pay attention to the issue of homosexuality on a scale hitherto unknown in this country. However, it remains a fact that almost all the 'gay supplements' which are put out offer nothing more than the same sort of trite explanations of terms used in the world of the homosexual sub-culture and focus on things such as what sort of sex and what sort of love lives homosexuals have. In other words they have a peek at that 'frightening other world' via the safety of a telescope and fail completely and utterly to address the diversity which exists amongst homosexuals. Likewise, the question of the journey, perhaps more accurately described as the struggle, for self-acceptance as homosexuals is totally ignored. Gay TV personalities are presented to viewers who are keen to be allowed a gingerly peek at the unusual creatures paraded before them. Such TV personalities do not go beyond ingratiating themselves to the majority in society.

Something we should never lose sight of is the fact that the reason the media took an interest in the subject of homosexuality in the first place was none other than because Occur, the Gay and Lesbian Action Association, instigated legal proceedings against the City of Tokyo. The members of Occur only took this action after a very long year of anguish and the investment of an absolutely tremendous amount of mental energy. Thanks for the current high levels of media interest must also be given to groups such as the Japanese chapter of the International Lesbian and Gay Alliance for the steady work they continue to invest with the aim of heightening public awareness of the existence and plight of homosexuals in this country.

Homosexuals must become politically aware and effect changes to mainstream society.

One hears it said that the younger the generation, the more tolerant they are of homosexuality. From my personal point of view, as someone who spends a lot of time socializing with students from the preparatory school, I can sense that the young generation today hasn't had its way of thinking or perception of homosexuality poisoned by straight-out theories of abnormality or heresy. Yet, on close observation of what is being said, I find that quite often their acceptance of homosexuals is because there were homosexuals whose existence was sanctioned in the schools that they went to. In other words, we can interpret from this that it is because certain teenage homosexuals were forward in coming out and were determined not to lead a lifestyle which was unnatural for them, that the grip of prejudice on the minds of the heterosexuals around them was somewhat loosened. These teenagers were determined to avoid following what for them would have been an unnatural pathway through life, a pathway set down in accordance with the predetermined expectations of the heteronormative environment around them. They chose to avoid a lifestyle where they would have always had to conceal their true feelings, despite the fact that the adoption of such a lifestyle would have readily met with the full approval of society.

It is virtually impossible to consider the lot of homosexuals improving if they remain silent. From the Education Department's charter quoted earlier, it is clearly pure fantasy to think the government or regional public bodies will, of their own accord, do anything for homosexuals. And whilst Japan is thought of as being an atheistic country, there are many religious organizations here which proscribe homosexuality. There is no predicting what actions such organizations might take to try to clamp down on it in the future. Further, there are still mountains of academics who refer to homosexual love as being an 'abnormal sexual desire'. Unless this changes, the day when we can walk through the city holding hands without embarrassment or apology will not come in a month of Sundays. I would like to see the energy expended by homosexuals in arranging to meet one another in hiding diverted into being used to redress, even partly, the inequitable situation that exists at present.

I believe that there is a need for homosexuals to join together and become politically aware and active. To illustrate what can be achieved by concerted effort we can look at the fact that the Gay and Lesbian Action Association, at the time of the 1991 general revision of the *Kōjien* Dictionary [Iwanami Shoten][9], was able to get the editors to change the definition of 'homosexuality'. The definition had previously read 'a form of abnormal sexual desire' but this was replaced by 'having a person of the same sex as the object of one's love and sexual desire'. This wording is uncomplicated and unambiguous. The revision of this dictionary entry was achieved through a proper written submission presented in the form of a series of questions, followed by negotiations with the editors regarding what constituted appropriate wording for this particular entry. I doubt very much that such a result could have been achieved had the approach been made by an individual with no support base. It is no simple matter to overturn the entrenched rationality of the majority. It can only be done with the backing of a group.

I would like to see the removal of institutionalized discrimination added to the list of successes already achieved. What a great source of confidence it would be if only we had a human rights clause in our constitution[10], such as the Dutch and French have in theirs, stating that it is illegal to discriminate on the basis of sexual orientation. The inclusion of such a clause in our constitution would mean that we would be able to freely build our lives as people and not be shackled to the deeply ingrained and inflexible mentality which acts to bolster and further perpetrate our society's dependence on the type of marriage arrangement currently existing. When heterosexuals get married they acquire all sorts of rights in relation to taxation, the acquisition of housing and many other things. I observe this all the time and would dearly love equal rights in regards to these things. If they say that formal marriage is necessary to acquire such rights, then I would like to see marriages between homosexuals recognized. I acknowledge that an almost incomprehensibly long journey is necessary for this to become a reality. I believe, however, that life is of a very poor quality if we discard our dreams. Be that as it may, the fact is that none of the political parties in Japan, not even the reformist parties, has the question of homosexuality on the agenda. They don't even have any proper policies in relation to AIDS, never mind homosexuality as such! Moreover, amongst the various political lobby groups, some display woeful levels of awareness and consciousness, particularly regarding sexual matters. As far as political lobbying is concerned, hoping for co-operation from such bodies seems to be out of the question. Simply trying to find someone with some interest in the issue of homosexuality is like looking for a needle in a haystack. One wonders if the only way forward is to produce a homosexual member of the Diet[11]!

If social recognition of homosexuals were to provide equality before the law, we would be able to liberate not only homosexuals but also heterosexuals from the existing deeply rooted, but narrow, interpretation of what constitutes rational norms endorsed by the majority in society. Such a liberation would provide an opportunity to discover a new approach to living. This new approach would go beyond just being able to escape from the often rigid division of labour in a household based on gender. It would extend to redressing the privations inflicted on homosexuals as a result of societal expectations in terms of the sorts of behaviour, attitude and mannerisms we are expected to display. We would witness a loosening of the concept of there being only a limited range of acceptable types of behaviour, attitudes and mannerisms which are attributed to, associated with and expected of a person as a result of his or her gender.

A society which is friendly to minorities will be a society which is far more friendly to all, including the heterosexual majority. To cite an example that does not pertain to homosexuals, we might briefly turn our attention to the design of the North Exit Plaza of the Japan Railways' Funabashi Station. This design gives priority to vehicles over pedestrians. With its underground car park, it is possible to go to the station by car, but this means you now find many more cars congregating around the station and intensified traffic jams! The outdoor plaza has a bus terminal underneath, but to get to the entrance of the station, the design forces you to go up a level before coming down again and escalators aren't provided for even half the flights of stairs. People in wheelchairs or who find staircases hard going have to take a hugely circuitous route. Just imagine how unfriendly this planning is for users! It ignores members of a particular minority group and is quite unfriendly to the majority too! I am simply flabbergasted by the politicians on both sides of parliament who are proud of this design.

We are prepared and willing to be a pioneering homosexual couple.

I have decided that I want to make a positive contribution to changing the level of public awareness society has in relation to the question of homosexuality by joining and working with the groups Occur and Taurus and, on a personal level, by surviving without apology and having the confidence to live my life as the homosexual I am. I would like to be instrumental in bringing about an acknowledgement that it is only natural for homosexuals and members of other minority groups to be found in all walks of life, holding whatever positions in society they might hold. For example, I am still pretending to be a heterosexual in the staff room at the preparatory school and am ever conscious of the need to fit the expected image of heterosexuality when there. At least that is the situation now. Who knows what will happen after this book comes out and it becomes known that I am of the minority sexual persuasion? This acting and trying to play a role which simply isn't natural for me is very trying. I'm doing this for the time being because my job is very important to me. It is a means of supporting myself. Also there seems no particular point in channelling my energies into what could be described as reckless valour.

Having said that, I am tired of replying, 'I am seeing someone but you know how it is…' every time someone with the best of intentions mentions to me that, 'Getting married and settling down is just what you need. It settles your mind and will do wonders in terms of clearing up the mental anxiety you suffer from' or 'Children are just so great. I wouldn't wait too long to start a family if I were you!' Only on very rare occasions would someone pry into my private life and ask, 'What sort of girl are you going out with?' Continually having to find the mental energy needed to dodge this sort of question and divert the conversation in an apparently nonchalant fashion whenever the topic of my personal life comes up has just become too much. It has become un-reasonable and absurd. How easy my life would be if I were able to respond openly and honestly and have the conversation run something along the lines of my saying 'My partner happens to be a man' and the other party simply replying 'Is that so?'

Whether in fact I will be able to do just that or whether, having written this book, I will be forced to leave the preparatory school and, if worst comes to worst, go to court to fight, is yet to be seen. A deciding factor will be just how many heterosexuals, regardless of whether they be teachers or students, I can win over as allies. I do not repudiate all heterosexuals out of hand, but by the same token I am simply no longer prepared to compromise my convictions. Having come to this major decision in my life, I affirm that as Nyāgo, Ryuta's partner, the confidence I have to face the future has never been greater nor has my morale ever been higher.

In stating this I fully acknowledge that any group action that hopes to achieve gay rights will, for the foreseeable future, have to rely solely on the work and support of homosexuals. Furthermore, let me – no, let *us* – record our names here. For Ryuta Yanase and Satoru Ito there is yet another aim. We want to be a happy couple, second to none. We believe that being born as homosexuals and leading our lives as homosexuals is normal and natural for us. We do not think that it should, in itself, be considered a source of anguish or unhappiness. Rather, our hearts beat with excitement at having discussed together the fact that we would like to demonstrate, as a couple, that we are able to form a new type of relationship, one overflowing with a vitality that even exceeds that known to heterosexuals. We will remove the fetters that accompany the male/female gender role distinction and interact with each other as two natural, unaffected and individual human beings who are not beholden to any precedent, established custom or conventional rationality. Ours is a relationship in which we support each other from the heart, yet in which we both are strictly committed to moulding ourselves to better suit each other. The fact that we have decided to embark upon such a dramatic course in our lives brings with it a sense of peace and comfort and a concomitant sense of excitement. And although I think that we will quite soon be overtaken, as it were, by the next generation of homosexuals, we would like to think of ourselves as being pioneers with presence! We take on the challenge of acting as role models to others. When they see us enjoying the relationship we have they should realize that, rather than being intimidated by the discriminatory eye of heterosexuals, they would be missing out if they were to fail to follow in our footsteps.

I will close on a quite different note. The present that Ryuta gave me for my birthday this year was a giant *manekineko*[12]. That cat now ostentatiously commands a presence beside the TV in our loungeroom as if to say he will ensure good fortune and attend the new dramas that will unfold in this household in the future.

Nuta and Nyāgo are now ready to accept the challenge which lies ahead. We take our places on the starting blocks, inspired.

4 A word from my partner

Before meeting Satoru I was a person without an identity to call my own, a person who didn't express himself.

I would like to introduce myself to all those reading this book. I am Nuta, alias Ryuta Yanase, partner of Satoru Ito, the main character described in this book.

Nearly seven years have flown by since the first day I met 'Nyāgo' Ito. In this seven year period there really have been all sorts of things happen in our lives. I would like to write something about what has occurred between the two of us from my own perspective. I will try, as far as possible, not to go over the same ground that Satoru has already covered.

Before I met Satoru I had never had a relationship with anyone for long enough to develop emotional attachments. I really didn't know how to handle relationships. I never divulged my emotions or inner feelings to anyone before meeting Satoru. My relationships with lovers and friends alike were non-committal and inoffensive. I didn't know what sort of a person I was as I never revealed my inner self to anyone. When I met Satoru I was twenty-four but I didn't have a personality I could call my own.

I now realize how fortunate I was to have met Satoru. I am glad to have discovered that love can be such a wonderful thing. As Satoru has written, many was the time we would have heated arguments. But this was because I had met him as he himself was and I had also met me as I myself was…an honest me that I hadn't known up until that time.

For most people it is probably the case that when they are children the persons with whom they can best be themselves are their parents, particularly their mother, and their siblings. However, in the process of growing up the person in whom you can best confide changes from being your mother or father to being a friend, and before long, a lover. Before meeting Satoru I really didn't know how I should interact with my partner or how I should express what I wanted to say. I didn't know how to argue either.

Even now that tendency remains. I always fall silent whenever I get mad. I really and truly say nothing for hours on end (okay, this might be just a bit of an exaggeration!). Satoru can't stand this tendency but I simply don't know how to let myself explode. I feel that I would like to shout something out but I can't vent my feelings aloud. That's why I keep quiet. I seethe with anger but remain silent. Satoru can't take this silence and begs me to speak, to say something – anything – but for some reason I just can't. It is probably more accurate to describe this situation as simply my getting into a bad mood and taking it upon myself to keep a stony silence rather than as an argument as such. Satoru gets dragged into this and simply doesn't know how to handle the situation. First and foremost, he was always on the receiving end because I absolutely never told him the reason why I was in a bad mood. Often I myself didn't know what on earth I was angry about. This set up a vicious circle in which I would get even angrier at myself. The first three to four years after we started seeing each other were dominated by arguments which followed this sort of pattern. For that whole period I gave him a very hard time. Looking back at it now, I really feel I did him a dreadful disservice. All I can do now is feel humility at the way he managed to endure such a selfish and highly strung person as I was.

Gayness is part of my make-up, my personality. Towards an acknowledgment and acceptance of myself.

When Satoru coaxed me into facing aspects of my personality that I didn't want to confront, I would selfishly vent my anger by retreating into my own world of silence. That approach, however, was clearly wrong. I was being forced to confront an ugly aspect of my behaviour, an ungainly aspect of my behaviour, square on. It was a wall I had to get over. There was no-one else who was able to get over that wall for me. I had to do it myself. Although I had not realized it, in the depths of my heart I hoped that Satoru would always be there to guard the wall of my ego and never allow it to crack. So, when he didn't move to protect it I couldn't control my anger. Clearly, however, that was not how I should have acted. I had to break down that wall myself. If I hadn't I would have ended up suffering every time it looked like it was being threatened.

Every time it looked like the wall might suffer damage I would let fly at Satoru. I admit that I was below criticism! And yet, albeit gradually, I succeeded in changing through my love for him.

Although clumsily, he put everything he had into laying bare his soul and tackling our relationship head on. Thanks to this I found myself, little by little, able to reveal my innermost self. Or it might have been that in the course of watching him, and without realizing it, I came to learn how to follow his example and lay my own soul bare. That 'me', whose soul had been bared in front of Satoru, was headstrong and willful. I would hide from myself the fact that I was giving Satoru hell by suddenly clamming up, because I didn't want to acknowledge it. And whenever it looked as though the wall around my ego was in any danger of coming down I would do the same. This is not to say, however, that I do not have a soft side! I am, in fact, a person who gets very lonely and craves companionship. I feel that the seven years since I first met Satoru were seven years in which I came to get to know that 'other me'. Perhaps they were seven years spent in recognizing just who I am and accepting myself.

It is often said that 'to know your partner is to know yourself' and sure enough, it is indeed because you have a partner who is able to bear his soul to you that you are able to come to know yourself. In this regard I will be forever indebted to Satoru for enduring such a willful person as I was. The most important thing, I consider, is whether or not you can take cognizance of yourself. We all have a facet to our personalities which we are particularly averse to scrutinizing, do we not? I feel that it is only when we are able to take cognizance of that part of ourselves, in other words to acknowledge it, to get to understand it and to accept it, that it ceases to be a failing. Yet no matter how well you might know yourself, unless there is acknowledgment of that self by both you and your partner it is likely that the same things will prove to continue to cause arguments between you. So you could say that accepting yourself is tantamount to accepting your partner, could you not? Conversely, people who can't accept themselves are not able to accept their partner. When you acknowledge your own shortcomings they gradually cease to be shortcomings. I believe we can say a similar thing about being gay: if you acknowledge your homosexuality it will gradually cease to be an issue for you.

Obviously this aspect of my self is very important to me and I recognize that acknowledging and accepting my gay self is one of the most pressing and profound challenges for me at the moment. I would like here to briefly mention how I came to accept, or am still coming to terms with, my gay self.

Declaring to my sister and mother that I was gay and building a deeper relationship with them as a result.

When I first met Satoru I was excessively conscious of being gay. I was forever on tenterhooks, fearing that others would find out. In the vast ocean which is society, I always pretended to be a heterosexual, feigning an interest in women. Through my association with Satoru, however, I gradually learned to gain confidence in the fact that I am gay. No, perhaps, rather than saying I became more confident, it would probably be more accurate to state that I came to realize that being gay is natural for me. It is nothing more than a perfectly natural part of my being.

Having come to this realization, I approached my sister one day, about five years ago, and admitted to her that I was gay. I told her that Satoru Ito was my partner. In my conversations with her until then I had only ever referred to him as a good friend. This was my first experience of 'coming out'. I made the admission with mixed emotions – a sense of hope and anticipation combined with a sense of anxiety and uneasiness. However I need not have worried because my sister's reaction was unexpected and actually quite wonderful:

'Thank you for sharing this with me. It must have been the most difficult thing for you to come out and tell me that'.

That was what my sister said to me! She even went on to say:

'I'll never look down on you Ryuta, just because you're gay. In fact, I think it is a wonderful thing! I'm so glad you've been able to meet a nice partner. You must look after him well'.

I must tell you that I have never known greater happiness than that which I felt when my sister responded in this way. I was so glad I had told her and felt this from the bottom of my heart. It was as though at long, long last I was able to set down part of the heavy burden I had secretly shouldered for the past twenty odd years. I would no longer have to pretend to be a heterosexual in front of her! I was glad that, at least in front of her, I would be able to be my true self, or at least be closer to being my true self than I had ever been in the past. After this disclosure the bond between my sister and me grew all the stronger. It deeply moved me that she was able to find within her an understanding of a set of values that hitherto had been foreign to her and further, accept me as a result.

In September last year I finally broke the news to my mother. I also told her that my partner was Mr Satoru Ito. As with my sister, I had portrayed Satoru to my mother as nothing more than a good friend up until then. It seems that coming clean about your sexuality like this is referred to as 'coming out'. However, when I think back to how I felt at that time, I can positively state that it was not a matter that the mere description 'coming out' does justice to. Certainly it is effectively a 'coming out', but I had never thought of it as such. I simply wanted my sister and mother to know me much better. I confided in them with hopes and prayers that they might come to better understand the person I was. I wonder if you follow the gist of my argument here. What it is that I'm trying to say is that I didn't come out for the sake of coming out. There was a need for me to tell at least these two people about that integral part of me which is my gayness. I begged from my soul that at least these two people might get to know me more fully.

My mother's reaction was surprising in the same way as my sister's had been. It was a truly wonderful thing for me. She said:

'I am very happy that you've spoken about this and not hidden that part of you away from me. And it is good that you've met a wonderful partner. Look after him'.

For whatever reason, she said exactly the same thing as my sister had! To be honest I was surprised at my mother's reaction because, after all, she was born a dozen or so years before the Second World War started. That she could be so broad-minded reconfirmed the respect I had for her in my heart. Not respect for her as a mother so much, but as a human being.

Confessing my homosexuality to these two people whom I dealt with on a daily basis brought about a big change in my life. I feel that this was a turning point in the relationship between my mother and me. We are better able to understand each other as a result. More than anything else, the reason I am glad I told my mother and sister is that I myself feel very much unburdened as a result. Opening up to them removed a tremendous burden from me. I never imagined in my wildest dreams that having just two more people who allow me to be myself and do not demand that I deny my sexual orientation in front of them would make me feel so different! Having unburdened myself I came to realize just how very restricted and closed the life that I had led up until that point had been.

At the end of last year I again unburdened myself, this time to a close heterosexual friend I had known since primary school. When I told him that I was gay he was taken aback momentarily, but he soon was doing his very best to try to comprehend my sexual orientation. Our friendship continues to this day, unaffected by my disclosure. In fact, if anything, perhaps the closeness of our relationship has been enhanced to the same extent that I have felt unburdened, since I no longer have to pretend to be a heterosexual when I'm with him.

Providing support and encouragement for each other and coming out together.

When you decide to reveal yourself as being gay, the important thing is the sort of relationship you hope to build with the person you 'come-out' to. There is no need to go to all the trouble involved in making a confidant of someone you aren't particularly bothered about having understand you. In my case, I truly wanted the people involved to understand me, no matter what, so it was nothing more than a case of revealing my homosexuality and taking these three heterosexuals, who meant so much to me, into my confidence. Regardless of the other party's reaction, it is you who makes the decision to come out and it is you and you alone who must accept the consequences of your disclosure. You must take responsibility for what ensues. The relationship you have had until then may well be shattered. You may also be made a laughing stock of by others. One thing that is certain is that the decision to come out has very serious implications. I have recently taken the position that, if irreparable damage results from taking someone into my confidence and disclosing that I am gay, then I just have to accept that. I consider it as a measure of the depth and sincerity of our friendship. If our friendship is so frail as to be shattered by my revelation, I won't be. Indeed this was how I felt when I came out to my mother, sister and closest friend.

As you are aware, this book represents another type of coming out. It is important to me that you know the reason why I chose to come out in this way. I did it because I love my partner, 'Nyāgo' Ito, from the bottom of my heart. That is the reason stated simply and clearly. Satoru was in two minds about whether or not he should use his real name for this book. It was only with the strong recommendation of the chief editor, Mr Asakawa, that Satoru decided to use his real name. When his decision was finally made and he was at the point of no return, Satoru seemed quite unsettled. 'If the fact that I'm gay reaches the ears of the director of the preparatory school and I'm fired, what will I do?' he asked, turning to me for advice. Without hesitating I responded to this man, whom I love unreservedly, that he should use my real name in the book as well. I explained that if he used both our real names the burden of any ensuing consequences could be shared. I was forthright in my response because the affection I feel for Nyāgo is limitless and I saw this as the very time he needed me to shield and protect him and help him come to terms with this difficult decision. Pretty good of me, wasn't it?!

My sister, whom I admire and respect very much, has a favourite saying which runs: 'You'll be alright, it won't kill you'. What do you think? Quite a good message, isn't it?! I like this saying very much, I really do. Of course, it shouldn't be used when hurting people. As far as the publication of this book is concerned, this saying can be understood literally. In other words, even if I come out in the public arena and announce myself by name as being gay, I'll still be right, it won't kill me. In fact if you can read between the lines here you'll probably realize that what I'm doing is trying to bolster my courage a bit because I do in fact feel a bit uneasy at the prospect of publicly declaring my sexuality, even though I know I haven't done anything wrong. All I am doing is turning to the world and making reference to the fact that I am the person I am.

So, why is it that Satoru and I should be made to feel ill at ease? It is probably because in society there are too many non-thinking people. Non-thinkers who cannot put themselves in the place of others and who are incapable of considering problems from the point of view of others. Non-thinkers who cannot sanction a set of values different to those they hold themselves. Non-thinkers who are just not happy unless they feel a sense of superiority over others. It is quite difficult for homosexuals to lead their lives in a way that is natural for them and without hiding who they are, in a world replete with such non-thinkers! Why is it that people who are just a bit different from others must be so pressured into conformity? The pressure mainstream society applies is certainly not restricted to gays. Discrimination is something that is known to many minority groups. AIDS patients (infected persons), single mothers, those of Korean ancestry, the *burakumin*[13], unmarried people, women and those of other races are but a few examples of the people who suffer discrimination at the hands of the majority in Japan. There is no limit once you start enumerating the various categories of people who suffer discrimination in our society. There can be no explanation for this level of discrimination and prejudice other than the fact that there are simply too many non-thinkers in the world.

Not living by the code stipulated by society but accepting each other as we are for what we are.

Japanese society as we know it is in quite a bad way. The men in control are to be pitied. They are men who are beyond help and who are unable to extricate themselves from the mindset of the stereotypical image males should fit. Men who seek a continuation of the mother-son relationship after marriage. Pathetic men who act high and mighty in the house, but when it comes down to it rely on their wives to do the jobs their mothers used to do for them in order to cope with the demands of life. To put it another way, we could say that married men are not unlike overgrown children. They tend to be incapable of handling any tasks other than those that relate to their work. Our society is run by men who make no attempt to take a step outside the gender role as stipulated by the heterosexual majority. They are comfortable with the notion of there being fixed gender roles defining fixed duties for them to perform. What on earth is meant by saying a man can only take on the mantle of respectability associated with being a fully-fledged member of society as a result of entering into the institution of marriage? It is beyond me. Society is run by men who allow themselves to be bound by the perceived need to fit the established male image. They fear, in the extreme, being thought of as effeminate and not living up to this image. They are men who are not capable of revealing the softer side of their natures to others. For them, close male friends would have to be completely out of the question. This is because they keep a part of themselves back and are unable to disclose any aspect of their character which might be deemed to be unmanly or anything about themselves which might be construed as a sign of weakness. Men who keep a part of themselves to themselves would surely never be able to become close friends with other such men, no matter how much they might associate with each other.

That is why I hate the set-up that allows society to be ruled by a mindset which dictates inflexible, stipulated gender roles and determines fixed images that both men and women are supposed to live up to. It isn't that I hate men or women as such. What I hate is the unwritten system that stipulates that 'a man (or a woman) has to be *thus*', in other words that there is a given gender mould which must be fitted. Where on earth do people's real selves go? The convention of the accepted image of what men are supposed to be like and how they are meant to behave and of what women are supposed to be like and how they are meant to behave leaves me wondering just where that part of the person which doesn't match this accepted image fits in. Conventional images can sometimes be far from the reality of the lives of real people. This can be the case for any group of people whether they be students, responsible adult members of society, the Japanese people taken as a group or even human beings generally. I cannot tolerate blanket societal demands and expectations based on nothing more than the group affiliation a particular person might have. If only we were all less bound by societal convention in terms of expected behaviour based on group association and far more able to reveal our real selves as the individual people we actually are, life could be so much more pleasant. We are surrounded by women who demand of their partners that they live up to the conventionally accepted image of manly behaviour and men who demand of their partners that they live up to the conventionally accepted image of womanly behaviour. But in my case I don't demand any such thing of my partner because I don't feel there is any need for me to do so. I don't see any point in Satoru or I demanding of each other that we live up to conventionally accepted images in our relationship with each other. That is also why Satoru demands nothing of me. Consequently, in one sense we are both free. When we are alone together we are free from all aspects of dependency on images relating to conventionally prescribed roles and associated behaviour and I feel very much at home with this freedom. I feel glad to be alive. I am glad to the depth of my being that Satoru came into my life.

In our association with each other, Satoru and I make no effort to conceal the gentler side of our natures or our weaknesses. Because of this we probably spoil each other in a way that would be thought of by others as inappropriate, perhaps off-colour and unacceptable, even disgusting. However, in our relationship we pay no heed to society's dictates in terms of how we are meant to act. We do not have to fear that what we say might lead our partner to think less of us because we are not living up to the conventionally accepted image of manliness. As partners we are able to fully let down our guards and relax in each other's company. I intend to live every single day as it comes, concealing nothing of my gentler nature, nor indeed anything at all from Satoru. I am quite prepared to accept the arrangement whereby he does things for me and we support each other and depend on each other.

All you poor, pathetic guys out there who are prisoners of the dictates of society's strait-jacketing, victims of society's inability to accept a wide variety of types of men – work away as you will every day! Never display vulnerability, never display your weaker side, your gentler nature to anyone! You might as well bury yourselves in your work as you have no life and nothing to build your lives on outside of it. For you there is no place other than where you are and that's where you will stay, in that socially sanctioned rut, for the rest of your lives! I truly believe that human beings who are bound hand and foot by societal convention as it relates to the narrow interpretation of accepted gender behaviour are thoroughly and utterly to be pitied.

How can a homosexual such as I am find acceptance in life? I consider this to be a lifetime question that has been assigned to me. It is a fact, however, that I perceive the gay aspect of my being as gradually moving towards having something of a diminished significance for me. Could this be because I have, albeit slowly, been able to come to terms with and accept my gayness? Whether this is the case or not, it remains a fact that it is necessary to have an absolutely tremendous level of determination if you are hoping to succeed in leading your life without camouflaging your real self or denying who you are to yourself. This is because leading your life true to yourself remains an extraordinarily difficult thing to accomplish in our heteronormative world. Accepting your natural orientation and living your life accordingly, remains a truly difficult quest in a society in which heterosexuals form the overwhelming majority. However, just having people in this world who accept me as the gay man that I am instills enormous confidence in me and allows me, as a gay man, to carry on with my life as nature intended I should. I hope in the future to increase the number of such people in my life. I believe that, more than anything else, it is necessary for me to associate with people who accept me for what I am and who I am. Such people provide positive reinforcement for the life I lead. This is essential for me if I am to reach the point where I can feel comfortable with myself leading the life that nature intended I should.

Postscript to Part One

by Satoru Ito

The other day my partner, Ryuta, told me something that he had
never told me before. It relates to an occurrence that took place
about a year or two after we had started going out with each other.
We were on board a ferry together, gazing at the sea from the deck.
I don't have a clear recollection of the incident myself but it seems
that I casually placed my hand on either his shoulder or hip. No
sooner had I done this than a group of men and women who were
some distance away started pointing at us and laughing derisively.
Ryuta was quick to notice this and nonchalantly moved my hand
away. Learning of this incident caused a familiar anger to rise
within me. Why should it be that two people in love must be
laughed at? Ryuta went on to tell more. He said that looking back
at it now he feels embarrassed and annoyed at the fact that he had
to remove his lover's hand. He added that he would like to be able
to act naturally in front of people even at the risk of being laughed
at. He said he believed that he should be able to hold my hand
without being laughed at because there is absolutely nothing
wrong in his doing so. Yet despite his believing this, the fact of the
matter is that he is still not able to hold hands with me in public.
He said that I should be patient in this regard, as one day soon he
will come right out and hold my hand at an amusement park or
some such place where there are people around. I was moved by
his saying this as it registered with me that both he and I were
displaying a definite determination to forge a new type of
relationship.

Although slowly, times have started to change. This is
evidenced by several interesting developments that have taken
place since the beginning of this year, 1993. Thanks to the input
of the Gay and Lesbian Action Association, the Education
Department has acknowledged that the view (referred to earlier),
that 'homosexuality is a sexual aberration', is inappropriate. It

is also noteworthy that the Ministry of Public Welfare has agreed to allow male homosexuals to donate blood, something that had not been allowed in the past on the grounds that the risk of HIV contamination was too great. Furthermore the Britannica and other encyclopaedias are revising the discriminatory entries they traditionally have provided about homosexuality.

This book was inspired by the encouragement received from a Mr Kaori Yamaki, and later a Mr Mitsuru Asakawa, to write about my experiences. The former was a member of the editorial staff of the magazine *Hito*[14]. He approached me and asked me to write something for the magazine. His request came immediately after I had resolved to lead my life as a homosexual and had 'come out' to my mother. So I decided without hesitation that I would take up his offer. Thus I embarked on writing a series of articles for the said magazine. Later, when it was suggested by Mr Asakawa that I expand on the series I had written and make it into a book, I again readily agreed as I believed that the production of this book would consolidate the position I had taken and in doing so act to help in settling my mind. Nonetheless it is true to say that in the course of writing this book I experienced mixed feelings and fluctuating emotions. I was able, however, to complete the manuscript thanks to the support and backup supplied by Ryuta Yanase, my partner. I wish to record here my thanks to Mr Yamaki, Mr Asakawa and my partner, Mr Ryuta Yanase.

6th June, 1993

Foreword to Part Two

It is very easy, living in a progressive Australian city as an openly gay mayor in a gay-friendly municipality, to think that prejudice and discrimination are no longer problems.

While most gay and lesbian couples in my own Town of Vincent hold hands in local parks, are valued as tenants by landlords and operate as equals in society, such tolerance and celebration of same-sex relationships is not universal, nor the norm.

Part Two of this revealing literary work by Satoru Ito and Ryuta Yanase shows how diverse the worldwide gay community is, yet also how similar our aspirations, needs and hopes are. The personal tales recounted here – of setting up house together, determining same-sex roles when all our modeling is heterosexual-based and even the everyday hassles of driving – all help to fashion a relationship.

But as detailed here, the illegal discrimination displayed by the City of Tokyo in the Fuchū Youth House case is eerily reminiscent of situations throughout the world, including Western Australia, where in the face of oppression gay and lesbian people have had to publicly fight discrimination. Such adversity also brings about strength in the local community and, most importantly, pride.

The relationship of Satoru and Ryuta gives a human focus to the political struggle. Legal acknowledgment that same-sex relationships are covered *per se* under freedom of association articles in the Japanese Constitution gives the personal relationship room to grow. There should be no limits to personal growth. Whenever some people in society try to hinder relationships on the basis of prejudice, that curtailment must be fought. Yet securing a legal victory against prejudice in the courts is only the beginning, as Part Two of this engaging story shows.

Mayor John Hyde
Town of Vincent, Western Australia
President of the Local Government Assoc. of Western Australia
April 2000

Part Two:
Our Partnership
by Ryuta Yanase and Satoru Ito

Preamble to Part Two

*The path I followed up until the point where I could state with pride
that I was a homosexual.*

One full year has passed since I reached the point where I was able
to state with pride that I am a homosexual.

Twenty five years ago, when I was in my 3rd year of junior high
school, I was attracted to a boy in my same class. He was very
tanned, fashionable in dress and good at sport. He always smelled
of sweet musk. I felt as though I wanted a friend. I had never been
good at making friends in my primary school years, years marked
by many changes of school. Looking back now I know that the way
my heart skipped a beat with the thrill of being with him was in
fact nothing other than proof of my having fallen in love. However,
it never occurred to me at that time that I could be a homosexual.
Nothing could have been further from my mind.

Twenty years ago, through exposure to gay magazines, it started
to dawn on me that perhaps I was homosexual. It seemed that, as
such, I would be unable to get married and have children. Also that
I would be forced to follow a shady path through life, existing in
a marginalized sub-culture. This prospect unequivocally made me
decide that I must change, because I didn't want to live the life of
an 'outlaw', removed from the comfort afforded by the acceptance
of mainstream society. I kept up the empty and lonely endeavour
to change myself for eight years. I thought to myself that I would
probably change if I were to go out with girls, but no matter how
many times I dated girls even the desire to hold their hand was
never experienced. By contrast, I was quite unable to control the
attraction I felt for the young men in the university circle that I was
in. One after another I fell for them in a succession of one-way love
affairs.

Day after day I suffered with a feeling of guilt as I dispensed
with my sexual urges, utilizing the soft pornographic pictures and

nude shots found in the gay magazines I bought. In my sixth year of university studies (I was officially enrolled for eight years, having taken two years off my studies) I fell head over heels in love with a student who was my junior. At that time, spending as much time as possible with him was my goal. This objective governed my behaviour and my whole life. I even went so far as moving into an apartment close to where he lived. I was simply unable to control the feelings that overtook me, even though it meant risking that my secret might become known to those around me. He was heterosexual, however, and there was never any hope of his returning my love. Still, he spent a lot of time with me as a friend. Indeed I'll never forget the kindness he showed me by inviting me to his wedding party in September this year! I was in love with him, but my heart was very heavy – believing that it would probably never be possible for me, a homosexual, to find a partner and happiness in life.

When, twenty years ago, with his graduation from university and his finding employment I bade farewell to the four year long, one-sided love affair, I at long last started to think that it would not be possible for me to live my life while denying my sexual orientation.[1] I realized fully and unequivocally that unless I chose a partner with the same sexual orientation that I had I would never be able to find a partner in life. So I started utilizing the services of the personal columns of gay magazines and frequenting the parts of the city with gay pubs and watering holes. Here my sexual appetite went wild. The sex was readily available but, since I didn't have the luxury of being able to spend time building up a relationship with anyone, I was unable to meet anyone with whom I could establish a long-term, intimate relationship. The more I tried to rush things the less success I had. I was even reduced to paying for sexual favours. On top of all this I received a blackmail threat. An anonymous person threatened to expose my homosexuality at the private high school where I was working. I fell into a state of deep depression thinking that perhaps it was my lot in life to have to continue hiding the fact that I was homosexual and accept the wretched existence my life represented.

Nevertheless, I continued in my search for a partner, utilizing the personal columns of gay magazines. It was through this avenue that I met my partner, Mr Ryuta Yanase. We lived near each other and had a common interest in Western music. We were also both good listeners. Generally we seemed quite compatible. Thus, it wasn't long before we started dating regularly. It took a considerable length of time for the 'love at first sight' that I felt to change into what might be described as our 'sharing thoughts and love'. Getting a deep knowledge of a partner is one and the same thing as clearly recognizing the differences between your value systems and ways of thinking. We went through a period in our relationship where we were forever arguing, sometimes so heatedly that I worried about our future together. Yet, somehow, we were always able to patch things up just before we reached the point of separating. This can be explained very simply. We would always talk things over thoroughly until we each gained an appreciation of the other party's position. For example, after a very long time (and only after many discussions and arguments), I finally came to appreciate the strain placed on Ryuta as a result of his being the only one able to drive. Having finally understood this, I put great effort into getting my own driver's licence so that I could assume some of this burden. Another example can be found in the way we studied Buddhism together in an effort to overcome our different approaches to religion.

Anyway, I had found a partner! Nothing could have imbued me with greater confidence than knowing this! I found that, as a result, I was able to give much more of myself to everything I was engaged in – my work and all other pursuits. This extended from the late night broadcasting work I was involved in through to the writing and publishing of user-friendly English reference books that were written from the point of view of helping students who struggled with that subject. My new-found energy was directed to all of my many pursuits. For example, the records I had kept in relation to the classical TV puppet show '*Hyokkori Hyōtan Island*' proved useful in the remake of the show which had originally been broadcast on NHK from 1964 to 1969. The role I played in assisting with the remake of the show (the storyline remained unchanged from the original) even made an item on the news! Even at that time, though, I was tormented by the fear of my homosexuality being exposed. I feared that if it were to become known that I was a homosexual, people would think less of me as a person and lower the value they placed on my achievements. I feared, in other words, that this would impact upon my livelihood and that consequently I wouldn't be able to make ends meet. I practically exhausted myself investing tremendous energy into making sure I said the right things whenever the topic of conversation turned to love or marriage when in the company of heterosexuals.

Two years ago a very slight change took place in my relationship with Ryuta. I refer to the time when Occur (the Gay and Lesbian Action Association) took on the City of Tokyo in a lawsuit. I attended the court hearings as an observer. The court action questioned the appropriateness of the city's refusal to allow homosexuals to utilize the public accommodation facilities provided at the Fuchū Youth House on the grounds that they might have sex together when staying in the same room. The father of Takashi Kazama, one of the plaintiffs, addressed a meeting after the hearing, saying that although it had been a shock for him to learn that his son was homosexual, he had come around to a position where he wanted to be in court to support him. At this his son wept. How dearly I wished that I might have my own mother say the same thing about me! I was nearly moved to tears as I witnessed Mr Kazama senior's announcement. I felt then that I had to move another step forward in life. Here in front of my very eyes the members of the Gay and Lesbian Action Association were fighting to create a place in society for us, giving all they had in order to make society a place where homosexuals would be able to lead their lives without the terrible stress we were all familiar with. At this point the homosexual who was seated beside me made some disparaging comments about the scene we were witnessing. Kazama's tears, he claimed, were nothing but a show – a mere charade. He went so far as to say that he agreed with the position the City of Tokyo was taking. This resulted in a real scene developing!

That evening I got into my car and flew around to Ryuta's apartment and we discussed the day's events in great detail. Since that day we have frequently discussed with each other not only the fact that we wanted to be a happy couple, but also how we might go about carving out a life for ourselves as homosexuals. We came to the conclusion that we would have to live together if we were to move our relationship the next step forward. What proved to be a major stumbling block here though, was the fact that we just couldn't broach the subject of our sexuality with our parents. As long as we concentrated on trying to keep our secret from our parents we would not be in a position to make any moves. We would have to resign ourselves to a continuation of the present situation where we were only able to meet for dates once or twice a week. We were faced with a real impasse.

A year and a half ago, as a result of an incident that had nothing at all do to with Ryuta, my life started to fall apart. I was suffering deep depression and wondering what the future held. I was so depressed that, on one occasion, I broke into tears when out on a date with Ryuta. I wasn't able to even get close to getting over my worries, despite having passed the night with Ryuta at my house. I was so depressed with everything that I felt a real sense of desperation. I had reached the end of my tether. In my desperation I made the decision to unload the burdensome secret I was carrying and tell my mother everything. She responded by saying:

'Although I can't personally understand it, your life is yours and mine is mine. You can only lead your own life. It won't be at all easy for you but good luck to you. You know – I've had an inkling of something like this for some time. You must feel quite relieved now that you've got it off your chest'.

Indeed it was just as mom had said. I tasted the greatest sense of relief that I have ever know in my life. Ryuta followed my example and soon he, too, announced to his mother that he was homosexual. In one almighty hit the circumstances in our lives changed dramatically, opening the way for our living together to become a reality.

Towards building a lifestyle for us – paving the way for a homosexual couple to live together.

About a year and a half ago I was approached by a Mr Kaori Yamaki of the editorial department of a magazine called *Hito* (published by Tarō Jirōsha) and asked to write some stimulating human interest articles for the magazine. I chose to write something of my own life history as a homosexual. The same company was later to publish the book 'My Gay Pride Declaration' based on these manuscripts. While I was involved in this work I was plagued with a series of fears and worries about whether or not I would lose the job I held at the preparatory school – whether or not the series of articles I was writing for the magazine would result in my dismissal – and whether word of my sexuality would reach the neighbourhood in which I lived, resulting in my being an object of scorn and the recipient of unwelcome attention. I was, however, buoyed by the words of my partner, Ryuta Yanase, who said:

'If you are that worried, why not publish my real name too? If you do that it might just be that much easier for you'.

The encouragement and support thus received allowed me to state unequivocally in the book 'My Gay Pride Declaration' that not only was I a homosexual – indeed a homosexual such as exists in all places and has existed in all ages throughout history – but also that homosexuals are not unusual and that they are neither abnormal nor perverted. I stated in black and white that they are simply nothing more than members of the minority sexual persuasion and certainly not something that deserves to be exorcised! I explained also that heterosexuals not only refuse to countenance a questioning of the 'rationality and common sense of society', which they themselves put in place simply on the basis of the fact that they form the majority in society, but also that they fear a breaking down of this 'rationality'. Because of this they, at times, refuse to acknowledge the very existence of homosexuals. Alternatively they feel comfortable placing homosexuals lower down on the social scale than the position which they themselves occupy. Sometimes, through prejudice and discrimination, they try to reject them or on occasions even obliterate them.

I was also able to convincingly introduce some findings of the most recent research which points to the fact that the prohibition of homosexuality by religion came about for no better reason than the fact that it ran contrary to the established practice of expanding the sphere of influence religion was able to command as a result of its promoting the birth of offspring and thus increasing the number of adherents it could claim. Further, by honestly, openly and painstakingly describing the clashes Ryuta and I have experienced over the past seven years (as at the time of writing), I was able to record not only just how difficult it was for us to come to understand each other and develop a love between ourselves, but also how invigorating it was to experience a new field of vision when we reached the point where we had overcome these difficulties. A whole new world opened up, so very different from the one we had experienced until then. In that book I was able, without dramatizing anything and without hiding anything, to pen the process which traced the long and circuitous path I had trodden from the time when I tried to deny my sexuality to myself, to eventually accepting myself for what I am and, finally, becoming confident that homosexuals are not excluded from the prospect of finding happiness in life.

While personally building a life for Ryuta and me, I found myself feeling very strongly that I would like to instigate some movement which would be instrumental in changing society in order to have it allow homosexuals to thrust out their chests and lead their lives with confidence, dignity and pride. This was not something which would be brought about through the example we were setting alone, although it would certainly have had a degree of influence in drawing attention to this issue. The appearance of our first book triggered an epoch-making turn in the Japanese media's treatment of homosexuals. The Asahi Newspaper, CNN and the Fuji TV channels introduced Ryuta and me as representing a new form of partnership rather than portraying us as an object of derision and ridicule or treating us as a laughing stock. I was also greatly encouraged by the many letters from readers who informed me that they had gained a new awareness and appreciation of the question of homosexuality from the book. There was correspondence from homosexuals who said the book had given them the confidence needed to move their lives forward in a positive fashion. There were even heterosexuals who came to reassess their understanding of their own relationships as a result of reading the book. Both Ryuta and I are excited and pleased with the fact that the book has been read and interpreted more positively than we had expected. This inspired us to strive all the more in our efforts to complement each other's lives and work towards becoming an even closer couple.

There are, however, always pitfalls. Having written a book which significantly highlights the plight of homosexuals and which brought about a considerable public response, we have to be careful not to overestimate the effect the book has had nor to overevaluate our contribution to the products of the networks of like-minded people who have come together through reading the book. We have to avoid the delusion of thinking that our books, or that we alone, can change society. We must always be vigilant not to alienate ourselves from, or tire of, working alongside those who operate at the grassroots level to improve the lot of homosexuals in society. We must not start thinking that we have established a monopoly in terms of being an 'authority' on this subject. We need to be careful not to pull the carpet out from under the feet of others or to work at cross purposes with those who share in the quest of improving the lot of homosexuals in Japanese society. We must never forget the uncertainty which plagued us in the early days. Similarly we must not allow fame or a desire to be seen as specialists take over our lives. We must never be so arrogant as to see ourselves as being the founders of a new philosophy. Ryuta and I have no desire whatsoever to see any such developments take place. What we want is to develop a lifestyle for ourselves as homosexuals, one in which we keep our feet planted firmly on the ground as we head out into the hitherto unknown and unexplored frontier that Japan is for an openly gay couple. We hope to do this bearing in mind the needs that will present themselves to us in our old age.

At the moment what homosexuals in Japan need is not a high profile gay TV personality couple. What is most urgently needed is to have, through the support of many people, plenty of actual examples of the homosexual lifestyle and demands being met where there are specific needs to be satisfied (even if they are demands on the country) to allow such a lifestyle to exist. This is a massive job and not something any one person can bring about. It is for this very reason that we have published these two books. We would like to offer our personal experiences and lifestyle to the public as something concrete to hopefully assist, to whatever degree they can, movements aiming to improve the lot of homosexuals in Japan.

There are two main themes dealt with in this book. One of these concerns the way Ryuta sees the earlier book 'My Gay Pride Declaration'. It was written from my point of view, covering the seven years from when we first met. Some parts of it were consciously written in a vague way, as there were some things which Ryuta didn't really want me to reveal.

Thus, in this new book we present an interpretation of our eight year history together through Ryuta's eyes, incorporating his undisguised and unabashed personal feelings. We have also included experiences that I was not able to disclose in the first book. Consequently the reader will be able to trace the paths we have pursued through the stormy vicissitudes of our life together. If this book is read in conjunction with the earlier one, you will become aware of the slight differences which exist in the ways each of us perceived various things and, perhaps, glean an appreciation of how interesting relationships are and how deep they can be. We hope that the reader might develop a more accurate and better informed understanding of the situation Japanese homosexuals are in through Ryuta's analysis.

The other theme of this book relates to our living together as a couple in one household. This stage of our life together started immediately after the publication of 'My Gay Pride Declaration'. Although we are living together as a couple, we share the house with my mother. This book also revisits my 'coming out' to my mother, relating it from Ryuta's perspective. He then picks up the story with us turning our minds to house renovations and his moving in.

His moving in was followed by a period when he was plagued by a series of unpredicted events and unexpected developments, the existence and effects of which registered only very slowly with me. Ryuta became increasingly stressed and we found that our life together was not the happy experience it should have been. Nuta and Nyāgo's relationship was in danger! There were concerns about our partnership, both in terms of its strength and how we ought to manage it. Would we be able to overcome the greatest challenge yet to our relationship? There was a massive and dramatic development lying ahead for us.

Let me give you some idea of where I am as I write this. It is late at night on the 18th of March 1994. Ryuta and I are by ourselves at home – that is to say, my mother is not at home with us. We are feeling pleasantly comfortable, having just prepared and enjoyed dinner together. In fact we prepared enough for three people in order to let mom taste the results of our culinary efforts. This has the added benefit of cutting down on the amount of work involved in meal preparation, something which mostly falls on mom's shoulders. We have one such day a week. The meal this evening consisted of broiled fish with stir-fried vegetables and *miso* soup[2] with peas and soya bean curd.

We congratulated each other on the improvement in terms of the culinary flair we demonstrated over previous efforts and after that we each retired to our own rooms to spend some time as we pleased. Then we spent about three hours or so looking at what we had each written for this book and derived considerable satisfaction and pleasure from both the off-the-cuff and the more in-depth discussion that ensued. As an important 'ritual' we had our goodnight hug and kiss, after which I retired to my own room.

Being able to enjoy such a warm partnership while respecting each other's privacy is something which, for us, only became possible in recent times – eight months after taking up residence together. I am reminded of just how the two of us (but particularly I) had underestimated what would be involved in living together. When one's mother enters into the equation circumstances become just that much more complicated and difficult to deal with. The future held colossal challenges, the likes of which we hadn't experienced in the seven years we had been together up until that time.

I hope you will compare the individual accounts of our lives together, which are provided to offer something of a balanced picture. Since starting our lives together we have discovered that our individual positions are very different. I expected to continue living my life much as I had in the past, whereas Ryuta had to try to fit into the routine of a new household. He had to get used to living in someone else's house.

This second scenario, Ryuta's assimilation into the Ito household, is one which is still unfolding. I expect that as it does, there will be further arguments and difficulties to be overcome. We will face these in the future. I can state, however, that I feel we have passed over the first difficult phase of our lives together. I am, at long last, able to honestly and frankly report that I have come to appreciate both how trying and yet how pleasurable running a household can be.

Compared to 'My Gay Pride Declaration', in which I un-equivocally declared and described the new relationship Ryuta and I were forging together, the reader may find that there is an element of 'crispness' lacking in this, our second book. I feel that it has been possible to portray Nuta and Nyāgo as the people we really are, warts and all. Accordingly it might just be that this book in fact offers more to its readers in terms of possibly acting as a reference source, irrespective of one's sexuality.

Just to re-cap: We are most certainly a homosexual couple. As such we are working hard, slowly but surely, at uncovering a path we can follow together in life. We are doing this with conviction and hope in our hearts. We are a couple who feel a quiet sense of delight and satisfaction that we have jointly accomplished the co-authorship of this book.

Satoru Ito

4 Our Love Notebook

The Genesis of Our Love.

1 Our fateful meeting
by Ryuta Yanase

Our first meeting. Satoru was just too great a guy.

The time was early April 1986. I cast my eye over the steady stream of people flooding through the turnstiles and out of the railway station. There was still five minutes before our appointed meeting time. I was waiting to rendezvous with a particular man. It was a man I had come to know of about three days earlier, through the personal columns of a gay magazine. I had been looking under the heading 'Seeking a Mate'. We had only spoken on the telephone so far, and hadn't as yet actually met. Thus neither of us knew what the other party looked like. It didn't occur to me at the time that the man I was about to meet would end up being my partner in life. This simply hadn't entered my head.

My state of mind was a mixture of expectation and anxiety. What sort of man would appear? He had written in his letter that he was thirty-one years old. His liking for music, particularly Western music, was something we both had in common. The voice on the other end of the line seemed to be quite a gentle one. You never know, this time we might hit it off. But what if he didn't take a liking to me? What would I do then?

My name is Ryuta Yanase. My trade is mould carpentry, in other words I'm in the building industry. I was twenty-four years of age at the time being described and was living with my parents, my elder sister and her son, my nephew. My sister had only 'come home', as it were, of late – having recently divorced her husband.

I am a man, yet there I was, hoping to meet a male partner. Yes

– I am gay, a homosexual. In order that we might readily recognize each other we had arranged for him to carry a blue shoulder bag over his shoulder and for me to wear a white, summer jumper. I wasn't waiting long before a man fitting the given description came down the stairs of the station. He carried a blue shoulder bag over his shoulder and he appeared to be looking for someone. My heart pounded loudly. Should I rouse up my courage and call out to him? This I did.

'Hello. Would you be Mr Ito?'

'I am, yes. Are you Ryuta?'

We had managed to correctly identify each other from amongst the throng of people on our first attempt. 'Should we perhaps first of all retire to a coffee shop?' I ventured and this suggestion was met with ready agreement – a very welcome development. This is how our first arranged meeting took place in a coffee shop near my house.

His name, he said, was Satoru Ito. He told me he was currently living with his mother, his father having passed away. He told me that he was an instructor at a preparatory school. He had really beautiful eyes and appeared to be a very gentle person. This was my first impression of him. Once we started talking together, however, my first impression crumbled away, raising some noise as it did. In the coffee shop he got quite carried away. I tried my best to keep the momentum of the conversation up and contribute to the discussion. I am sure of that much. However, the things that he was talking about were things which, at that time, were difficult for me to accept. In the surrounds of the coffee shop he repeatedly used the word 'gay' quite openly and without reservation. What was more, his voice was quite loud. I felt my face burn with embarrassment just being there.

At that stage I bore a severe sense of awkwardness and harboured a distinct sense of guilt and shame about being homosexual. Could you expect otherwise? It was an age in which male homosexuals were called 'poofters' and 'homos' and constantly scorned with derisive laughter. In those days I felt tremendous shame. Because of my sexuality, I felt as though I should apologize to society for being who I was.

He, on the other hand, was quite different. He kept using the word 'gay' like a machine-gun, with no hesitation whatsoever. It was as though he was asking everyone in the shop to stop and listen. What a great man – but perhaps too great! For someone on the timid and cowardly side like me he was just a touch over the top! For this reason I made up my mind there and then that I probably would not seek a repeat date with him.

He kept on talking about gays in a voice which was not only loud but audible to others. This made me so tense that I had to visit the toilet. When I said to him 'please excuse me for a moment, I have a stomachache and need to be excused', he responded 'Oh I see. You're quite a shy type then!' I was able to manage only a wry smile in response to this. I felt as though I had reached my limit and couldn't take much more. Fortune was not smiling on our relationship at all at that stage. We talked for about an hour and then, as we were about to part, agreed on another time to meet. Just as we were about to head for home, he said 'It looks as though we two might get along just fine!' I managed a response which indicated agreement while smiling faintly. From the bottom of my heart, however, I heard a voice screaming 'You have to be joking! No way!'

Starting to feel that this person had something that I didn't have.

Later in April 1986.

I received a phone call from Satoru two or three days after our first meeting in the coffee shop. He invited me over to spend some time at his place, saying he wanted to talk more, and in a more relaxed setting. For a moment I was on the point of declining the offer on the phone, thinking to myself that there was nothing else to talk about, but then I decided to meet him and tell him face to face that I wanted to finish our relationship. For one thing I was alone that day and had no plans to meet anyone. For another, I felt that regardless of whether I was to break it off with him or not, perhaps I would be able to tell him things about myself which I wanted to tell him. It had been all I could do to keep myself listening to what he had been saying the other day in the coffee shop – never mind contributing significantly to the conversation. Even so, I was in two minds about what to do because I was thinking that I would tell him that we could build a relationship as friends and not as lovers.

Soon after I arrived at his house he started telling me about his life history. He told me how he had changed schools many times and never been able to make friends properly. He reported how he hit upon the idea of seeking the attention of the teachers when he became resigned to the fact that he was unable to make friends amongst classmates. He also reported how he realized that the teachers wouldn't be interested in him unless his school grades were good. For this reason he put his heart and soul into his studies, never doing anything contrary to the teacher's instructions. He reported that he himself chose to work hard and obtain excellent grades in order to be considered a top student. He told me how, having achieved the required level of academic excellence, he had pleased everyone by managing to earn a place in Kaisei Junior High School and how subsequently he had obtained magnificent grades in Kaisei Senior High School and even managed to be offered a place at Tokyo University!!! Was I hearing correctly? This remarkable level of academic achievement was indeed most impressive. And yet that same student who had proven himself capable of pulling in such excellent academic grades was telling me how very much he regretted sacrificing his youth to academic pursuits. More than anything he now lamented the fact that he chose to try to be liked by the teachers and be popular with them.

I was quite taken aback by all that he was telling me. He had a completely different set of values from mine. In fact, in retrospect I should say that I didn't have anything which could have been called a set of values as such in those days. I had certainly never had social interaction nor been involved with anyone to an appreciable extent before. Nor had the friendships I had experienced ever progressed beyond being anything other than superficial, non-intrusive and non-confronting. For this reason I didn't know what sort of person I was myself. I didn't have anything which could have been described as a 'face' of my own. Being 'faceless', as I was, meant that I was in no position to respond in any way to him. I must say though, that I couldn't comprehend why he regretted his student days as much as he did. I felt an indescribable type of shock at his pronouncements. Looking back at it now I can state that whereas he was doing his level best to lay his soul bare to me, I don't think that I was able to reciprocate. You see, in order to bare your soul it is necessary to have one. Since I didn't have a soul as such at that time, there was no way I could have reciprocated by bearing it to him. All

I was able to do was act as a listener. I began, however, to feel that this person certainly had something which I lacked. At the end of the day I was unable to tell him that I only wanted to be Platonic friends from that time on.

Getting irritated with Satoru; arguing with him over his behaviour in public – his not caring what others might think.

Late April 1986.

A month flew by while my heart continued to tell me that my association with Satoru was not going to work out. That stage of my life, however, was characterized by an irresoluteness, a lack of decisiveness, and I sensed that the feelings I had in relation to this man were starting to undergo a change. Little by little I felt an attraction for him.

We are now in Yokohama. Today represents the first real date we have had with each other. We decided we would stroll through the famous gardens on the hillsides overlooking the harbour and then wander through the Chinatown district of the city. Young couples surround us. Just looking at them makes me seethe with anger. I feel like coming up from behind and giving them a good whack about the ears but this is not possible for a timid soul such as I. Some couples are holding hands, others walking arm in arm. But for my partner and me this is not possible. The reason why is simple enough. It is because from the moment we join hands we will be laughed at and become objects of society's scorn and derision. As long as we pretend to be heterosexuals we are allowed a comfortable place in the workings of society. From the instant we were to hold hands with each other (even though in fact we, too, are lovers) we would be confronting society by announcing that we were homosexuals. By announcing that we were a homosexual couple we would put ourselves directly in the firing line of society, one which is defined by society's blanket consideration of gays as fitting the 'homo' image, equating the term 'gay' with 'poofter'. We would end up being on the receiving end of ridicule, derision, scornful jibes and sneering laughter.

I am now in a position to interpret the situation we faced back then differently. But at the time, just simply walking together with Satoru was quite a difficult thing for me to do, wondering whether or not two men walking together in an area almost exclusively frequented by young heterosexual couples would be thought of as being beyond the pale. What should have been a really enjoyable date wasn't, because I was totally unable to relax.

I was a very sensitive person and quite cowardly. I was almost excessive in my fear that others might discover that I was homosexual. I hadn't accepted myself as a homosexual. I felt a mixture of loathing and guilt about being a homosexual. I was aware that in this regard Satoru was, even at that stage, streets ahead of me. At the very least I can say that he had opened the door to accepting himself as a homosexual. I wonder if you are able to imagine what sort of a date a pair such as he and I were able to have.

Satoru was keen to hold my hand when we were on a date. He always wanted to walk close to me. It was a natural desire and a reasonable request. I had to refuse his advances, however, for the simple and clear-cut reason that I had no desire whatsoever to choose a course of action which would make me the laughing stock of all those around me. Neither was I sure that I could withstand being in such a position. Whenever we were walking and Satoru would get close to me I would, quietly and without fuss, move away to set a distance between us. When he would try to hold hands with me I would nonchalantly move his hand away. It wasn't that I was dating a man I disliked. In fact I was walking with someone for whom the beginnings of an indistinct love were germinating. Nor was it as though I were a popular singer or a TV idol whose love life was public property. Why did I have to be so concerned about what those around me would think?

At any rate our date in Yokohama ended without incident. Satoru had to control his desire to hold hands with me and I had to put up with the discomfort of wondering what the people around us were thinking. That was our memorable first date. It already hinted at the prospect of difficulties lying ahead for us and was followed by a period in which we found reason to quarrel and argue almost incessantly.

On our way home from a date together in July 1986 we dropped into a *sushi* shop where, initially, a quiet and enjoyable conversation took place in a convivial atmosphere. Before long, however, I just felt too awkward and uncomfortable to enjoy being there. We were seated at the counter where the chef was privy to our conversation while he prepared the food in front of us. Satoru turned to me and said, quite earnestly, '*Sushi* is just so much more delicious when you share it with someone you care about'. Looking back at it now, I realize that it was really a very mild comment, reflecting the affection he felt for me. But at the time I simply could not stand it. I felt as though this comment was tantamount to our turning to the chef and declaring our homosexuality to him. I wanted to leave the premises at the very earliest opportunity, but I couldn't communicate this to Satoru. He continued devouring the *sushi* with relish, displaying as he did an innocence and naivete attributable, perhaps, to the sheer joy of being in the company of the person he was attracted to. I, on the other hand, felt completely ill at ease, fixing my eyes on the counter in front of me and not looking up except when it was unavoidable.

We launched into an argument about the experience soon after leaving the shop. The foul mood I was in remained with me for the rest of the day. Yet despite this, Satoru didn't seem to comprehend what I was angry about. I found myself thinking that I would really prefer not to continue going out with such an artless man.

As simply continuing to be angry and not explaining anything wouldn't help in bringing the two of us closer to any kind of mutual understanding, I told him how his choice of words in that one statement made me feel so very uncomfortable. I also told him that I hoped in the future he would be a little more circumspect about what he pops into our conversations.

Satoru apologized over and over again, finishing off with the comment 'Why is it that we must be so guarded about what we say? The world is wrong, we're not'. In my heart I knew that he was indeed correct, even without it having to be stated. But to tell the truth, I actually knew nothing; nothing that I could be certain about or that I could articulate. I had always taken the full blame for my own inability to fit in squarely. The notion that blame should be attributed to society was foreign to me. I blamed myself for the fact that I was homosexual and accepted that it couldn't be helped that society had no place for homosexuals.

I simply couldn't keep up with Satoru on dates when he would try to act, if anything in a rather natural way, as though our partnership as a homosexual couple were sanctioned by society.

As it transpired, my anger was not being directed towards society at large, but rather towards Satoru. I asked him why he couldn't tailor his behaviour in such a way as to conceal the fact that we were a gay couple from those around us.

I was unable to face the world unless I was at all times, and in all situations, wearing the mask of heterosexuality. I never queried why it was that I was unable to face the world without my heterosexual mask. It seems it was easier for me to attack the approach to life Satoru Ito was taking than to face myself as the homosexual who had taken knocks all his life and was downtrodden.

It was through the strategy of blaming others that I managed to avoid looking at myself and recognizing myself as the person I am. It had become a survival strategy of mine well before Satoru came into my life. It was a habit which had become part and parcel of my life. Single-handedly I had to find some means of accommodating the homosexual that I knew I was, while simultaneously accommodating the expectations of society at large.

Working for my uncle as a carpenter. Despising him for the harsh treatment he meted out to me.

I would like at this juncture to explain a little more about the sort of person I was when I first met Satoru. I worked as a mould carpenter from about six months before I met Satoru until May 1993. My boss was my uncle, my mother's younger brother. I was never an outgoing type, always disinclined to want to meet new people, and after starting to work for my uncle I found myself all the more frightened of people I didn't know (I will go into the reasons for this a little later on). This cast a very dark shadow across the relationship I had with Satoru.

My mother was one of three children. It was the younger of her two brothers who was my boss. He previously had worked for his older brother for a long time, until the older brother suicided. I am not sure why he took this course of action. Maybe the pressure of work was too much for him or perhaps he felt he had reached the limit of his physical endurance. Nobody will ever know, now that he is no longer with us. It goes without saying that my remaining uncle keenly felt the shock of this suicide. It is even possible that he thus became mentally unstable. I am sure that he suffered a considerable amount of stress from being suddenly thrust to the forefront of the business, particularly given that he had, up until that time, always 'played second fiddle', as it were, hiding in his brother's shadow.

When I started working there it was plain for all to see that my uncle was jittery and not quite on top of things. Those working for him had all been employed by his brother on the same basis as he had, so although he was now their boss, as far as they were concerned he was still an equal. In fact he was the boss in name only. Nevertheless the full responsibility for the work fell squarely on his shoulders. Under the circumstances, I was the only outlet he had to exert his authority. And, naturally enough, I was initially inept at the jobs I was given to do. So, I suppose it is not surprising that he repeatedly took me to task.

I felt that learning to withstand this amount of pressure was a necessary part of becoming a fully-fledged carpenter in my own right. That was why, when I first started working there, I never challenged what my uncle said. Or perhaps it was because I wasn't able to challenge him. In hindsight I appreciate that this was the wrong tack to have taken. I should have found the courage to confront him about the most unreasonable way that he told me off.

Being told off for mistakes or ineptitude on a job is not unreasonable. But my uncle tried to exert his authority in front of the other workers by lecturing me. To put it another way, he used me time and time again to salvage his own pride. This was a way of trying to protect his own reputation and to escape awkward situations with his pride intact.

I always felt great resentment about this, a resentment that soon turned to hatred. And yet I found it difficult to talk back or argue a point with him. Indeed I was never able to. In a nutshell I guess you could say that I was unable to break down the barrier between us.

Eventually I ended up using him, too, so that I could hide, become 'invisible' as it were. In the end I used him as a tool to blend into the background and not stand out, though I never planned it that way and didn't do it consciously. I simply chose the easiest route that presented itself for coping with the circumstances I was confronted with; the 'path of least resistance', so to speak.

I couldn't question my uncle or resist his directives because, ultimately, I craved the feeling of reassurance that came from hiding in his shadow. And this was despite the fact that I despised him. Nonetheless I never attempted to emerge from my invisibility. Rather, by way of recompense, I continued to 'offer' myself as a 'tool' to be used by my uncle to allow him to save face and ensure his ego was protected.

I worked for him for seven years. The whole time I tried to remain invisible – not wanting to stand out or have attention drawn to myself – simply wanting to keep a low profile. Deep in my heart I always felt that at the end of the day I would be able to rely on him to somehow look after things for me. My uncle, for his part, continued to use me as a tool to shield his ego. For these seven years I worked to the best of my ability and, not surprisingly, became quite proficient at what I was doing. However, trying to keep a low profile by availing myself of my uncle's protection somehow managed, over time, to bring about a sense of guilt – the sort that is associated with doing something a bit underhanded. I ended up leaving the job, without ever coming straight out and confronting my uncle.

Continually being told off by my uncle. Suffering anxiety attacks – fearing being looked at by others.

On a construction site there are many different tradesmen to be found. Apart from the mould carpenters there are electricians, plumbers, scaffolders, labourers, iron-workers and site supervisors to name but a few. Each plays his own part in the construction of a single building. As already mentioned my uncle was forever picking on me. As a person not naturally given to being the centre of attention or to associating with many people I found this very hard to bear. It wasn't being told off *per se* that I found so bad. It was having my clumsiness drawn to the attention of others that I found hard to take. With my uncle running me down in front of the other site workers every day, day in day out, I got to the point where I eventually feared other people even looking at me. This wasn't restricted to the worksite, but spilled over into my private life as well. For example, when I heard someone laughing as I walked along the street I would suspect that they were laughing at me and I couldn't get away quickly enough. Likewise I was dreadfully conscious of being in the full view of people sitting opposite me on the train. I felt as though I was being made fun of. Eventually I reached a point where my blood rushed to my head and I broke out in uncontrollable cold sweats. When this happened I would rush off the train and head straight for home. No matter where I went, mere glances from people would pierce me. There were even times when I felt that my grasp on a normal level of mental stability was precarious. At these times I was hardly able to walk outside due to my being so very conscious of the existence of other people. I became a terribly pusillanimous person when it came to dealing with other people looking at me.

As it happened, the first time I met Satoru was when I was going through a bad patch and things didn't look set to improve. Despite this I was loathe to acknowledge myself as being such a sorry and woeful person. With the discomfort I experienced when out in public you can imagine how trying it was for me to leave the house every time we arranged a date. And more than anything else I feared Satoru would see what a troubled person I was.

Back in the days when Satoru and I first met he didn't have a driver's licence, so the job of driving always fell to me. Now as anyone who drives will testify, there are times when, for no particular reason at all, your eyes meet those of the driver of the car in front, behind or beside you. When this happened to me I would experience a most unpleasant and unwelcome sensation. In those days, once this sensation appeared on the scene I was unable to control it. I would imagine that someone was looking at me through the rear-vision mirror and I couldn't stand it. But you can't stop the car and get out to seek refuge anywhere when you are driving. All you can do is remain in your seat.

When I found myself in this situation I would start to have a panic attack which I then tried to hide from Satoru. I tried for all I was worth, as I didn't want him to know what was happening. Blood would rush to my head, and though I might want to speak I was quite unable to do so. Then I would get angry with myself. In other words, with Satoru being totally unaware of it, I would descend into a state of extreme anxiety. By the time he realized something was up I was already infuriated with myself.

It goes without saying that he was quite taken aback by my sudden bad temper. It is only natural that he was surprised at the way I scowled and would keep a stony silence when he spoke to me. He would ask what was up and what I was angry at, begging me to tell him, but I was unable to do so. I couldn't explain it to him. I felt that I couldn't afford to let him perceive me as the sorry and wretched person I really was.

It took me the extraordinarily long period of seven years before I could properly explain my circumstances to Satoru and thus account for my behaviour. I know that throughout those seven years I gave him a very hard time but I simply couldn't explain my mental state to him. It was exactly as if there was another 'me' within me who was manipulating me. I was repeating the same mistake *ad infinitum*, realizing as I did so that I was making things harder and harder for Satoru.

It is quite understandable that he would start wondering whether he was to blame for my foul moods and, naturally enough, this concern made *him* anxious. He later suffered anxiety neurosis, no doubt at least partly as a result of this situation. Whenever I got into a bad mood he would press me for the cause. He was himself greatly affected and uneasy at such times. It was only after he was able to clearly establish that it was not his fault that I behaved as I did and that he was not to blame for my outbursts of anger that he was able to escape from the anxiety and uneasiness that afflicted him.

Our dates proved to be a source of anguish for him in many ways, as they did for me. When on dates I unwittingly caused him great stress. It was only when I was able to ascertain the true nature of this other 'me' that was governing my life that Satoru and I were released from this pattern of interaction which dominated our relationship. Up until that time I was unable to be in control – obstructed by a barrier surrounding me – and repeating the same act of folly, namely dropping into seemingly inexplicable moody bouts of silence. This was a far cry from what I needed to do if I were to stop making Satoru anxious. Our dates, which for an ordinary couple might have been enjoyable experiences, turned into something perhaps best described as 'grand encounters'.

Fearing people's looks all the more. Dates take the form of take-away dinners in the car.

April 1987. Approximately one year has passed since I first met Satoru. Our date today is drawing to a close and it is dinner time.

We will be having a hamburger patty TV style dinner this evening. At the moment we are not at home, nor in a restaurant, but in my beloved car, a Honda Civic. Why, you might be wondering, are we eating a TV dinner in the car? Let me explain!

As mentioned earlier I first met Satoru when my mental state was taking a turn for the worse. Initially I was able to somehow manage to eat out but eventually that proved to be a trying experience. The thing I dreaded most were the looks I received from other people. As for eating a meal in full view of others, I found this very hard to cope with. I had even thought to myself that if our going out together meant that I had to continue eating out as we were, I would prefer to leave him.

I was starting to feel that at some stage I would have to tell him this, but a couple of things held me back. For one thing I felt that it would hardly be fair on him, given that it was not his fault that I suffered from anxiety attacks, and for another my pride got in the way, preventing me from being able to explain my unfortunate circumstances to him. But unless I could explain my fears and anxieties to him, I would be condemned to continue eating meals in restaurants and other public places every time we went on a date. And this, for me, was too terrifying a prospect to contemplate.

There was a terrific tug-o-war between my pride and my fear of being forced to eat out in public for evermore. This was a fear that embraced my heart. In the end it was my fear which emerged victorious. I decided to explain my situation to Satoru. No, I didn't 'decide', but was rather driven to the point where I had no choice but to offer an explanation. And still, this was easier said than done. How was I to get him to understand my torment? How was I to communicate to him a terror that he had not experienced for himself? It seemed to be next to impossible, yet somehow I had to get my feelings across. Unless, by whatever means, I could get Satoru to comprehend what I was going through, the very continuation of our relationship would be in serious jeopardy.

I feared being with people. My fear of catching the eye of others had reached abnormal levels. I hated people and I thoroughly hated myself. I dreaded crowds and was unable to stand the gaze of others. I detested the gutless person I was. When I explained this and the mentality which underscored it to Satoru I became quite emotional. This was partly because, initially, Satoru had great difficulty understanding where I was coming from; particularly when I explained that I couldn't face going out amongst crowds of people or that it was not possible for me to enjoy a meal when I was exposed to the public gaze. I finally unequivocally declared that I would be prepared to put an end to our relationship if he insisted we eat out together.

He replied in a most grieved tone of voice, asking me if that meant that we'd never again be able to eat together in a restaurant. I was unable to say there and then that I believed that would be the case, because I loved him too much. I was quite unable to say anything in fact, confused as I was with a mixture of guilt, exasperation and regret for having hurt him by being so pathetic. I was the focus of this exasperation. I was exasperated with myself for not being able to extricate myself from the darkness I was in, no matter how much I struggled to do so.

After a while he turned to me and said, 'I'll put up with that. I'll put up with that arrangement because I don't want us to separate. I absolutely don't want that'. His voice was very weak as he spoke these words. I had hurt him again. And again I blamed myself for hurting him so much simply by being a gutless, pathetic creature.

And yet, while I came down hard on myself, I never made any attempt to challenge my own position. The fear and hatred I felt towards people was that strong! I wanted to set myself free! I wanted to be free to live my own life! Such were the cries echoing deep in my soul, but there was always something holding me back. It was as though I was being bound hand and foot. I wondered if that was to be my lot in life – if I was to ever be able to break free. I was being controlled by a sense of hopelessness.

From that time on our dates were planned to take us to deserted spots in the country where we could share our meals in the car. This resulted in our mealtimes becoming flat and monotonous. Certainly these were not the sort of dates we would have chosen if there had been an alternative. The other 'me' within me wouldn't allow me to be free. This other 'me' would always be there telling me 'You're the scum of the earth. There's no way you'll ever be happy. You're nothing but a filthy poofter. Hate! Hate people more! Hate yourself more!' He would always drag me back to the depths of Hades if I even so much as tried to seek happiness. The conflict between me and this other 'me' was set to continue for some time.

Through my association with Satoru I tried to dispel the hatred I felt for my uncle.

March 1988. Satoru obtained his driver's licence. It became apparent that Satoru found it very hard going with such a self-centred and self-absorbed person as I was at the wheel. He could do nothing but sit in the passenger seat and take what was dished up. I was prone to clam up and take my frustrations out on him whenever we were caught in a traffic jam or experienced any similar annoyance. There was no escape for him. What's more, he had to fall in line and sympathize with me whenever a stupid driver suddenly cut in front of me. And it didn't end there. If he didn't get sufficiently mad he would find himself the target of my wrath, though he himself had done nothing wrong. When I got tired after driving long distances he would have to endure sarcastic comments from me of the 'Why is it I have to do all the driving?' ilk. How the poor man suffered with such a cutting and spiteful person as his partner. I felt sorry for him and wanted to do something to help him, so I put it to him that if he found my driving so terrible he should learn to drive himself. And at the age of thirty-five he made the decision to obtain his own driver's licence.

This was a major decision and earned him my high regard. Not only did he resolve to get his licence, he actually carried through and got it – wow! He felt pleased, believing that this would be instrumental in reducing the number of arguments we would have. I also believed this initially – but the reality was to prove otherwise.

I turned into a devil of an instructor who picked on the newly licensed driver at every turn and end. His lack of driving finesse made me angry. Whenever he encountered an even slightly dangerous situation I would sling off at him and give him a most vehement tongue lashing, after which I would grumble incessantly. Even for Satoru there was a limit to how much he could take. When he reached it he would come back at me with 'Why must you always be angry at me even though I went to such lengths to get my licence?' There are limits to human patience. It was only natural that he should feel that his limits were being tested. Whenever I rode with him his driving would get very clumsy because he felt tense with me in the car. The harder he tried to not make me lose my cool, the worse mess he would make of his driving. I was putting the poor man terribly on edge.

The situation can be compared to when I was still very new at the carpentry trade and was constantly being told off by my uncle. He never let up. He was on my back the whole time. I used to think to myself that he was such a gutless man – always trying to make himself look good in front of others, worried only about his own ego and not my feelings. But then it dawned on me that I was guilty of doing to Satoru just what my uncle had done to me. Here I was doing exactly the same thing as the man I hated! In other words, when I looked at the situation in as detached a way as possible, I realized that I too was a despicable, gutless person who persistently tried to show himself in a good light.

I was quite incapable of controlling my own emotions. Indeed I wasn't aware of the cause of my anger. Perhaps my anger wasn't directed at Satoru at all. In fact I began to feel that perhaps it was an anger more directed towards my uncle – an anger that could never be dissipated whilst ever I was unable to confront him head on. The anger within me had no focus and I ended up directing it at Satoru, expending it on him. I am ashamed and embarrassed at both the part of me that was not able to express anger at my uncle and at the part of me that could take it out on Satoru. After I came to appreciate this we witnessed a drop, albeit a slow one, in the number of arguments we had.

2 Finding the courage to announce to my family that I have a lover
by Ryuta Yanase

The first time ever I announced that I was gay – coming out to my sister.

A day in December 1989.

This proved to be a day I will never forget as long as I live. It was the day I first divulged the fact that I was homosexual to a heterosexual person. The person I made this revelation to was my sister.

As mentioned earlier, I used to live with my parents and my divorced sister and her child. There were five of us living together in a three bedroom condominium with a lounge room and a kitchen. The lack of space was a contributing factor in my sister's decision to move into a flat of her own. She moved out with my nephew towards the end of last year, taking up residence in a nearby apartment.

Living under the same roof as my sister and her son had proven to be a very positive thing for me. They were a source of support and comfort for someone who had, by and large, lost faith in people. In particular my nephew, Gen, taught me many things. He used to say 'People can only act silly in front of people who will allow them to'. For me, Gen was one of just a handful of such people and I always felt very relaxed in his company. I would feel as though I was on top of things. Yes indeed, I had forgotten that there had been a time when I had been known as a bit of a joker, before I became overly conscious of my sexual orientation. Gen, for his part, was a real wag whenever he was with me. We really got on well and felt comfortable acting the goat in each other's company.

At one stage when I was shunning contact with people, I was on the verge of forgetting how to laugh and how to make people laugh. But Gen reminded me of these things. I would often be given the job of putting him to bed at night when my sister came home late. He would not, however, go to sleep quietly – this came at a price! He would insist that I make up a bedtime story for him. He was particularly partial to the story about one of the most natural of all bodily functions. The main character was an old man who went off to the woods to relieve himself. The old lady in the story likewise went down to the river to answer the call of nature. For some reason or other kids just love this sort of story. Anyway I would get carried away with this theme, the story being rendered all the more interesting for Gen, coming as it did from a twenty-six year old man speaking in baby language! I guess, looking at it objectively, those bedtime stories must have been a touch on the weird side, not so much for what the stories were about as the sight of me telling them!

Nonetheless it was simply wonderful how, though I would tell these weird and wonderful tales, Gen never thought of me as being weird. On the contrary, he just accepted me as I was. He was mature enough to do that. It is probably the case that Gen, and other children too, have an intriguing ability to let me be myself and be natural in front of them.

In the same way, it is a strange thing that, though I might be physically tired when I get home from work, I feel mentally invigorated when Satoru comes out to meet me. I feel an acceptance as though my inner soul is being set free the moment I see his face. This is because he is totally without socially induced, preconceived ideas about who I should be and how I should act. He is totally without prejudice in relation to me. He is again the precious person he was before he became aware of his sexual orientation, back at the stage of life when adopting society's preconceptions and difficulties about homosexuality – its prejudice against and loathing towards it – were foreign to his experience, something he simply could not conceptualize. That is why his presence was so important to me. In his presence I was able to be free from the sense of being with people 'from the other team', as it were. It is extremely sad to reflect on the fact that once he was to start to become aware of his own sexuality the blank canvas (which represented his true self, his inner being) would get painted over with a hatred and loathing for homosexuality.

I told myself that I must never let such a thing happen to Gen. I had a duty to inform Gen of the fact that I was homosexual. If telling him this were to distance him from me, I would have to accept the consequences because I cannot change the fact that I am gay.

After her divorce my sister was exhausted from trying to do battle on two fronts: holding down a job while at the same time raising her son. Her exhaustion was a concern for the entire family. As previously mentioned, she had moved into an apartment a mere 300 meters from our parents' house. Now there was talk of a second marriage. This was certainly welcome news and cause for congratulations. But if she remarried, she and Gen would, naturally enough, move to her new partner's house. She would be much further away.

As the day of her second marriage approached I found myself experiencing many different emotions. Talk of her remarrying seemed to come out of the blue. I was seized with the fear that I would lose an irretrievable opportunity to confide in her and disclose my secret if I didn't seize the moment and act soon. The fear was also that Gen would, for me, become an unbearably distant figure once he became aware of his own sexual orientation if I couldn't take my sister into my confidence and come out to her.

I made up my mind that I would come out to my sister before she moved. I was unsure just what I would do, however, if she had negative feelings towards homosexuals. I just wouldn't know how to face her in the future if her reaction were something like 'Not you Ryuta...a *homo*? Tell me you're joking. Yuk!' I knew that even if she were to turn against me I would still have to deal with her for the rest of my life. Although I had made the decision to come out to her, I was tortured by concerns and anxieties. Making the decision, though, rendered me a somewhat different person to the one I had been before that. I thought to myself that even if a wedge were driven between us I would still have Satoru. I wouldn't be left alone in this world. I kept my spirits up by asking myself the question 'Is it wrong for me to be a homosexual?' and telling myself that it definitely wasn't. I was able to find such words of encouragement thanks to my having met Satoru.

It was with great trepidation that I made the decision to ring my sister and break the news to her. I told her that I was homosexual, that this was a terribly serious issue for me and that I had been troubled by it for a long, long time. I explained that being a homosexual was certainly not something which people have any say in and that I would never marry, as I was unable to muster any interest at all in the fairer sex. I told her that I had a partner in Mr Satoru Ito, and that I planned to maintain the relationship I had with him. I got all this off my chest in one go.

Far from what I had feared might be her reaction, I found her response almost off-puttingly accepting. It was wonderful. She didn't come back at me with 'Don't be so silly – find a girl and get yourself married' or 'That's disgusting', but instead offered support for my position, saying 'It's good you have found yourself a partner. It doesn't matter to me one iota whether you are a homosexual or not. It's up to each individual to find his or her own partner in life. It has got nothing to do with anyone else and likewise no-one has the right to question it. You've done very well to find such a good man as Mr Ito. Make sure you do the right thing by him'. My sister had no problem accepting me. This development proved to be a tremendous source of joy, providing a huge boost to my self-confidence. For a while after I put the phone down my spirits soared with ecstasy.

Before this wonderfully uplifting sensation began to subside I rang Satoru, then headed over to his place where we shared the joy together. I told him that I had 'taken the plunge' and come out to my sister. He asked what her reaction had been and I proceeded to relate the whole incident to him. I had been extremely tense as it was the first time in my life I had ever come out to a heterosexual, but that just served to heighten the sense of joy I experienced when I found acceptance as the homosexual I am. In fact the sense of rapture was so great that it took me by surprise! Satoru was also elated at my finding acceptance with my sister, no less so than he would have been had he been the one in my position. He said 'That's great. That's great!' over and over again!

I wonder what would have happened if on that occasion my sister had rejected me. I guess I would have experienced a sense of being cast into the darkest depths of Hades. You see, at that stage I had virtually no self-confidence regarding my homosexuality. Looking back I realize how very servile and lacking in moral courage I was then. When I came out to my sister there was still a large element of obsequiousness in my attitude, the 'Oh great heterosexual, could you somehow see your way clear to accepting me?' sort of thing. And for this very reason the exhilaration I felt when I found acceptance was tinged with a sense of subservience, again of the 'Oh great heterosexual, thank you. Thank you for accepting me' ilk. Of course there was much more to the joy I experienced than there was to this 'obsequious aspect' of my consciousness.

Yet, it would be fair to say that because of this attitude of subservience I greatly feared rejection. I harboured a simply tremendous anxiety about being hurt. Whenever a homosexual lacks confidence in himself as a homosexual he will feel that he has to justify himself to the heterosexual party he seeks to come out to. The heterosexual party, on the other hand, will always command the stronger position in any negotiations, representing, as he does, the socially accepted and endorsed position regarding what constitutes a 'normal' sexual orientation. Although things happened to go well in my case, thanks to my sister being an open-minded and tolerant person, I have come to appreciate that whether you feel joy and elation as a result of coming out or whether disclosing your sexuality results in your being thrust into the darkest depths of depression depends almost entirely on the other party. This is a strange situation when you stand back and think about it. Both the initiative to come out and the ability to direct the result of this action should be with the homosexual.

Let us suppose for a moment that the other party were to come back and say 'Gays are disgusting, despicable. I could never accept them'. I wouldn't allow myself to get depressed over this, for the simple reason that no-one is able to alter the fact that I am homosexual, irrespective of whether this is sanctioned or not. I would like to become a person who could shamelessly respond:

'I am a homosexual. Whether you accept me or not has no bearing on the validity of this fact. You are not able to change my sexuality. Similarly you are not able to change the fact that you are a heterosexual. I remain the same person after making this admission to you as I was before making the admission. I'm still me. If your opinion of me changes as a result of my admission, that is because of the prejudice you harbour. In other words, your ability to accept me as a homosexual, or your lack of such ability, is a question for you yourself to come to terms with. If you cannot accept the homosexual I am, please ask yourself why not; why is it that you despise homosexuals?'

Leaving my parents' home and moving into an apartment. Continuous arguments about the telephone.

March 1990. Four years have now passed since I met Satoru. There are still interminable arguments taking place between us but our lifestyle is about to undergo a change. I am moving away from my parents' house and setting up my own home. As a matter of fact my sister's remarrying had something to do with this. She was the first of the children to move out of our parents' home when she got married the first time. After divorcing, however, she moved back and got herself a new job but found that with all she had on her plate she was not having an easy time of it at all. About a year ago she and her son moved out of our parents' place and into a nearby flat where they started their life together as a two person household. When she got married for the second time she moved out of her flat, thus providing me with the opportunity to take over the lease.

The accommodation consisted of two bedrooms, a combined dining/kitchen area, a bathroom and a toilet. She even left me the fridge and washing machine. It was still quite a new building and very smartly appointed and I would have been a fool to let the opportunity to move in slip by. My head was abuzz with all sorts of ideas about how I might organize the interior of the flat. I rather fancied that I might keep a few tropical fish – something I had wanted to do since I was a young lad. I could be quite the man about town using indoor plants and what have you to dress the place up! Here was a chance for me to display a bit of flair as an interior decorator!

I felt a bit sad leaving Satoru out of things, but being the self-centred person I was, my mind was focussed on how I would decorate my own room and nothing else. A little while later I turned my thoughts to how moving away from my parents and into a flat of my own would affect my relationship with Satoru. First and foremost, if I was living away from my parents I would be able to meet him anytime I wanted to, day or night, without feeling constrained in any way. I would be able to talk on the phone as much as I liked about whatever I liked without being ever conscious of the 'satellite dish' ears of my parents! I would be free to leave gay magazines lying about if I wanted to, and what's more I would be free to have sex without concerning myself about others! This would be great!

With the support and backup of both my sister and Satoru, and the fact that at work I was becoming confident in my ability as a carpenter, I was able to make the decision to move into the flat without too much difficulty. The one who was most pleased for me was my partner, Satoru Ito. In fact, he might just have been even more pleased than I was myself! There was no doubt that while living under the same roof as my parents I had to find enormous reserves of inner strength and mental energy in order to maintain the relationship I shared with Satoru, since it was a partnership neither endorsed by my parents nor approved by society.

My moving out represented a big change for Satoru, too. To illustrate, let me cite the circumstances surrounding our telephone conversations. Being ever conscious of the presence of my parents, I couldn't for the life of me bring myself to say such a thing as 'I love you' on the telephone. I always had to make out that I was talking to just an ordinary old friend. It was only natural that Satoru would feel frustrated at the contrived contributions I made to our telephone conversations. So I would often use public phones in order to be able to speak freely.

There were also problems with this arrangement, however. Often, for example, I would get mad when I had gone to a public phone but found I couldn't get through to Satoru, either because he happened to be already talking to someone else or for some other reason. This would lead to a huge argument. To address this problem Satoru came up with an unusual birthday present for me – a cordless phone – which considerably alleviated the issue of a lack of privacy.

Another change that resulted from moving out of my parents' house was that I no longer had to hide things away. When I was living at home I always had to hide gay magazines such as *Barazoku* or *Adon*. Why was it that I had to be so concerned about the people around me? I look back now in horror at the restricted lifestyle I used to lead in those days. If someone were to tell me today that I had to go back to that same lifestyle I'm sure I would go mad. Anyway, all that aside, the fact was that I launched into an independent life on my own.

After moving into the apartment I became aware of several changes, both in myself and in my relationship with Satoru. Firstly, the length of time we spent on the phone increased dramatically. But even more important was what we were able to talk about. We were able to speak lovingly to each other without any restrictions. We were able to express our thoughts freely. This was especially the case when the topic of conversation turned to homosexuality. There was nothing to interfere with our arguments! Furthermore, we were now free from restrictions on being able to meet. It used to be very difficult for us to meet at any time other than the weekend. If we did manage to meet at other times there was no venue available for us to relax and talk. There was now no need to search for a time or a venue in order to arrange this.

Of course, being able to meet at anytime and being able to use the phone as much as you like whenever you like can themselves develop into new sources of friction. To illustrate this point I should mention that being a carpenter is quite physically demanding. It is quite common, when you've got a lot of work on, to just want to sleep after you've got home and had something to eat. As Satoru wasn't in my position he could hardly imagine how exhausted I was after work. At such times, when the phone rang I would have a sense of foreboding, thinking to myself 'We're in for another argument here' and sure enough, nearly every time, we were.

Often all I wanted to do was to finish the call quickly and get some shut-eye, so my telephone manners left a lot to be desired. Sometimes when I was really tired the only words to escape my lips would be three carefully selected perfunctory expressions – 'uh huh', 'really' and 'that's good'. These constituted the sum total of my contribution to the conversation. And after I had given him free reign to talk I would put the lid on it by saying 'You'll have to excuse me, I have to go now' and immediately getting ready for bed.

Wishful thinking! My partner, Satoru Ito, is someone who has to be handled properly. About thirty minutes after hanging up the phone I would hear the doorbell, would I not?! Who else could it be? Who else would come visiting at midnight? My attempts to close off by saying 'Goodnight I have to sleep now' just did not work. Very gingerly I would open the front door and there he was, out of breath and looking concerned. He had dashed over in his car, angry at having been hung up on. He claimed that when I was tired my manner on the telephone was dreadful. It was curt and even frightening. I know that I used to become extremely self-centred and think only of myself when I was dead tired. I would not spare so much as a thought for Satoru or how he might feel, my only concern being how soon I could end the phone call and settle down for the night. Not long into the phone calls Satoru's sermons would commence: 'Is that the best you can do as a conversationalist? I understand that you are tired but it wouldn't hurt to pay a bit more attention to what the other person has to say, would it? There are times when I'm whacked but that doesn't stop me from putting everything I have into following what's going on'. I was hardly able to find an argument to respond to this. Everything he said was both right and reasonable. How sneaky of him to come up with such rational arguments which I couldn't counter! It was such a pain – his arguments all held water! This would itself exacerbate my bad mood, due to the lack of balance in the equation! After I moved into my own apartment arguments along these lines cropped up frequently. We followed a pattern of inane discussions and arguments, sometimes until two in the morning, torturing our exhausted bodies in the process.

Through these arguments it came home to us just how hard it is to give in, to be conciliatory and willing to compromise. Is it the case that people become more and more self-centred the more they are pushed to the limits of their endurance? Do they, as they reach the point of exhaustion, find their concern for others receding into the distance? I felt that there was definitely a tendency for this to happen, but the essence of the problem was to be found elsewhere. Every time we had an argument over the telephone we would sit down and have a thorough talk about what we needed to do in order to avoid the same argument occurring again. Over time, as we discussed these matters again and again, the frequency of the arguments we had in relation to the telephone gradually decreased.

Both Satoru and I tend to be quite strong-willed people. I imagine that I would get infuriated myself if, when I had plenty of bits of information I wanted to pass onto Satoru, he had the attitude that I displayed when I was tired. Perhaps he was also a bit lacking in consideration for me and my exhausted state. I have no doubt that, had we both shown more understanding and consideration for the other's position, we would have been able to avoid repeating these futile arguments. In those days, however, neither of us could really see ourselves for what we were, nor were we able to look at the situation from the other party's perspective. We had been going together for more than four years and may have developed an element of arrogance that led to our presuming that there was no need to state certain things since the other party would automatically understand anyway. We came to realize, however, that there are many things which do have to be said in order to be understood. For example, I often wanted to get away even before I answered the phone. I didn't have it in me to even attempt to honestly explain how tired I was. So it was only to be expected that Satoru wouldn't fully appreciate or unquestioningly accept my physical exhaustion. No matter how dog-tired one is, it should be possible, if one is sincere, to at least explain oneself to one's partner. Had I done this, Satoru might have been able to yield a little. But instead, I was acting the part of the North Wind in Aesop's fable[1]. I went better than that, though. I added thunder and torrential rain to the plot, just to be sure! In this situation, just what were we to do? There was really nothing for it but for us both to turn our attention to playing the role of the sun in the said fable.

Now 'accepting' this is all very well and good. But understanding something in theory and applying it in real life are quite different things. Even now, what can be likened to typhoons or major earthquakes sometimes appear in our relationship, but at least we hold ourselves in check and concentrate on trying to keep the feelings of the other party in mind. We no longer entertain the arrogant notion that 'there is no need to say anything because the other party will understand'. We tell each other things that we know may result in arguments, but it is precisely through such discussions that we learn to appreciate the other party's position better and understand each other better. If you always avoid clashes you will lose sight of both yourself and your partner before you know it.

August 1990. The plan was for my sister to move to her new place at the same time that I moved into her old apartment. But with her workload and exhaustion, she decided to put off her move until Gen's summer holidays. Since I couldn't wait any longer to begin my new life, I ended up sharing the apartment with them for a short while.

Today was the day my sister and Gen moved out. For the most part the big items to be moved had been shifted earlier, so my sister and Gen really only had to take themselves to their new condominium in Tokyo. When they did, I was left behind. I missed them very much and found myself terribly lonely. You see, they were a pair of fun lovers. It didn't take much for them to turn on the sun! There wouldn't have been anyone in the entire Yanase family (distant relatives included) who would have come close to them in terms of their ability to bring fun to a situation. In fact, it was hard to tell which of them was better at it! No doubt about it, they were a couple of real characters who, if ranked on zest for life and a sunny outlook, permanently monopolized the top two positions in our family.

It is no exaggeration to say that the two of them were responsible for eighty percent of the life (and noise!) that emanated from our house. Little Gen used to make his presence felt, thumping and crashing about the place, while my sister would say to him in deep and threatening tones 'Genki (his nickname), time for bed, don't you think?' She would say this with such impressive conviction that others present would feel that they, too, should obey!

Now when I go back to visit my parents I find their house a garden of tranquillity. In the absence of my sister and Gen, I find the place unearthly quiet. There is certainly a big hole where they used to be.

I missed them very much but felt very glad that I had come out before they moved. It was strange that even while feeling a certain loneliness I did not feel isolated. I felt a bond existed between us which could never be broken, no matter how far away they might move physically. My sister and I are more than just siblings, we are close friends, even bosom friends. Having said this, I suspect that it was because we were siblings that there had been something of a mental barrier separating us. I believe that my coming out to her broke down this barrier.

Whilst society differentiates amongst people by doing such things as bestowing titles on some or placing letters after their names, I very firmly believe that the distinction society makes between people bears no relevance to the ability they have to become a true friend. Any person at all who allows me to be myself, be that person a primary school student, a centenarian or a sibling, would indeed be capable of being a true friend of mine.

From the legal action instigated by the Occur group and the tears shed by Mr Kazama to my thinking about gay pride.

February 1991. It was just about this time a year ago that representatives of Occur (the Gay and Lesbian Action Association) were invited to attend the Fuchū Youth House and talk about their group at a Leaders' Meeting. The Youth House is a municipal facility that provides public accommodation facilities and is run by the City of Tokyo. It is made available to various community groups and is used as a venue for encouraging social contact between community groups. At the Leaders' Meeting the Occur members announced that theirs was an association for homosexuals and then went on to explain about their group in more detail. Immediately following this they started experiencing harassment from the members of other groups staying there. They found themselves, for example, being called 'homos' and 'poofters' without any provocation and quite out of the blue. People took peeks at them while they were in the bath and there were knocks on their doors for no reason. It was very much a case of their being subjected to insults which it would be impossible to conceive as being anything other than intentional. When they complained to the administrator of the Youth House their protests fell on deaf ears. The management took no heed of their objections whatsoever.

Not long after this event, when they attempted to utilize the premises again, they were served with an absurd notification from the City of Tokyo stating that 'having people who are homosexual stay in the same room together would pass the wrong message to others' and 'accommodating homosexuals would subject children to an undesirable influence'. Accordingly, they were told, 'the Youth House refuses the use of its accommodation facilities to homosexual groups henceforth'. Naturally enough, as far as the Occur group was concerned this was hardly a satisfactory response.

Yet they did not decide there and then to take legal action. To take the matter to court they would need money, for one thing. There had never been a precedent for this sort of situation so they had no idea how to go about taking on the City of Tokyo. They would have to start preparing a legal case totally from scratch. They had some idea that being involved in a court case would require tremendous effort. Thus it took more than a year of exhaustive discussions amongst the members of Occur before it was decided to follow through and instigate legal proceedings.

My knowledge of all this came through Satoru, who is a supporter of the Occur group and who, from time to time, attends their meetings. At that stage he was, slowly but surely, deepening his involvement with them. By contrast, at that time I was very sceptical about the movement to liberate gays. To tell the truth I tended to think, personally, that there was no need for them to get involved in a court case. I actually felt some antipathy towards Occur because of what they were doing. Every time it was reported on the news that they were mounting a legal challenge against the

City of Tokyo I couldn't help thinking to myself that I was a
hopeless case. Not only was I doing nothing to help the movement
along, I was unable even to accept myself as a homosexual. Whilst
I knew that it wasn't necessary that all homosexuals get involved,
nor had the members of the Occur group ever suggested this, at that
time I constantly felt an incomparable jealousy, anger and
resentment towards them. I just felt compelled to disparage their
efforts. I felt a need to run them down. I just couldn't help it. It may
be that I was doing my utmost to avoid acknowledging my own
homosexuality. Having confidence in myself as a homosexual was
a totally alien experience to me.

Approximately one year after the Fuchū Youth House episode
(February 1992) Satoru attended the court hearing and the
subsequent meeting organized by Occur. This meeting was
attended by Mr Kazama, one of the plaintiffs in the court case, and
his parents who had come along to support him. What happened
there was that Mr Kazama's father made an announcement to the
meeting in which he stated 'I don't understand homosexuality but
I want to offer my son my support from here on in. In the future I
hope to come to the point where I can comprehend just what
homosexuality is'. It was at this announcement that Mr Kazama
found himself unable to hold back his tears.

There is no greater joy for homosexuals than to find acceptance
for themselves with their parents. I have no knowledge in relation
to the tension and discord that may have existed between Mr
Kazama and his parents but I would say that his tears spoke
eloquently in this regard, would you not? No sooner had Mr
Kazama shed his tears, however, than the homosexual sitting next
to Satoru said in a low voice, and to no-one in particular, 'What a
farcical display of tears. And Occur supports such productions,
eh!' Satoru, however, had been genuinely moved by Mr Kazama's
tears, and the emotion he felt had been totally destroyed by this
comment. He reported that he felt a great sadness at hearing the
comment in question. At that stage he hadn't as yet come out to
his own mother and felt that the hope he held in his heart, that one
day he would be able to receive his mother's blessing and
acceptance of him as a homosexual, was being contested. He felt
as though he had been personally insulted and that his mother had
been insulted too. This made him see red.

That night he told me in no uncertain terms about the anger he felt. He told me how that fellow had made his stomach turn. He queried how anyone could even say such a thing. His voice was quivering with anger the whole time as he described the incident to me. However, joining him in his anger was simply more than I was able to do. Though I knew in my head that it was an offensive comment, my heart simply couldn't go along with his expression of anger.

Satoru couldn't handle my lack of sympathy, nor the dullness of my reaction, and started to get angry at me for not joining him in his anger. The most I could offer was to say 'I am angry. If I say I am angry, I am'. The fact was, however, that contrary to what I was saying I began to sense an impatience with myself for not being able to get angry. We carried on until two in the morning debating and arguing the Occur case and the 'Kazama's tears' incident. This forced us to seriously think about what it was that prevented me from getting mad. Our attention was focussed upon the 'me' who was unable to join his partner in his anger, the same 'me' who was unable to feel genuine anger towards the City of Tokyo.

It seemed, however, that I was not alone in interpreting Occur's action of instigating the court case in a negative light. Many people, regardless of whether they were homosexual or hetero-sexual, seemed to see it that way. I had heard homosexual acquaintances express the opinion that members of Occur were using the courts to make a name for themselves and, if I am to be quite honest, I must admit that the same thought had, albeit momentarily, crossed my mind too.

For homosexuals, revealing one's identity to society carries with it enormous risks, and these risks are greatest for those who belong to heterosexual organizations. Being set up as a target of derision or ridicule could spell the end of one's career in a Japanese company, as such organizations place tremendous importance on everyone getting along with everyone else. It is a fact that there are homosexuals who have had things made so difficult for them that they found themselves with no choice but to resign from their jobs. In this regard I refer you to the article *Homosexuals* by Makiko Ida, published by Bungei Shunjū. On the other hand there are those like Osugi[2] who use the fact that they are gay to make a living, accepting the benefits to be gained from cashing in on their gayness. Most, though, have jobs in heterosexual organizations and for them the court case has nothing at all to do with their personal job security, as their sexuality is something which is permanently concealed.

The court case was being carried out based on a conviction the plaintiffs themselves had as homosexuals – a conviction that the question of homosexuality was one of human rights. Think about it. Is there anyone who would point to a disabled person and openly laugh? Would we ever permit someone to call a Japanese of Korean ancestry 'Korean' to his face? Why then is it that people are not even allowed to protest when a homosexual is treated with scorn, laughed at and called a 'homo' or a 'poofter'? Why are homosexuals singled out in this way? What the City of Tokyo was saying was that 'Homosexuals have no rights, so it is alright for them to be treated as a laughing stock. Furthermore, we don't like to have our municipal facilities utilized by people who are scorned by others. This is an imposition on the heterosexual majority'.

I will be a homosexual for the rest of my life in just the same way as heterosexuals will remain heterosexuals until the day they die. This being the case, I would like to live my life as a homosexual, acknowledging this at all times. That is what is meant by the right to lead one's life as a homosexual, is it not?

If I were to say to someone of Korean ancestry 'Uh – a Korean!' that person would most likely not take kindly to this. This is because such people have a certain pride in their Korean ancestry. They had parents who passed on a certain pride to them in relation to the identity they were to inherit.

For homosexuals, however, there isn't anyone, anywhere who teaches us to have pride in our sexuality. Not our parents, not our teachers at school, not our seniors at school. There is no-one at all who might tell us how we might lead our lives with pride. No-one provides any positive imagery and there are no role models anywhere. The members of Occur have found pride in themselves as homosexuals by dint of their court action, instigated through their own efforts. I must learn from this how I should lead my life with pride. Having had my eyes opened to this, I feel a great joy in the fact that I am leading my life in the same age as the Occur members. I admire them greatly for being able to get angry at having been subjected to discrimination. I am envious of them because they definitely have pride in themselves as homosexuals. They have '*Gay Pride*'. They were the first people to teach me the meaning of gay pride and how wonderful it is to have it. The incident relating to the tears of Mr Kazama finally forced me to question myself and my inability to have pride in myself as a homosexual. From this experience Satoru and I were able to glean one truth: that those who are unable to have pride in themselves are unable to get angry when they are made targets of public derision. I used to be such a person.

My partner comes out to his mother and I am introduced to her as his lover.

A day in September 1992.

On this day, after we had been for our drive and finished our dinner, we went upstairs to Satoru's room to relax. The expression 'to relax' may sound somewhat grand, for in fact we were rather like a giant fat cat and an elephant seal as we sprawled out on the floor! We had both become accustomed to our drives in the country and we welcomed the break from the jobs we had to do all week. In the daytime we would drive somewhere that took our fancy, then have dinner in the evening with Satoru's mother. We would bring home hot meals from outside and the three of us would eat them together. Satoru's mother seemed happy with this arrangement. In fact I was sure that she was happy not to have to prepare the meals herself. She was quite elderly. After dinner Satoru and I would retire to his room upstairs and laze around like a couple of sea lions, relaxed in conversation. And we would have sex if the mood took us. Of course this couldn't be achieved with both of us acting as lazy sea lions – a degree of application was required!

We started thinking that the way we were running our lives at the time wasn't really the way we wanted to. When you think of it, the pattern our dates took indicates that we had been hounded to the outer edge of society. This had a great deal to do with the fact that I had reached a point where I hated people and dreaded associating with them. This hatred and dread was caused by my desperate need to conceal my homosexuality. I had fear and hatred in my heart for the daggered looks people in society reserve for homosexuals.

Even if I had been able to love myself as the homosexual I was, Satoru and I would still have had to be very guarded about what we said whenever we went out to a restaurant. We have to pretend to be just friends and nothing more. We are not able to present ourselves as lovers or partners. If we were to join hands and walk together in a public place people would certainly look back over their shoulders at us. There would also be some who would laugh and point. When you walk with someone you really love there are moments when you feel particularly close to them and want to put your arm around them, but this is not possible for us. And this is something that can't be righted just by our changing. Whether I could accept myself as a homosexual or not wouldn't alter the fact that, as a homosexual couple we represent nothing more than a curiosity for the great majority in society. It is likely that we will always be on the receiving end of harassment from homophobes, harassment such as occurred at the Fuchū Youth House. Even when we meet other homosexuals I am not able to get into any meaningful conversation until I can ascertain just what level of conversation the other party will feel comfortable with.

For reasons already explained, our dates and the meals afterwards began to fit a pre-determined pattern. But of course, from time to time we would also enjoy dates that were of a more spontaneous nature. For us, however, to have an unplanned, happy-go-lucky date still involved being many times more aware of what we said and did in public than the average couple. Even now this awareness severely restricts the kind of dates we can have.

Anyway, let me get back to the time we were up in Satoru's room and enjoying some serious relaxation after our meal! It happened that on that occasion, out of the blue, he said to me 'I might just take the bull by the horns and come out to my mother today'. He took me somewhat by surprise with these words, but knowing him as I do, I knew that unless he were to make the move when the mood took him he might never find the courage to actually go through with it. Moments marked by such confidence and courage don't come every day. I advised him that he should make the move if he felt that he could and assured him that things would go well. With this encouragement he went downstairs.

Left alone, I felt a little awkward and embarrassed at the thought of having his mom know that I was his lover. It was a strange feeling, hard to put into words, something akin to that which I imagine a newly married bride would experience when she had to meet her mother-in-law the morning after the wedding night. There was of course no guarantee that Satoru would be able to find acceptance with his mother, and if she couldn't accept him she would certainly never accept me. Thus it was with a complex mixture of hope, expectation and anxiety that I waited for him to return.

In a while he returned to the room looking very happy. I had already gleaned a general idea of what had gone on, as to a certain extent voices carry up to the second floor from downstairs. It appeared that he had managed to gain his mother's acceptance of his homosexuality. The first thing he said to me was 'This is great. I'm so happy'. Of course, I was delighted to hear this. He had told his mother that he was a homosexual; that he felt sexually attracted to men; that he had no interest in women whatsoever and that consequently he had no intention to marry; that his partner was Ryuta Yanase and that he intended to spend his life with me. There can be no doubt that his sudden coming out would have been a shock for her, but it seems that she did her level best to try to understand him.

The degree to which she was actually able to comprehend homosexuality is not relevant. Rather we should appreciate the effort she put into trying. I felt very moved by this woman who was putting everything she had into trying to understand and accept her son, though she herself wasn't able to properly understand the nature of homosexuality. At the end of their meeting his mother commented that his homosexuality would mean the end of the family line and the disappearance of the family name. I must admit to having had somewhat mixed feelings upon hearing this.

As I was about to leave that evening the subject of our relationship was brought up again, and I was introduced to Satoru's mom with the words 'Ryuta is my lover. I hope you will both get on well with each other'. I admit to feeling a touch of embarrassment at that time, and she also seemed a little shy, but this was only to be expected I suppose. For most mothers this would be news that would knock their socks off! The sight of this woman who was doing such a fine job of coming to terms with the news she had just received, was wonderful and yet at the same time a little saddening. I was moved.

Such were the events of that night. They allowed me to hope that one day the time would come when I would be able to tell my own mother about myself. As things turned out that moment was to arrive unexpectedly soon.

My mother fully accepted me, though she struggled with the pain involved.

A day in November 1992.

There were many opportunities for me to go back to my parents' place to have dinner when I was so tired I couldn't be bothered cooking for myself in my apartment. As you can imagine, working on a building site is physically demanding and having to start preparing a meal after getting home is a most unwelcome prospect. I started off making my own meals several times a week but I still used to have mom's home-cooked dinners often. I would tell myself that cooking for one person was just not economical and I would remind myself that mom kept telling me to go back there for dinner. It was handy going back to my parents' place to eat, as for one thing it saved money on food bills. It suited me as I really felt that I shouldn't be expected to get a meal going when I was as tired as I was. I was very fortunate. I only really appreciated having meals at my parents' place after I moved out. When I did prepare a meal at home I used to find that after I had done the cooking, the laundry and had a bath, I just didn't have the energy to do the washing up. When you stop to think of it you would have to conclude that Japanese society is a bit strange. Five hours a day would be about the maximum one could work in order to have time to prepare meals, do the laundry, take a bath and finally tackle the washing up before possibly taking in a TV drama. It is quite easy to understand how my sister's health was affected by her over-working, given that she had a child to look after on top of all the rest.

Be that as it may, on the evening in question I was at my parents' house having dinner with my mother. There were just the two of us at home, my father being away on night shift at the freeway toll-gate where he worked. After the meal we chatted about my sister and her family. Then for no particular reason the topic of conversation turned to Satoru. He had been introduced to my family as a 'good friend'. The circumstances seemed just right and it suddenly occurred to me that the timing was appropriate to come out to my mother. Strangely enough, I didn't feel the sort of tension that I had felt when I came out to my sister. In my mind's eye I could see Satoru coming out to his mother. Perhaps I had been immunized in a sense, having already come out once and having been there when Satoru had come out to his mother.

I surprised myself at how calm I was when I broke the news. It may well have been due to my inability to explain things properly that she wasn't quite able to grasp the concept of homosexuality, but this didn't stop her putting everything she had into trying to understand me. There is no doubt that she tried to come to terms with the situation and accept me. However, her life had been devoid of the information, experiences or contexts necessary to render the word 'homosexuality' comprehensible for her, or to enable her to come to terms with it or afford it a place in her value system. I feel a sense of real gratitude to her now, for the effort she put into trying to understand me. In the twelve months following that day in November 1992, the two of us have been able to discuss a whole range of issues. It took me more than two decades to accept myself as a homosexual. It was just too much to hope my mother would comprehend all this in one go. No matter how well she understood the idea that her son was a homosexual, much more time was necessary before she could accept this in her heart. It was a lot to try to come to terms with. For a start she would have to give up on the idea of my marrying and providing her with grandchildren.

Recently I found myself responding sharply when she asked me a truly preposterous question. At such times I have to remind myself that it can't be helped that she doesn't understand the issue of homosexuality well. The fact of the matter is that I am the only person who can explain to her just what sort of a creature a homosexual is.

No doubt my mother would have hoped to live to see the grandchildren I might have produced for her, as indeed most people in her situation would. She must find it hard every time relatives or friends ask her when her son is going to get married. Indeed it was for this very reason that I needed her to understand how important it is that I live my life true to myself and how wonderful it is for me to be able to do so. It was no less than my duty to try to have her understand because otherwise coming out to her might have been effectively nothing more than cruelly inflicting pain on her. She would suffer enough simply in order to try to come to terms with the fact that her son was homosexual.

Exactly one year after I had come out to her my mother said something quite wonderful to me. She said that if she were asked 'What about your son, when is he going to get married?' she intended to respond by saying 'My son is a homosexual and he has found himself a wonderful partner, a Mr Ito, so he won't be marrying a girl'. I was so happy to hear this that tears came to my eyes. It was clear that she had struggled greatly in her desperate attempt to somehow or other accept her son as a homosexual ever since the day I had come out to her. Hearing these words defined for me just how hard this had been for her and how deadly earnest she was in trying to come to terms with my sexuality. Looking back I now feel ashamed at the behaviour I displayed at times, like getting impatient and being confrontational when she was unable to fully grasp the explanations of homosexuality I offered to her. I now sincerely appreciate the effort my mother put into accepting me in my entirety, inexperienced and unpolished as I was at trying to get my point across to her.

The fact that both our mothers accepted their homosexual sons proved to be a source of great encouragement and confidence for Satoru and me. When he and I first met we simply couldn't have imagined coming out to them. The fact that something that we couldn't have imagined at that time had now come to pass started us thinking that perhaps further plans that we didn't dare to imagine could also become a reality. These plans involved starting to live together with the blessing of our respective parents.

3 Moving towards setting up house with my partner
by Ryuta Yanase

In order to break the chains of hatred which bound me I had to take stock of, and accept, my own failings.

May 1993. A few days after the Golden Week[3] holiday I quit the carpenter's job I had held for seven years. I had made up my mind a couple of months earlier that I would do so, so I was in quite a settled frame of mind when the time came. The only thing that was not settled was the personal enmity and animosity I felt towards my uncle. As mentioned earlier, when I first went there to work he used me as a tool to protect his pride and avoid losing face. The bitterness I felt towards him for this was still very much alive. It is very easy to feel hatred towards someone but very difficult to forgive. I just didn't know what I should do to release my heart from the acrimony which arrested and imprisoned it.

In fact my uncle's scolding virtually ceased after I reached a certain proficiency at my job. Even though I might have wanted to confront him head on about the unreasonable treatment he had meted out to me, it was a little late by that stage as my uncle had changed along the way. In fact the situation when I quit the job was quite different to what it had been earlier in our working relationship. If anything, my uncle was going out of his way to be nice, in fact unpleasantly nice to me. Consequently I no longer had an object at which I could direct my anger. Nevertheless, in my heart of hearts I still felt a hatred towards him and I suspected that if I were to quit the job whilst harbouring this resentment I would probably carry it with me for the rest of my days. Thus it was with apprehension that I made the decision to leave that position. I did so without confronting him. I would be less than truthful if I were to say that there hadn't been any times when I relied on my uncle to make sure all went well for me. I always knew in my heart of hearts that he could be relied upon to bail me out if ever I got into trouble on the job. I can't deny that I used him to allow me to keep a low profile and be virtually 'invisible' on the job. He also relied on me to a certain extent to disguise his own ineptitude and shield his pride. I always resented this. I guess you could say that, in a sense, there was an element of interdependence in our working relationship.

I quite hated him before I left that job but I think I might now have reached a point where I can find it in my heart to forgive him. Looking at my overall situation objectively, I have to acknowledge that I also am guilty of using another person, my partner, as a shield to protect my own pride in exactly the same way that my uncle had done to protect his. I used Satoru as a buffer when my mental state was at its worst, that is when I hated myself for dreading other people looking at me and for trying to escape their looks. For the first three or four years of our association I vented my anger on Satoru in a most unreasonable way.

The fact that I detested my uncle's failings meant that I couldn't sanction them. But my uncle and I were two of a kind. To put it another way, my uncle's failings and my own failings were one and the same. My intolerance for his shortcomings was identical to my intolerance for my own shortcomings. Because I had managed to keep a lid on my own failings for a while it never occurred to me that I was doing to my partner exactly what my uncle had done to me. I was causing my partner the same pain my uncle had caused me.

In the midst of alternating surges of hatred and anger I eventually came to realize the stupidity that continuously drove this cycle. But even though I realized this, I had tremendous difficulty in forgiving my uncle. How was I ever going to manage to do so? I could see only one way to find forgiveness for my uncle. I would have to face my own failings fair and square, no more avoiding them.

First, I had to find the courage to stare hard at my own shortcomings. But simply staring at them would do nothing more than make things increasingly difficult for me. No, what I had to do was 'forgive' myself. I had to face up to my shortcomings and forgive myself. If I were able to forgive myself from the bottom of my heart I should then be able to honestly accept my failings. I would never be able to forgive anyone else until I was able to forgive myself. It was only when I came to properly understand this that I felt I would be able to really and truly find it in my heart to forgive my uncle and put all the rancour and ill-feeling I felt towards him behind me. For a long time I had been living in the shadows of my own shortcomings, always aware of them and never able to put them out of my mind. I continuously blamed myself and could see no way of interpreting things such that I might be allowed to forgive myself. So I continued to inflict pain upon both Satoru and myself. And I continued to hate my uncle.

I am a very selfish person. I only came to realize this from clashing with Satoru. When I finally came to this realization I found myself overwhelmed by how many failings I had. Perhaps that is why facing my own failings was such a terrible job. But I knew there was no way I could ever forgive my uncle if I remained ignorant of my own shortcomings. My uncle was but a mirror image of me. My reflection was always to be seen in him. I was confronted by my own shortcomings whenever I looked at him. This made me all the more angry. As I watched my uncle doing all he could to maintain his pride and protect his ego, I also saw myself doing the same things. To hate someone is an exceptionally easy thing to do. It is hell itself, though, when one's heart is held prisoner by that hatred.

I continued to hate my uncle for a full seven years, while the whole time wanting to be released from that prison of hatred. Forgiving my uncle was one and the same thing as forgiving myself. It was something I would have to continue to do until the day I died.

Anyway, having left my job, I had to consider the question of other work and my financial future. I didn't relish this prospect. Of course my income dried up, but being a bit on the slack side in these matters I wasn't keen to find another job straight away. That attitude, however, didn't stop the rent from being demanded every month. Although I did have some savings put away, it looked as though I couldn't afford to continue living where I was for very much longer. At this point the idea of moving in with Satoru once again flashed through my mind.

Preparing to make cohabitation with Satoru a reality: renovations.

It would have been about the autumn of 1992 that the question of taking up residence together arose. As ours was a partnership that was not recognized by society in any way, shape or form, we had to confront a whole raft of new issues. As I have already said, we had both already come out to our mothers and were fortunate that neither of them had rejected us. The road forward, however, was fraught with uncertainties. Satoru's mother had yet to agree to my moving into the Ito household. She had to be made aware of all the implications surrounding this proposal. And I still hadn't yet told my father! I had to make both my parents aware of the nature of our relationship in order to explain our planned living arrangements. But perhaps the biggest question was whether or not we could find the courage to actually go through with our plans.

To be perfectly honest, I had my reservations. Would I be able to get along with Satoru's mother? Where would I fit into this household comprised of Satoru and his mother? To what extent would I be able to join in the household without imposing or intruding? I simply had no idea what the answers to these questions might be. The number of questions to be resolved was daunting. What would we do about laundry arrangements? What arrange ments would we have for bathing? For eating? What room would be best for me to use? It wasn't as though Satoru were bringing home a bride. Would it, then, be beyond the pale for me to take on the housework? There simply was no precedent to guide us. There were no examples of couples who had been down this road. There was nothing for it but for us to try to work our way through these questions as best we could.

Satoru's father had been a dentist and had run his practice from home. Satoru and I talked it through and decided that the downstairs room that had been used as the dental consultation room (and was now being used only as a storeroom) could be renovated and I could move into it. Initially we thought I might be able to use an upstairs room that wasn't being used, but the house was designed such that it was necessary to pass through this room to get to the area where the washing could be hung out. There would have been no privacy for anyone if we had used that room.

The former consultation room was about the size of four-and-a-half *tatami* mats[4]. Adjacent to it was another room that had been used as a waiting room which was approximately four *tatami* mats in size. We figured that if the dividing wall were removed we would end up with a floor space of nearly ten *tatami* mats. The resulting room would have its own toilet and small sink and also its own entrance, separate from that leading to Satoru's mom's room. With this arrangement everyone would have a degree of privacy.

Once we had reached the point where we were discussing these details, all that remained was to get a renovator in to do the remodelling. Oh yes...we had not yet got Satoru's mother to agree to this proposal. The plan that Satoru and I had come up with to live under the one roof (albeit with his mother) was moving into its final stages.

With the blessing of both our mothers we commence our lives together in Satoru's house.

July 1993.

Things seem to be moving forward very quickly. It is now approximately two months since I quit my job. In that two month period we have received the approval of both our mothers to live together. We have also both introduced our partners to our respective mothers. In addition we have approached a renovator who has agreed to do the renovations we have in mind. We are spending our Sundays clearing out all the junk from the former consultation room that had become a storeroom. I must say that I find sorting stuff and clearing it out in an attempt to get this room into some sort of order quite a pleasurable and enjoyable experience, ever conscious that this will be the room where I will be able to live with my partner. We have somehow managed to get ourselves to this point and it is now as though a mighty wind is precipitating a great haste.

It would be no overstatement to say that the room in question had been jam-packed with things. There were seven or eight hundred old magazines and books alone. Plus there was a whole array of old fashioned dental surgery implements and collections of study materials dating back to Satoru's father's university days. One could hardly come into contact with such a collection of things without stepping back in amazement that so many things could have accumulated in one room.

We crammed the rubbish into black polythene rubbish bags. By any estimate we would have made at least thirty trips to deliver these to the local rubbish collection point. You can imagine that it was no easy job to get rid of everything and leave the room empty in time for the renovations to start. It was at the beginning of June that we decided the renovations could start sometime in July. This meant that there were only four Sundays for us to clear out the entire room.

Of course, at the same time I had to clean out the flat I was vacating. The room I was moving into had only about half the floor space of the flat I was moving from, so of course I was not able to take everything with me. Now I was staring in awe and amazement at all the things that had collected in my own apartment. It was hard to tell which was the more challenging, the apartment I was leaving or the room I was moving into! I was certainly in no position to criticize others for being hoarders.

It is strange how satisfying it can be to turf things out once you have made up your mind to do so. I set to clearing out my stuff like a man possessed. Every item I threw out meant one item fewer to carry. This was the way to look at it! No-one can suggest a better way for settling one's mind than to have a good clear out! I had to congratulate myself for my efforts, because there was no-one else there to do it! Apart from the washing machine, wardrobe and desk, which I sold to a second-hand furniture and appliance store, and a few selected magazines that I really felt were necessary to keep, I disposed of everything. It was then that I realized just how many unnecessary things I had accumulated – clothes I never wore and knickknacks and gadgets I would probably never use. It seemed a bit of a waste but I had to close my eyes and ruthlessly throw things out. If I had attempted to take even half of the things I owned I would have only been making a rod for my own back.

When I saw the finished room after the renovations were complete I was really very surprised. It was hard to believe that it could look so good! There was nothing left to suggest that it had once been a consultation room. And it seemed so spacious now that the partition was gone! All the wallpaper was fresh and clean! It really didn't resemble the former room at all. I gaped at the scene in front of my eyes for a few moments in astonishment. All this had been made possible through the goodwill of Satoru. I could not find any words to express my gratitude and appreciation. My old flat was a very nice one but it couldn't be compared to this! It was hard to believe that only a month ago this area had been a storage room. And now it was transformed into a beautiful room befitting me!!! Alright then, it was time to move in! I felt a renewed sense of vigour and was really looking forward to making the move.

Everything was in place. I had finished the sorting and packing. The electricity, gas and telephone companies had all been dealt with and I said goodbye to the landlord. All that remained now was to wait for the removalist's truck.

As luck would have it, it was a rainy day on which the move took place. In the building industry we used to say that rain was good because it compacted the ground, but on this occasion the heavens opened up. There was torrential rain that, in a sense, symbolized the love fraught with difficulties that Satoru and I shared. In spite of this, though, the fact that there wasn't much to be transported made the move to the new room quite smooth.

I got my mother to help with the house-moving. She might have felt as if her son was moving to somewhere a long way away, I guess. I realized that she might be feeling a sadness similar to that felt when losing a daughter to another family, but that wasn't what was happening. It was rather that I was gaining my independence and setting up my own home, living in a corner of the Ito household. The new relationship that Satoru and I were to share was about to commence. Something that we thought could never happen was about to become a reality. I will never forget the gratitude and the emotion I felt as I undid the string on the boxes in my new room.

That evening we invited both mothers to join us for dinner. Satoru served some *sushi* that he had bought. The conversation started a bit stiffly with introductions being made before moving on to general topics. During the evening the genial conversation rambled from one topic to another. Finally, the two mothers finished the evening off on something of a formal note, each acknowledging the situation before them and asking for the other party's acceptance of, and support for, us in the future.

Now that I think of it, that conversation represented the first time ever a blessing had been given to our union. Up until then no-one had openly sanctioned our relationship, not our friends nor our parents. So the time spent over that meal represented a very precious moment in our relationship. It's not that we love each other because we hope to gain public approval, but by the same token, to go through life and not have anyone be happy for you as a couple would be a very lonely and isolating experience. The fact is, however, that that is the situation for most homosexual couples. They live their lives silently in a corner of the world, even though they have done nothing wrong, hurt no-one and caused no anguish, pain or trouble.

It took me thirty years before I reached the point in my life where I could come out to my mother and another year before my partner and I could live together. What a very difficult thing it is to live your life true to yourself. I mean really true to your feelings without falsifying anything. Indeed in this regard I haven't yet reached my goal. I prefer to see my real start in life as coming up. For many years I have been obliged to be deceptive and pretend to be something I am not, and I now want to learn how to be open with myself.

This new house is the place where my new life will begin. It is not as though I am doing anything extraordinary. I am doing nothing more than what is perfectly natural for me. My partner is also in this house. I am living with the person I love with all my heart. I can no longer suppress the urge to live honestly and be open with myself. This is how I am and being told that I am disgusting, being pointed at and laughed at won't change that fact. This is me. This is my new lifestyle and at last I am able to take my place at this new starting line. From now on I will be able to be myself as nature intended I should be.

After my mom went home Satoru and I stayed in my new room and we talked in a very deep and meaningful way right through the night. The following comments are typical of those which were made that evening. They were made with heartfelt emotion:

'At long last we are able to live together'.

'It's hard to believe if you think back to when we first met'.

'Ryuta will be here in the house whenever I get back from work from now on'.

I doubt that I had ever experienced, in all my thirty-one years, such a quiet sense of gratitude as I experienced that night, knowing that from then on I would be sharing my life with the person I genuinely loved. When you think of it, this shouldn't really be such a big deal, as I was only doing what was perfectly natural. The only thing was that my partner happened to be of the same sex. Why should we have to agonize and suffer so much on account of this?

People dread isolation and loneliness. They fear being different from everyone else and being rejected. However the difference between homosexuals and heterosexuals contains an element that can't be passed off simply as a 'difference' as such. This is because the difference embodied in the very existence of homosexuals is something which is not sanctioned by mainstream society. In terms of imagery the very, very best one can hope for is the very occasional TV appearance of a gay in drag. He will be used as a comic item, a source of humour in a program designed to provide light relief and make people laugh. For most heterosexuals, homosexuals remain the source of a good laugh. They always have to be portrayed as being a form of life of less intrinsic value than heterosexuals. They must be despised and detested in order to allow heterosexuals to always enjoy a sense of superiority. I fully acknowledge that this sort of prejudice-laden 'illogical logic' remains the realm of the heterosexuals in society. However, in order for me to accept myself as a homosexual it will be necessary for me, at some stage, to come to terms with this 'illogical logic'. In other words it will be necessary for me to be able to accept as a fact of life that heterosexuals might consider me to be a lower form of life than they are and not be fazed by it. I must lead my life fully recognizing and acknowledging this reality. If I didn't have a partner I would most likely still be leading my life without having disclosed my sexual orientation to anyone. I am not strong enough to face the world's prejudice alone. It is not easy to have the confidence that will allow you to stand up and say 'I am not wrong in what I feel'. It is only through my association with Satoru, and in an environment where all sorts of clashes ruled in our relation-ship, that I have come to discover myself and finally learn what my real feelings are, free from falsification, pretence and deceit.

It took a long time to come out to my mother and a long time for me to take up living with my partner. But through this I have come to acknowledge what my real feelings are. I am still not able to hold my partner's hand in public without being conscious of the looks we would receive. I am not able to hug him when I want to. Everything I have at the moment I have thanks to two things: the support of my partner and the very natural desire which any human being has to live his own life in accordance with what nature decreed for him. For me this natural desire is a very fragile thing which would crumble in an instant if it were not for the support of my partner. For this reason I would like to take this opportunity to record here my gratitude to Satoru.

5 Life Notebook

Building a Life for Ourselves.

1 The bewilderment which accompanied our living together. The curtain is lifted on a stormy time
by Satoru Ito

Intoxicated by the joy of living together, I was under the illusion that anything and everything would go well.

In the seven years and three months leading up to our taking up residence together both Ryuta and I would often feel a sadness come over us at sunset when we were out on a date. We knew that later that evening we would each be going back to our separate homes even though this wasn't really what we wanted. Our only contact again before the next date would be on the telephone. I couldn't bear the pain of separating from Ryuta, even though it was only temporary. As things stood I couldn't see any prospect of our relationship going beyond what we already had. However, once we had both come out to our parents, our plans to move the relationship forward – to have Ryuta move into the Ito household – progressed very quickly.

It would not have been possible for my mother to live on her own in the house nor to move out and live elsewhere, so it was decided that Ryuta should move in with us. His room would be the unused room downstairs. It was then time to organize the renovations and to this end the two of us had spent every Sunday in June clearing out all that was stored there. The renovations went on from June 28th until July 16th and included the provision of a bath for Ryuta's use. The cost ran to a figure of three million yen [1], of which the bath and associated plumbing costs accounted for two million yen. But this was money well spent.

On July 19th Ryuta's mother visited. During the conversation she said to my mother 'Thank you for all you have done. I know I can rely on you to continue to provide the support Ryuta and Satoru will need in the future'. I felt a truly tremendous sense of happiness knowing that both our mothers gave us their blessing.

On July 25th Ryuta moved in. I cannot describe how ecstatic that made me. I knew I would always have Ryuta near me from that day on. I felt a tremendous peace of mind knowing that Ryuta would be sleeping in the room directly below mine. The thought that Ryuta would be there waiting for me when I came home every day meant that any fatigue that I felt as a result of my day's work would start to lift as I approached the house. Every night we would be able to discuss the events of the day at our leisure. We were free to choose the hour of these discussions and there were no restrictions on how long we could talk. It was a real relief not to have to worry what I should do if I weren't able to get home to put a call through at the usual time. I would no longer find myself cutting short incoming calls from other people because I was expecting Ryuta to call. Living together would make it much easier to ensure that communication was maintained.

All of this made me deliriously happy. I imagined that everything would now just automatically go right for us, without my having to shepherd our relationship along at all. Strange as it may seem, I experienced a rapid improvement in my health, particularly in relation to the anxiety neurosis I was suffering. Consequently the dosage of medication I was required to take was halved.

It was evident that Ryuta was doing all he could to ensure that he and my mom got on well with each other. On days when I had to work at the preparatory school he would do things like take her along to the masseur for foot massages and even accompany her on shopping trips. On occasions he would even do the shopping run for her. Whilst I was very impressed by the way he was putting himself out, and I was thinking what a kind and considerate fellow he was, I failed to realize that he was actually taking on duties that I should have been shouldering. Mom hadn't always shown delight at the prospect of Ryuta moving in with us but she apparently soon found herself quite delighted with the fact that now at least there was someone in the house to have a word with and, unlike her son, Ryuta didn't flare up when asked to help with the shopping even when he was busy. Indeed it wasn't long before she found herself becoming more and more reliant on him, first for one thing and then another.

As for meals, Ryuta and I didn't alter the existing arrangement of eating with our respective families. This suited Ryuta, who seemed keen to catch up with his pet cat, a really cute pedigree American short-haired tabby (with all the papers), at least once a day. It was also a good way of doing the right thing by his mother who, early in the piece, had expressed the sentiment that having Ryuta move out of their house to come and live with me was like losing a daughter to an in-law's family. Having Ryuta join his own family for dinner on weekdays was also good because it spared my mom from preparing dinner for three people. As for breakfasts, mom used to wake Ryuta up after I had gone to work in the mornings because he would take her to the masseur, and it ended up that the job of preparing his breakfast fell to her after a while. I let things ride for a while, happily thinking that things would work themselves out nicely as on Sundays Ryuta and I intended taking on the cooking together. That plan came to an abrupt end after we cooked curry and rice on August 8th, meat and vegetable stir-fry on 15th and fried *gyōza* dumplings on 29th.

After Ryuta moved in, instead of our life together being the enjoyable experience we had expected, there was a sudden upsurge in the number of arguments we had. Four in August, four again in September, one in October, three in November, two in December, six in January and five in February – of which two were big ones. For the first two months I put these down to 'teething problems', with most of the arguments involving my mother in some shape or form. For example, when Ryuta and I were busily working away in the kitchen my mother couldn't help but interfere, giving advice on this and that. Her interference was such that Ryuta told me that he no longer wanted to prepare food together with me, by which he meant 'together with my mom'. On another occasion when my mother was trying to work out how to use the new bus system that was being introduced, I got very frustrated with her and fell into a moody silence. This would affect my relationship with Ryuta who, in turn, got mad with me for bringing the frustrations I felt as a result of my relationship with my mom, into our relationship. All I wanted was for Ryuta to sympathize with me and help relieve

the frustrations I felt by allowing me to grumble about how hard
it was for me to deal with my mom – at least that was how I felt at
the time – and I couldn't understand why he refused to go along
with this.

**Underestimating my partner's level of stress. I believed that
everything would work out somehow; it was just a matter of our
getting used to things.**

While things were bubbling along, Ryuta pointed out that he didn't
think that I was pulling my weight as far as the housework was
concerned. I considered that I was busy enough with the preparatory school and my work as a writer, and hadn't bothered to turn
my attention to acquiring any knowledge of cooking skills. As for
the washing, about the most I would ever do would be to collect a
bundle of dirty washing in the evening and virtually drop it in front
of my mom. It was the same with shopping. All I ever did, and even
this only on the very rare occasion, was to go with my mom to the
supermarket and collect the necessities of life. Mom found it hard
to ask me to do the shopping because I would get into a bad mood
if I were pressed for time. She would then say something like
'Ryuta would have done it for me'.

Now I couldn't argue with the fact that on the odd occasion
when, instead of Ryuta, I would take mom to the masseur I would
show my displeasure if she were to ask me to organize to buy
something which was troublesome to get and which required more
than just a quick and easy shopping sortie. When she tried to open
the car door before the car came to a complete stop I would see red.
The tendency to flare up grew stronger the busier I was at work.

Initially I was taken aback by Ryuta's accusation that I wasn't
pulling my weight with the housework, but after a while I agreed,
after a fashion, with what he said. In a sense it was just as though
my mother and I were playing out the roles of a heterosexual
husband and wife. I was the personification of the typical
'husband', going to work and leaving all the housework to
someone else to do. I behaved as I pleased at home and there was
always someone to pick up after me. I never questioned this 'man's
role'. At that stage I was so slow to catch on that I hadn't realized
that I had to seriously address the situation at hand or face dire

consequences. Although I made a conscious effort to do the shopping and put the rubbish out on Monday, Wednesday and Friday evenings (up until then Ryuta had always done this) whenever I was able to, and had managed to cook a hamburger for Ryuta on December 5th almost without help, I still felt deep down that there was no particular urgency to change the way things were. I thought that I would have a chance to move in that direction at something of a leisurely pace once my work slowed down a bit.

The end of the year was closing in. It was the busiest time of the year at the preparatory school and it didn't help matters that I was laid up with the cold that I catch every year, regular as clockwork. The question of my helping with the day to day running of the household was still not a pressing issue to my mind. For one thing I thought to myself that if I took all the housework away from my mother she would go downhill and lose her faculties very quickly. So I felt it was better, to a certain extent, to have her continue to look after certain jobs and do things around the house.

Now while this was both a sensible and rational argument, I didn't properly grasp the fact that allowing mom to continue to do some housework was quite a separate issue from learning how to do it myself. This was why the significance of an important argument with Ryuta in November escaped me.

The argument came about as a result of Ryuta not being able to eat the breakfast of mixed fermented soya beans and whitebait that my mom had prepared for him. He said he just didn't fancy the soya beans with something as out of place as whitebait. He was only used to eating it with finely chopped spring onions. I reproached him for not showing any appreciation of the fact that mom had gone to considerable trouble to prepare him breakfast. However, after I had calmed down, I realized that I should have respected the differences in the ways people enjoy food, and I decided to tell my mom about Ryuta's likes and dislikes. But on that occasion, in response to him saying 'I don't want any more breakfasts', I steamrolled him, arguing that he should try to eat the breakfast in front of him because mom had made it to thank him for taking her to the masseur.

There were other rumblings of discontent from Ryuta at this time, too. He felt very conscious of my mother's presence sometimes, for instance at mealtimes or when he went upstairs, because that was where my mom spent a lot of her time. He told me that he felt a hesitancy to go upstairs. I got quite frustrated by the fact that he would never do his washing at our house. Although I told him he was most welcome to use the washing machine, he continued to carry all his dirty laundry back to his parents' place. He continued this practice until January of the following year. Even though my mom would be kind enough to say things like 'the clothes line is free, you can use it if you like', he felt that he was intruding on her domain if he used the laundry or the kitchen, or did any of the housework. Taking up residence in another person's house and feeling at home and comfortable there is not a feat which is easily achieved. Yet I didn't pay much attention to his concerns. I just went about my business while treating Ryuta's concerns lightly, naively believing that it was just a matter of him getting used to our new living arrangements. In fact I was quite blind to the constraints Ryuta felt living in the Ito household.

As for me I was just so happy to have Ryuta living under the same roof that without even realizing it I had effectively established a 'memorandum of understanding for living together' that went something like 'living together is just so wonderful that we should each be able to withstand any pressure and overcome any difficulties that might arise, in order to ensure that the progress we've made in our relationship and in moving towards the goal of sharing our lives together will not be eroded'. So, every time Ryuta complained to me about things that annoyed him I would tell him, in not so many words, that he should just make himself at home and stop feeling as though he didn't belong or didn't have the right to treat the house as his own. He responded by visiting his parents' house several times a week and having cooking lessons with his mom. He kept notes about the different things he was learning as he went.

At one point he said to me 'I'll never cook the meals that I am learning to make in this house. But in the future I would be prepared to make them just for you'. I wasn't pleased by this and told him so. This led to another argument and his threatening to move out of the house. He didn't really mean it – it was just being said to goad me – but nevertheless it certainly strengthened his arguing position. His threatening to go would provoke an overreaction on my behalf. I would cling onto him and, in a crazed manner, beg him not to leave.

As you may have noticed, both Ryuta and I tend to be quite fierce when attacking each other. I would accuse him of hating me and suggest that perhaps all would go well if I were to do away with my mother! This was my way of rebuking him with extreme arguments and contorted and convoluted reasoning. Ryuta would come back at me with things like 'You are mad. You've got a screw loose. All I said was I would leave this house. I didn't say I'd leave you! If you killed your mom you'd be a criminal. What would that do for our relationship?' As you can see we both let fly with things that would be sure to hurt the other.

It wasn't long before Ryuta found himself unable to bear my failure to properly understand why he was getting so stressed. He started to lock himself up in his room and virtually stopped visiting the upstairs room which was for our shared use.

His downstairs room catches no sunlight and is like a veritable icebox in winter. Thus Ryuta bought a very powerful electric heater, only to find that the electric circuit breaker would trip whenever he turned it on 'high'. But the tension between us was so great that he put up with living in the cold, little, cramped room which was full to capacity with his things. And still, I made no attempt to give proper consideration to his circumstances.

Ryuta rejected my unwritten memorandum of understanding. He claimed that living by that edict alone just wouldn't work. I was pushed to arguing that he should bear in mind that I had spent a million yen renovating that room. Of course, my reference to this was really only a ploy to bolster my own arguing position. I was really very slow to realize that I had, for all intents and purposes, replaced the part of the unwritten understanding which referred to 'both Ryuta and I', with the idea that 'Ryuta should be able to put up with any challenges that came his way'. It took until early in the new year for me to realize this.

All of the onus for adjusting to the new living arrangements was foisted onto Ryuta. My own personal daily routine and lifestyle remained virtually unchanged. Things such as the sort of meals I had, the timing of my bath and how I utilized the rooms in the house remained as they had been before Ryuta joined the household. Ryuta, on the other hand, was thrust into a new world, one to which he was completely unaccustomed. It was a world that already had established rules about the use of space in the house, and now

Ryuta was expected to fit himself in. It is as plain as the nose on your face which of us was being required to make the greater adjustment, is it not? It was pure fantasy to suggest that we should be able to get over that hurdle simply through the love we had for each other.

Ryuta breaks down in tears as he opens up to me. Things seem to be looking up as a result.

Ryuta's stress reached a climax in early 1994. I had just assumed that things would somehow work themselves out. I thought that we could work things out so that there would be two households living together under the one roof. He had his own living space, my mother and I had ours and the two of these co-existed. However, under this arrangement there wasn't any possibility of Ryuta and Satoru creating a personal space together, at least not in the short term. Could our relationship develop under these circumstances? Could we possibly be satisfied just living together under the one roof? I took it upon myself to blame Ryuta for my uncertainty about this, presuming that since he was prepared to go along with the existing arrangements I would have to accept that I should pretty much give up on the idea of our doing the shopping, cooking and laundry together.

It was only to be expected that Ryuta's stress level would greatly increase through dealing with a person such as I was. Whenever we had an argument he would make comments like 'I don't really feel like I'm living here' and 'It's as though I'm trapped in my dingy, lonely room'. And yet I didn't see what was happening.

Finally, on January 24th, Ryuta was reduced to tears. We had set out in the car for a date but then, out of the blue, Ryuta fell into a foul mood and suddenly turned for home. He went to his room and tried to shut himself in. As always, I pursued the matter, trying to find out what was behind it all. I found it impossible to just leave him be for a while. I made him come up to my room. The two of us flopped down on the *futon*² in stony silence. Suddenly Ryuta crumbled. Raising his voice, he said 'I'm sorry' and started crying. Until then he had been unable to express how depressed he was and had acted very coldly towards me. Now he came to me for comfort and asked me to embrace him. This took me by surprise, but even greater than the surprise was the sense of appreciation I felt at his opening up to me. In the eight years we had been together this was the first time he had completely opened up and fully exposed his weaker side to me. He had always tended to go on the offensive with me and close off his personal feelings. So his opening up like this was a source of real delight for me.

I would go so far as to say that this was the first time he had properly sought soul comfort from me and, after all the time we had been together, only now did I feel truly loved by him. Until this moment I had always been the one seeking his comfort and help when something was troubling or depressing me. By contrast, Ryuta had kept everything to himself, no matter what it was, and this meant that ultimately there was a clear distance between us. Nuta was Nuta and Nyāgo was Nyāgo. But this new development marked our stepping out onto a different plane in our relationship. It embraced what could be described as a tremendous sense of vividness for us. Before I realized it I was telling Ryuta that if he would continue to turn to me for comfort and reassurance we might just be able to find the answers to the problems that dogged him and that it might just be possible for us to find the strength required to face the future together as partners.

Immediately following this incident Ryuta went out and bought some clothesline to allow him to hang up his washing in the upstairs shared room. He did this because he felt loathe to have to share the washing line on the verandah with my mom. This way he could hang up his washing whenever it suited him. He then started doing his washing whenever he wanted to, provided mom wasn't using the washing machine at the time.

Again I had been blinded by Ryuta's display of emotion and once again I failed to look deeper into the reasons for his suffering and depression. Now that he had had a good cry, got it off his chest and started doing his washing at our house, I felt that everything would go well. My feeling that the awkward period was behind us was reinforced when the preparatory school went on holiday in February and I took over the job of taking mom to and from the masseur. I also took on all the shopping. I got mom to write down all the things we needed to buy and I took it from there. I also took on the whole of the washing process. I was using the washing machine, hanging out the washing, bringing it in, folding it and putting it away. I also polished up my culinary skills and took charge of disposing of the rubbish. I had come to realize that I would never learn how to run a household unless I actually got down to doing some of the housework myself.

Taking a more active role in the running of the household seemed to bring about a reduction in the number of clashes I had with my mom. When Ryuta commented that at long last I had taken to helping with the housework, I was lulled into a sense of believing that everything was on an even keel. That illusion was shattered with the eruption of three late night battles, on February 19th, 26th and 27th. The argument on the 26th went on for twelve hours, including breaks. We had not had clashes such as these for quite a long time. They were very serious arguments. I was afraid that they might have been nails in the coffin of our relationship – that was how bad they were. Things had come to a head for Ryuta, who couldn't find a sense of belonging, or a sense of a place for himself in our house. He claimed that he couldn't stand the complete lack of privacy; always having to worry about where my mom was and what she was doing. He said he wanted to be able to go upstairs without having to encounter her. He also wanted to be able to cook in his own room but he couldn't because there was no gas connection. He said that he wanted a kitchen and wanted to feel free to be able to use the washing machine at anytime without feeling that he was imposing or depriving my mother of the use of it. He said that he regretted having disposed of his books, washing machine and wardrobe to move in with us. He declared that he was going to buy another bookcase and wardrobe and put them upstairs. He said that if the roles were reversed and I had moved in with his family I wouldn't want to be in the position he was in now.

During the first of these arguments (on February 19th) I was unable to respond to all of the things that he claimed were stressing him, but I managed to tie things over somewhat by providing him with a bookcase and promising to clear a space for a wardrobe. On February 21st I gave him a microwave oven so that he could prepare some food for himself. Ryuta then said that he had overstepped the mark by demanding too many things. This effort to pour oil on troubled waters seduced me into believing that things would now settle down. Only after all this time was I starting to get something of an appreciation of the difficulties Ryuta was facing. In my naiveté, however, I again thought that Ryuta would now be able to put up with our situation and manage in accordance with the 'understanding' we had for overcoming the difficulties we faced in living together.

Ryuta took his mother's advice and bought a simple gas ring to use in his room. He already had a tap in his room and with the microwave oven I gave him he was now set up to prepare food there. He got right into the swing of things and took on the challenge of making a sweet and sour dish, using chicken instead of the usual pork. He went out and did a major bout of shopping and proved his culinary prowess by producing a very tasty dish indeed. The only drawback was that the room filled up with smoke. There was no exhaust fan, and thus no getting rid of the cooking smell even when the windows were left wide open all through the night and until the following afternoon. The smell just wouldn't go away. It permeated our clothes. Here again I was insensitive, thoughtlessly commenting that our clothes smelled while failing to address the ventilation problem. This caused Ryuta's anger to smoulder again.

On the 26th Ryuta said to me 'I'm going to leave and go back to my parents' place and when I get enough money together I'll rent a flat near here'. I overreacted again. The exchange between us ran something along the following lines:

'I want a much bigger room. I'm not able to treat this place as my own and laze around if I want to. I can't properly relax. I want you to add a staircase so I can go upstairs without your mom seeing me. I want you to install a proper kitchen for me upstairs. I want you to arrange an increase in the amperage so the electric circuit breaker doesn't keep tripping'.

'OK. I'll do it all. I don't care how much it costs, I'll fix all those things up. Just don't leave me!'

'I don't want you to have to fork out a fortune'.

'I owe that much to you surely, having put you through what I have'.

'OK. I'll stay on the condition that the renovations get done'.

'Is that the only way you can put it? Couldn't you add something to the effect that you want to stay with me...?'

'You just don't see what I'm going through, do you?'

Later that night Ryuta broke down crying once again.

'The fact of the matter is that I miss you too much. How come we can't eat together? I thought that I would feel that I was part of the household even if I did my own shopping and cooking and ate by myself, but it just isn't working. I feel an emptiness in my soul, a sadness. I live in the hope that you will invite me to eat with you, Nyāgo. I want to feel that we are really living together, not that we are living separately under the same roof'.

The next day I went out and found an exhaust fan which simply hooked onto an open window and didn't necessitate putting holes in the wall. We decided that once a week we would cook and eat together in Ryuta's room. With this arrangement in place I thought that things would settle down but, that night as we were about to turn in, Ryuta turned to me and said that if we were to swap rooms for a while I would start to appreciate just how he felt. This set me off, and I accused him again of being too demanding. Another round of arguments ensued. But this time we finally managed to step back and look at the situation objectively. We managed to completely open up to each other and thoroughly discuss our individual points of view. The channels of communication remained open for several days after that. I came to realize that our desire to live with each other was not enough, by itself, for him to manage the stress he was experiencing. Even though by rights I should have been Ryuta's first line of defence against such stress, it was brought home to me that from his perspective I didn't fully appreciate his situation in spite of all his efforts to explain it to me. He said that the only person who would lend him an ear was his mother. I was at last able to come to something of an overall appreciation of Ryuta's feelings. The two of us then reconfirmed that our aim was nothing other than to build a life for the two of us together.

Coming to the realization that I had been pushing all the cooking, shopping and washing onto my mother.

I sometimes wonder why it took me so long to be able to see things from Ryuta's point of view and also why I had imagined organizing our lives together would be a simple matter.

My mother and I had been sharing the house together for approximately twelve years since my father died at the end of 1981. During this period I had earned the money to run the household mostly by working at the preparatory school, supplementing my income from time to time with work received as a freelance writer. I provided for my mom financially and she, in turn, looked after me and all the housework. This seemed like a reasonable sort of arrangement, as I had no free time in which to do housework. I was too busy with lesson preparation and getting through the mountains of manuscripts I had to look at.

The living arrangement we had in place suited me just fine, although it was very clear that the relationship I had with my mother was not the sort of relationship a mother and son usually have. I was the man going out to work and she was the woman staying home and looking after the house. We were acting out the roles of a typical heterosexual married couple, were we not? All the ingredients were there. I would work overtime and then bring work home. I overworked myself and left the running of the house totally to the woman in the house. Never mind lending a hand preparing the meals – I actually complained about them!

Basically I was acting like the lord of the manor. For the past twelve years I had been following the male heterosexual tradition of knowing nothing at all about housework. The result was that I found myself getting angry now that my mom was getting on in years and no longer as efficient as she had been in the past. Five or six years ago she began to complain that the housework was starting to get on top of her and the situation developed where I would scream at her and rebuke her for this. It was not beyond me to complain about the way things were done. For example, there was a gradual move away from freshly-cooked meals to ones featuring frozen foods, including frozen vegetables. I would gripe at this, being accustomed to more tasty meals.

Gradually things went from bad to worse. I would come home late, tired after a day's work, and clash with my mom. I started to be very demanding, not unlike the typical husband who considers himself to be the lord and master of the household. For example, when mom would ask me to help her out with something (partic-ularly shopping) I would always be too busy and never be able to find the time to get round to doing it. What was worse, I would tend to blow my top when she asked me to do something in the morning when I was hurrying to get off to work.

I rationalized what can only be described as giving mom a

terrible time and displaying a deplorable lack of compassion and understanding, glibly excusing my actions by telling myself that I was frustrated at watching her grow old. I had observed both her hearing going and then her legs. Yet, I expected her to be capable of still doing what she used to be able to do. Initially we had rows because of this. But mom was no match for me when it came to shouting, logic or persistence. She would cry or snap and wring her hands saying 'I know. You don't have to say any more'. I was in the stronger position in all our confrontations. Our clashes could never have been described as occurring on a level playing field.

Looking back at it now, I grew very impatient in response to her growing old. I was too anxious to solve any health problems the moment they presented themselves. For example, I thought of a hearing aid the moment mom's hearing went, and the treatment a masseur could provide as soon as her legs started to give her trouble. Of course these things were necessary, but all I really wanted was for her to get back to normal so that she could continue looking after me.

The fact of the matter is that if I had faced mom and spoken calmly to her, paying attention to both how I said what I wanted to say and my body language, we would have been able to communicate, even without the use of her hearing aid. This is still the case today. When what she says doesn't make a lot of sense I find it is basically better to listen for the gist of it rather than to pick her up on each and every query I have, as I get frustrated in the process of attempting this. It would have been better for all concerned if I had been satisfied with just catching the general gist of what she was saying but I wasn't able to find the time, nor did I have the patience (or the experience), to communicate with her any better than I was. I had become just like a typical married, male Japanese office worker.

Ryuta and I have never tried to pass housework off as something unimportant. In my previous book, 'My Gay Pride Declaration', I addressed this matter in somewhat grandiose terms stating how in our lives together Ryuta and I were not going to be held captive by the dictates of society in terms of perceiving certain jobs around the house as being 'men's work' and others as 'women's work'. I talked of how we planned to enjoy rising to the challenge of forging a new type of relationship with each other, one free from gender-based role stereotyping.

Over the course of the twelve years I had been sharing the house with just my mother, I decided that when she passed on I would get into the housework in a serious way. I thought to myself that as long as I knuckled down to it, it shouldn't pose a problem for me. I managed to underestimate just what running a household entails. I only came to appreciate very recently how housework cuts into both work and leisure time. I was hoping for a bit much when I thought I would suddenly be able to build a relationship with my partner which was based on the idea of our being equals, when the lifestyle I had led for the previous twelve years reflected an attitude which was typical of the heterosexual husband who considers housework to be something below him, someone else's domain.

In order to work things out with both my partner and my mother I am obliged to start to learn how to help run the household.

Without realizing it, the idea that Ryuta was coming into the household as a 'bride' (or 'groom'?!) had found its way into my consciousness. As discussed above, in my understanding of what 'we' would do to overcome any difficulties or trials we encountered on the way to creating a happy life together I had – somewhere along the line – unconsciously replaced 'we' with 'Ryuta'. I only fully appreciated how dangerous this situation was as a result of some chance discussions with a number of heterosexual males.

First there was Mr 'A', a white collar worker whose job entailed numerous changes of postings. He was always moving house. He claimed that he had no idea about housework and no inclination to learn, either. He reported that the only thing he had in common with his wife was his children. I learned from what he said that it is possible for a relationship between two people to change into something which is nothing more than a source of stress, something with no evident potential for development. In other words, it is possible for two people in a relationship to find themselves in a rut which is defined by the gender roles society dictates: the man going out to work and 'bringing home the *sushi*', as it were, and the woman staying at home and running the house. This situation can result in the wife's becoming subordinate to the husband and forming a dependency on him.

There was also a Mr 'B' who spoke about his family relationships. Mr 'B' had had three changes of job in his career and was
currently working for a publishing company while freelancing on
the side. He said he fully understood the difficulty Ryuta had in
terms of using the bath. He explained that it was perfectly
understandable that Ryuta should feel awkward in this regard. He
pointed out that Ryuta was in no position to demand he be
permitted to bathe whenever he wanted and suggested that the only
thing to do would be to put a bath in upstairs. This would be for
Ryuta's use and his room could be joined to mine by a spiral
staircase.

He went on to say that his own family would only stay with
either set of in-laws if there was a particularly good reason for them
to do so, and that it rarely ever happened. He said he couldn't
imagine living with them on a daily basis. Furthermore, he
explained how, in consideration of how little storage space there
was in the house, he had to cut down on certain things, like how
many CDs he could buy, in order to ensure there was still enough
room to store things belonging to his wife and kid.

It was no wonder Ryuta didn't believe the promises I made to
do something about the stress he was under since I put no thought
at all into ensuring there was space set aside for us to share. I am
a bit of a hoarder and would not think twice about adding to the
number of possessions I had by bringing home whatever I felt
inclined to buy. I owe a debt of thanks to Ryuta for his patience
and advice in relation to the appropriation and use of space within
the house. I admit I was wrong in my interpretation of what was
appropriate in this regard.

If I had continued behaving as I was, treating the whole house
as though it was for my personal use and not concerning myself
with the needs of others nor the fostering of an environment which
would nurture a relationship, I would have become the personification of the self-centred, bombastic male image that is
generally accepted as defining the man's role in the Japanese
household. This was the very role I professed to reject whilst
paying lip service to the idea of advancing homosexual rights.

It would be no exaggeration to say, particularly at that point, that
the future of our relationship was dependent on the degree to which
I could appreciate the difficulties and trials Ryuta was exper-

iencing. Ryuta said that we would have to do whatever we could to find some way of making a success of our venture to live together in the same household as my mother. He warned that I should bear in mind that if things got to the point where they exceeded his tolerance threshold he would be prepared to temporarily move out – into an apartment of his own near to our house.

It was necessary for me to revisit my relationship with my mom and arrange things so that it was not a cause of friction in the household. I feel now that perhaps at that time I had actually given up on the idea of having honest dialogue with my mother, her advancing years being the excuse I proffered for the *ipso facto* position I took. I was in fact guilty at times of acting in a quite inconsiderate way towards her. I should have been able to treat her better than I did. I recall the happy time we had in January at Ryuta's house when he and I and both our mothers sat down and enjoyed a duck casserole together. The picture of my mom singing in the car on the way home flashes across my mind's eye.

I must take it upon myself to arrange things so that, little by little, I take over the main responsibilities in relation to the running of the household. If, for example, I were to fix a time when I was to do the washing, Ryuta would feel less hesitant to use the washing machine.

I must arrange things so that we move away from the existing situation where my mom is in charge of the running of the house and where I act only in an assisting capacity, to the situation where the roles are reversed and I take over the main responsibility for the running of the house, with mom carrying out a 'supportive role', as it were. That would be the most appropriate plan of action, given mom's advanced years. By getting mom to take on the role of 'teacher' we might be able to escape from the sort of relationship we have at the moment, one which is based on the 'male (husband's) role' and the 'female (wife's) role' mentality. By challenging this established idea of there being a demarcation of work along gender lines I would be better placed to appreciate all the work my mother had done in her house for more than fifty years. We might even be able to build something of a relaxed, enjoyable and stress-free relationship. It is never too late to try to rectify a situation.

It was necessary for me to come to this realization and to assume the main responsibilities for running the house if I were to qualify as Ryuta's partner in life. It was only after Ryuta and I actually started living with each other that we were able to see past the restrictions imposed by society's gender based categorizing of work, behaviour and expectations, and picture the form our lives together might take.

Not concealing things reduces the level of discrimination at work and in the neighbourhood where we live.

We were fortunate in that, while we were going through the exhaustive process of coming to terms with the roles we might each play in the household and examining our personal levels of consciousness in relation to just where we might be placing ourselves *vis-a-vis* the existing structures of society, we were not subjected to any direct harassment as such. Because of this we had the opportunity to both thoroughly discuss with each other and argue about just what our lives together should be like.

Meanwhile, in the Spring of 1993, a new man was appointed to the position of principal at the school where I worked. As he had indicated from the very beginning that he sympathized with the students and shared their feelings on a range of issues, I felt that he might be a person I could come out to. Thus it was that, late that autumn, I took the opportunity that presented itself one day when we were in a coffee shop and produced the book 'My Gay Pride Declaration'. Whilst trying to control my nerves, I broke the news to him that I was homosexual and that I was living with a partner who was of the same sex. I am delighted to be able to report that he accepted this as being a personal matter and assured me that he would not fire me on the basis of my sexuality.

Further, I disclosed my homosexuality to a colleague whom I knew I could trust. He responded that he would be supportive of my position. As for my students, when they asked 'Do you have anyone you are going out with?' or 'Are you married?' I would, after establishing a basic sense of trust, be completely open with them. These days I almost never find myself being avoided or experience antipathy directed towards me simply on account of my being homosexual. I find that as people come into contact with me as an individual and we engage in lively debates, the prejudices that they hold in relation to homosexuals by and large disappear. One chap said that he was delighted that I had been able to open up to him.

There were good-humoured drinking parties at which I was asked in jest 'Which of us here would be the type that appeals to you?' There was even one bloke who reported that he had shown a newspaper article about me to his mother who replied that I must be a great man!

The main problem we will face appears to be in the immediate neighbourhood. As I write this, however, I must report that as yet I haven't met with any harassment, nor is it evident that any nasty rumours are circulating about me. I don't know how much the couple in the house to the right of ours knows but they seem to be as nice to my mom as they have always been. They give a cheery 'hello' not only to me, but to Ryuta as well. We surmise that if we just come out and publicly state that we live at such-and-such an address in Funabashi City there will be no basis for rumours to start. If we come right out and state, bold as brass, that there is a homosexual couple living here, all that people would be able to say would be 'So it seems'. We believe, on the other hand, that if we were to try to hide, or keep our whereabouts secret and live without drawing attention to ourselves, we would be setting ourselves up for scandal-mongers who love to pry into other people's business.

Although ours is a residential street the people living here tend to keep to themselves and have never had very much to do with one another. In fact no-one really knows anyone else. It might just be that because of this there appears to be an air of normality in the neighbourhood. If it was somewhere where everyone knew everyone else's business it would be a very much more difficult situation for my mom to have to cope with. When my mother met one of the local housewives and mentioned the trouble she was having with her legs, her friend took her by the hand and, as if meaning well, said 'Just wait until your son brings a wife home who will be able to look after you'. It must have taken all the courage she could muster, but in response my mom said 'My son is a little odd. He reckons he's not ever going to get married'. The pluck she demonstrated on that occasion meant a lot to me. If only there was a guarantee that life wouldn't become more difficult for her if she were to come out and respond to such comments in a straightforward way, stating that her son had a partner who was male and that they had found happiness living together! It remains a fact that for Ryuta and me even without experiencing harassment or having to deal with rumours flying about the place, there is a hesitancy – indeed an inability – on our behalf, to come right out and state that we are living together as a couple. That would require tremendous grit.

When I had almost completed the manuscript for this book I realized that things are perhaps not quite normal around here. Visitors to our house are subjected to the stares of a married couple who live in an apartment across the street. Even our visitors have been taken aback by the audaciousness of these neighbours. Also, I discovered that our neighbour to the north was pulling his blind down whenever Ryuta left the house. We are subjected to this sort of non-violent harassment.

A young friend of ours succeeds in doing away with the prejudice his family displayed in relation to his associating with us.

Let me take this opportunity to introduce to you an emotional incident which involved a friend, a Mr Tokizawa, who lives less than a minute's walk away from my house. (He is now twenty-five years old and working as a part-time teacher at a local state school.) He came to the private high school in Chiba Prefecture as a first year student when I was in my third year of employment there. It was the year that I was sacked upon the appearance of my book entitled '*Sir! Being Slapped is Offensive*'.

Anyway, I met Mr Tokizawa through the class on Modern Society which I was responsible for. He later organized with his parents for me to act as his home tutor. It turned out that this job was to continue until he graduated from high school. We discussed many different things at all times except when he was fully occupied cramming for the usual rounds of examinations. He told me about the complex he had about his elder brother and the path he was tracing for himself through life and love. We also talked about social problems and my life history. Whenever I had an interesting friend come to visit me I would always invite Mr Tokizawa to join us. His presence would ensure a lively and enjoyable discussion. With the exception of Ryuta, Mr Tokizawa was the friend who visited me most often.

We could discuss the difficulties we faced in a very down to earth way. And we offered each other encouragement and advice in relation to the difficulties we faced. He was one of the unusual heterosexual friends I had. Anyway, when his mother saw a newspaper article about Ryuta and me she told him that she didn't want him coming to our house anymore. He took offence and asked why. It transpired that she feared that her son might be a homosexual (or that he might become one) and whether he was or not, she didn't welcome the prospect of nasty rumours to that effect starting up. He counted to ten and suppressed the desire to ask caustically if she would disown him if he were to claim he was a homosexual. Instead he chose a compromise path that didn't really sit comfortably with him. He told her that if someone were to raise the subject all she needed to say was 'My son is heterosexual but he is a close friend of Mr Ito who is homosexual. Mr Ito is a person who is to be respected and, even though there is an age difference, he treats my son as more of an equal than anything else. He is someone whose acquaintance I value very much'.

This message seemed to get through to his mother. From then on she was happier seeing him off whenever he came to visit me than she ever had been before. Later it seems his dad also came on board and said 'It's alright. Don't make an issue of such a thing. Times are changing and we mustn't be left behind'. When Ryuta and I heard this a sense of joy touched our very souls. We regarded it as a near miracle that we found such a strong ally as Mr Tokizawa in a heterosexual. No matter what trials and tribulations might await us in the future, just the knowledge that this man is living nearby will prove a very great source of reassurance and encouragement for us.

2 The loneliness of living in a room that represents a fortress of isolation in someone else's house
by Ryuta Yanase

Being ever aware of the presence of Satoru's mother prevents me from doing my laundry or taking a bath.

It was in July last year that I moved into Satoru's house. More than six months have flown by since then. From this vantage point I can

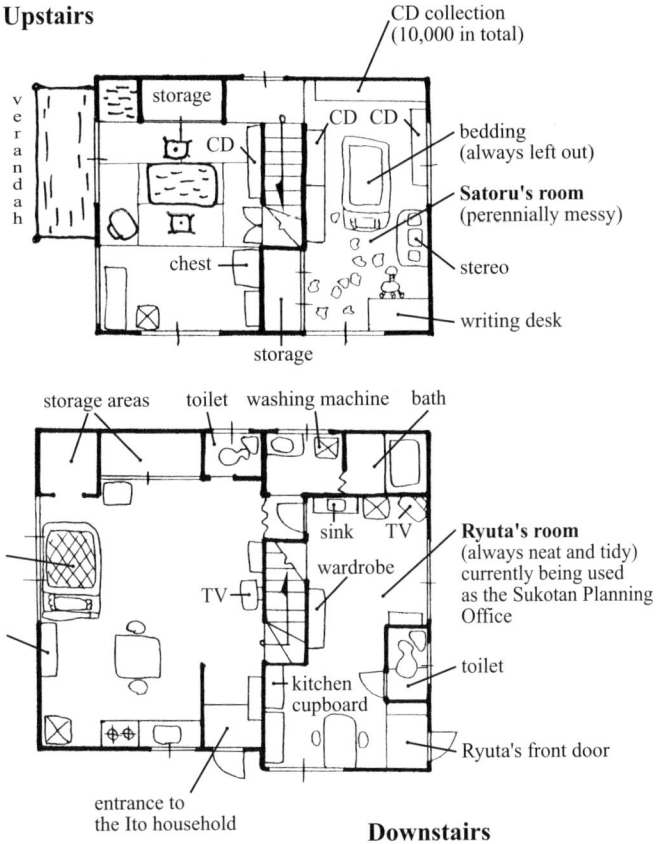

Figure 1: Sketch of house floor plan

see that our early notion that 'things would somehow work themselves out once we started living together' contained a large portion of wishful thinking. Allow me to briefly outline our living arrangements before turning to the main theme of this section. As I have already made clear, we have adopted a lifestyle, currently very popular, in which two separate households live together under one roof. The renovated room that I live in is pretty much self-contained. Although it is not a large room it has both a sink and a toilet. In addition it has a separate entrance, its own front door. There is also a door that connects to the main part of the house. I share the main bathroom, but other than that it would be fair to say that we have virtually achieved our objective of ensuring that we respect each other's privacy. Moreover, in order to maintain a sense of equality in the relationship, I pay rent to cover the electricity and gas bills.

Initially I underestimated what was involved in setting up this sort of living arrangement. I felt that simply living together would allow things to work out for us. As time went on, however, it became clear that the situation developing was giving rise to certain seemingly insurmountable problems. I will go into this a little later. The immediate problem at that time was that I felt very much like an outsider where I was. I felt considerable pressure to get on well with Satoru's mother as soon as possible. Accordingly, I initially put everything I had into trying to foster a friendly and informal relationship with her. Of course, even before my moving in the three of us had shared a meal together once a week after our date, but it is quite a different kettle of fish when it comes to actually sharing your lives as members of one household. Mrs Ito and I would both have to 'give' a bit if things were to go smoothly and we hadn't yet mastered that side of things. I was fully aware that unless we hit it off and learned to feel at home with each other my life under the same roof as her would be very difficult.

When I first moved into the Ito residence, the only place I felt I could be myself and act in an unconstrained manner was the one room which Satoru had renovated for me. It was the only haven of privacy to be found in the house. This was inconvenient in a great many ways and it was by no means easy to deal with. For example I found myself overcome by a sense of isolation and solitude, accompanied by a sense of being subjugated, as though I was being locked in my room by myself. It was very lonely.

The first week had been great. I had been immersed in finalizing the move. I had been buying things which I needed and tying up loose ends. However, once that stage passed I started to settle in and found myself with time on my hands. Indeed the days seemed interminably long. I should perhaps have turned my attention to doing something worthwhile with the time I found myself with, but I simply couldn't bring myself around to looking for a new job. Instead, I wasted my days in discontent. Naturally, any person would be affected by such a situation. I found my mental state deteriorating. I spent my time just waiting for evening to come because that was when Satoru came home. He was at work all day, teaching at a preparatory school. As a consequence, I was home alone all day. On occasions, as a diversion, I would get into my car and head off somewhere for a drive, but I had to watch what I spent as I was out of work and had no income. At that stage I hadn't managed to develop a close relationship with Satoru's mother. I found it very difficult to have a conversation with her without going through Satoru.

As time went by I found coping with the daytime increasingly trying. Or rather, I found restricting myself to my room when Satoru wasn't home very trying. My room became an island both isolated from society and separate from the mainland of the Ito household. I just couldn't handle being in that room all the time. Plus, I had to cope with the fact that we were a homosexual couple totally lacking society's approval. I would be less than honest if I were to say that I wasn't bothered by how those in the neighbourhood looked at me. Hoping to be accepted by the neighbours as a homosexual couple was probably quite out of the question. Even if I were to live in this house for ten years I doubt if the man next door or the lady across the road would ever smile and greet me when they saw me. It was more a case of their treating me with contempt and displaying an aversion to even the suspicion that possibly Satoru and I might be a homosexual couple. These thoughts played on my mind and did nothing to improve my mental state. I ended up being very conscious of being outside whenever I left the house. I always hoped that I wouldn't meet anyone when walking the thirty-odd meters along the street to put the rubbish out or when going to the car bay I was renting.

As for life inside the house, the door from my room to the rest of the house was a source of fear and dread when I first moved in. I felt very awkward approaching it. It was okay when I knew Satoru was home, but considerable courage was needed to open it when he wasn't. The living room, where Satoru's mother spent most of her time, was on the other side of that door, so I could be pretty sure that once I opened it I would be directly in her line of sight.

Before I moved in I had fully intended to do as Satoru suggested and treat the washing machine as my own, using it whenever I wished. Likewise I intended to bathe whenever I felt like it. In practice though, it just didn't work that way. Satoru had to be there in order for me to be able to do anything. When he was late coming home I would wait before using the bath. I wasn't able to do my washing during the day, although this was not because his mother had ever indicated that I shouldn't. Rather, the fact was that, for me, not being comfortable with her was the same thing as not feeling at home, and therefore feeling that I shouldn't treat the house as my own. That things might turn out this way was something which hadn't occured to me before I actually moved in. It may seem obvious that living with other people means losing your privacy but, having never experienced it myself, I hadn't properly realized all the implications involved. Meanwhile there was no denying that my pile of dirty laundry was growing day by day. If I didn't find a way of doing it soon I would be in danger of running out of things to wear. Consequently, it wasn't long before I gave up on the idea of doing my washing at what was now my home in favour of the quickest and most efficient means of getting it done: carting it all back to my parents' place and getting my mom to do it. Once there, I stayed around for dinner as I always had in the past.

Serving the household as though I was Satoru's bride.

I knew I couldn't live forever on this island. Or rather, I couldn't go on forever treating my room as an island. As for our awkwardness with the reception we were getting from the neighbours, there was nothing for it other than for us to consciously bear in mind that the fault for society's not accepting a homosexual couple lay with society and not with us. We were doing nothing wrong at all. However, as for my relationship with Satoru's mom, I could see no way to get around the feeling of isolation I had in the Ito household other than to break the ice with her. One means of doing this came to mind as I pondered the situation. It seemed that what was required was for me to do everything I could to help her, just as a new bride in the family would. By this means I hoped to win her acceptance and then, as the next step, feel that I could treat the family home as my own.

The first plan I came up with was to take her to the masseur, as Satoru has already mentioned. She was seventy eight years of age and her legs weren't very good and she wasn't able to manage shopping very satisfactorily. She was going to the local masseur for a leg massage two or three times a week. It so happened that she slipped and fell one rainy day two or three months before I moved in. Because of this she had lost the confidence she had always had in her ability to get around by herself. She had, in recent weeks, said she wasn't able to walk to the masseur's practice anymore. His practice was only a five minute walk away for a young and fit person, but Mrs Ito reckoned it took her thirty minutes to get there. She had to stop and rest along the way in order to be able to make it.

So, I took it upon myself to drive her there and back. I would put her in the car and take her there every Tuesday and Thursday. Chauffeuring her to and fro had a surprising effect. Actually, I was taken aback by the effect it had. I was the recipient of tremendous expressions of gratitude. Thanks were being lavished upon me! I couldn't possibly have imagined how much she would open her heart to me as a result of my doing this for her. It was a delightful miscalculation on my part!

She started preparing my breakfast on Tuesdays and Thursdays in an effort to reciprocate. I was a little embarrassed, and perhaps felt a touch sneaky, but I treated it as a give and take situation and accepted her kindness with gratitude.

At 9 am she would knock on my door and wake me. The conversation would run something like:

'Mr Yanase. Breakfast's ready!'

'Thank you. I'll be down in a minute'. This would be followed by:

'Good morning'.

'Breakfast is on the table so let's eat together before we go'.

There was nothing particularly striking about the substance of the conversation as such but it meant a lot to me. It offered tangible proof that the ice had been broken and that we were getting on well with each other. I got the feeling that she was delighted to have someone to talk to, as for the most part she was alone the whole day. Taking her to the masseur paid off handsomely. The distance between us decreased dramatically.

With time, as we got to know each other better, she prepared my breakfast every day, regardless of whether we were going to the masseur or not. She was rarely visited by anyone and I had plenty of time on my hands as I was still out of work. Satoru and I were about the only people she got to talk to on a daily basis. A strange bond of solidarity began to form between us, borne of a shared sense of isolation. Our topic of common interest and conversation was Satoru. Allow me to introduce the following as an illustration of the sort of conversations we would have:

Mrs Ito: 'I guess you feel I spoiled him as a child. He was given his own way quite a bit because his late father used to tell me to go easy on him and not tell him off too much. Being the only child in the house, he had no-one to play with'.

Me: 'I guess you're right. Sometimes I think Satoru could be a little more careful with his choice of words. He tends to be just a little quick tempered at times'.

Mrs Ito: 'You're not wrong there!'

Our conversations seemed to always begin with our saying unflattering things about Satoru. From there we would move on to talking about the tropical island she grew up on and then on to the Great Kantō Earthquake[3] which she experienced as a young woman and from there on to the *haiku* poetry[4] which she had been writing for forty years. She never ran out of things to talk about. She simply wanted someone to talk to, that was it. She seemed genuinely delighted to have someone around with whom she could converse. I had come into the household and was able to play that role. I am sure that this was a positive thing for both of us.

As we got to know each other and became comfortable with each other, she gradually started to ask me to do the shopping. When she said 'Mr Yanase, we've run out of vegetables and meat' I could hardly respond 'Oh, that's too bad!' Sometimes I would think 'Oh, not again', but actually I did owe her for making breakfasts for me. So I learned to respond cheerfully and say 'Oh, in that case shall we go to the supermarket together?'

Initially I got a bit carried away with the gallant 'daughter-in-law' role I was pursuing. Every time I was asked to do something my heart was filled with a sense of being useful and carrying out a positive role in the household. I felt a real sense of satisfaction. I firmly believed that playing the role of a dutiful 'daughter-in-law' would allow us all to get along comfortably in the same household.

The problem was that the number of jobs Mrs Ito asked me to do soon became limitless. It started with requests for me to nip out and buy some side dishes for meals, but soon escalated to include requests to change fluorescent light tubes, fix leaking taps and take down curtains. Soon I was washing the curtains I had taken down, airing the bedding, buying replacement kitchen appliances, putting out the rubbish three times a week, on Monday, Wednesday and Friday...the list went on and on and on.

The most surprising thing about all of this was that her son didn't lift a finger to help. For example, she told me that her bedding hadn't been aired for more than a year. I thought she couldn't be right, but when I checked with Satoru, he confirmed it. He was aware of this but hadn't done anything about it. And the reason she would ask me to pop out and buy some side dishes to complement the dinner table was because Satoru would fly off the handle if asked to do the shopping when he was pressed for time – and he was usually pressed for time. He just didn't think shopping was a job he should be expected to do. It seemed very much as though Satoru intrinsically considered the housework, shopping and cooking to be things his mother should do. Thus it was that his mom would approach me with requests. She didn't want to be shouted at.

Interestingly, before I came to live in the Ito household, Satoru had once commented that the quality of his mom's cooking was deteriorating and he didn't know what to do about it. Perhaps, he thought, his mom was getting a bit old and unable to cope. He added that she used to be good at making all sorts of tasty meals.

In hindsight, it seems the decline in her culinary prowess was only to be expected really. No matter how good someone might be at preparing appetizing dishes, it is not possible to make decent meals without the necessary ingredients. Looking at it from Mrs Ito's point of view, she couldn't get out of the house that much so she would ask her son to collect the ingredients she needed. After he responded sharply too many times she felt she couldn't easily approach him with this sort of request. This meant that she didn't have what she needed which, in turn, led to the meals she served being rather poor in quality.

As I gradually came to understand the sort of lifestyle Satoru and his mother led I started to become somewhat dissatisfied with

Satoru. All the things I was doing for his mom were things he really should have been doing himself, were they not? Once this thought took root in my mind there was no erasing it. I started to resent the incompetence Satoru displayed in regards to the jobs around the house.

There was also a discontentment welling up in me related to the sort of relationship he, his mother and I should be having. I felt that if I was to continue being at his mother's beck and call there was a strong likelihood that, with human nature being what it is, this would very quickly become the norm. I would be expected to carry out this role in the household for evermore. It wasn't a case of my holding any ill feelings as such towards his mother, nor my not wanting to help her. Basically she was a very broad-minded and amiable person for whom such a trivial thing as keeping track of who does what for whom didn't warrant attention. This is why once it started to become the expected course of events that I would do whatever needed to be done in the house she thought nothing of relying on me for any and all such jobs.

Losing faith in Satoru who seemed oblivious to the housework, just expecting it to be done. I set about learning how to cook.

Gradually Mrs Ito's requests became increasingly burdensome. When she asked 'Mr Yanase, have you noticed that the fluorescent tube isn't working?' she really meant 'Go and buy a new fluorescent tube'. And when she said 'Mr Yanase, shall we air the bedding today? It is such nice weather...' this could only be interpreted as 'Air the bedding please'. Although I started to feel burdened by these requests it wasn't easy to tactfully say 'no' to her. And while I might have thought to myself 'What a demanding old hag', I continued fostering the relationship, which was founded on the understanding that I would do whatever I could for her. However, all I was actually doing by being party to this arrangement was grinning and bearing the consequences. I was making a rod for my own back.

Eventually the stress got the better of me and I exploded. About two to three months after I moved into the Ito household I found that Satoru and I became repeatedly engaged in non-constructive, pointless arguments. These arguments proved unproductive because, having bottled up my stress for a very long time, I would get emotional trying to explain to Satoru how I felt. My tone of voice, however, was apparently too sharp. He invariably became defensive. With emotions running high on both sides we were unable to achieve anything constructive from these exchanges.

He displayed an amazing inadequacy, indeed a complete blindness, to the jobs that needed doing around the house. He just very conveniently left the whole lot to his aged mother – the cleaning, the washing, looking after the meals – everything. He never hung the bedding out for airing nor did he ever do any shopping. His blindness and incompetence in this regard demonstrated an intrinsic lack of understanding of the needs of those doing the housework.

I felt that my frustration was not getting through to Satoru. As time went on I developed a sense of hopelessness. I began to feel that there was absolutely no point in trying to discuss anything with him. Soon my sense of frustration and hopelessness reached a crisis point. I was determined to not allow myself ever to fall into the situation I witnessed Satoru and his mom in. I watched as, from time to time, he would fly off the handle at his elderly mom, telling her she should be able to prepare much better meals or that she couldn't expect him to go shopping with her when he had other things to do. Yet he remained quite unable to prepare even the simplest of meals. What a joyless future awaited the man! It would be hard to imagine a more pathetic situation. It was a most unhappy situation for both of them. Witnessing their relationship made me determined to become *au fait* with at least the rudiments of cooking. I knew that if I didn't, I could end up in a most unenviable position in the future.

Standing back now and looking at the situation more objectively, I was really in no position to judge Satoru. In the first place, I had hardly ever made my own dinner when I was living in the flat by myself. I would go to my parents' house for dinner. And after moving in with Satoru I continued going to my parents' place to eat mom's home cooked dinners. This arrangement still continues today. Nothing has changed in that regard. Even though I had everything I needed to cook for myself in my flat, the most elaborate things I ever managed to put on the table were simple vermicelli noodles[5] and a plate of rice with curry poured over it. In terms of the day to day running of the house the only things I could actually boast I was any good at were organizing the washing and keeping the house clean and tidy. I could hardly expect to be eulogized for that!

Even before I was a homosexual I was a member of the stronger sex, a male, an *otoko*[6]. Now what I mean by this is that, although I am homosexual, I was expected to match society's image and fit into the role of 'the Japanese man'. I was forced into a mould which society had created – a mould which included a particular value system. Without realizing it I internalized this value system. It was inculcated without my even knowing it. Indeed, my unconscious acceptance of this value system – which defined the interests men are meant to have and stipulated the behaviour they are meant to exhibit – was reflected in the way I interacted with my own mother.

Being a 'man' I wasn't expected to be in the kitchen. In recognition of this, my mom found it very easy to invite me over to eat. And, of course, it was very convenient for me to have her prepare and serve my dinner. That is why it was very easy to accept that it was appropriate for me to go. However, seeing the dynamics between Satoru and his mom so graphically portrayed before my eyes made me realize that I couldn't afford the luxury of living by the gender based role code of society and being kept out of the kitchen.

Realizing that I would be heading into difficult straits myself if nothing were done, I spoke to my mother about what I was witnessing Satoru and his mother go through. I asked her to give me some tips on cooking. She warmed to this suggestion and immediately said 'Leave it to me. I'll have you mastering all the kitchen skills you need. You'll be able to cook anything you want to!' She accepted my request with an almost eerie degree of enthusiasm. She was very happy to be able to contribute something worthwhile to my future. Thanks to her input, my cooking repertoire these days is quite extensive.

She was initially quite self-effacing about her ability to be a cooking teacher. But taking on the job gave her a sense of purpose. It wasn't long before she felt confident enough to announce that she was really quite an ace when it came to things such as cleaning and preparing fish, for example. This had a very positive effect on her morale. She developed a self-confidence hitherto unknown to her. Conversations along the following lines would flow between us:

> Mom: 'When you stop to think of it, poor old Mrs Ito is in a most unenviable position. She is not well herself and, let's face it, she's hardly in a position to show Satoru how to cook anything. She's got enough on her plate just looking after herself I would imagine'.
>
> Me: 'I suppose you're right on that score'
>
> Mom: 'You know, you and I are much better off in that regard, thanks to your new insight into what might have been in store for us'.
>
> Me: 'I guess that's a good way of interpreting things'.

Initially I simply felt anger towards Satoru for his inability to see and take control of what was happening around him, but eventually that anger turned to something like pity for him and his mother. I came to appreciate that he had never really had a chance either to learn how to cook or to realize the importance of his doing so. The fact that his mom was now quite elderly and not in good health didn't help matters either.

Satoru is now doing what he can to rectify things. He takes it on himself to ask his mom what shopping needs to be done and then goes off and does it. He has taken to doing the laundry and has even been known to prepare breakfast for me on occasions. Furthermore, he is working on his skills with the kitchen knife, although he still has quite a long way to go in this regard. But hey, never mind, he is doing his very best and improving as he goes! He is doing his utmost to wrest himself from the role society stipulates 'men' should fulfill. At the same time, he is striving to gain independence from his mother.

Being unable to cook for myself or do my own washing in the house: losing the sense of leading my own life results in my stress levels exploding.

Under the living conditions described above, I developed a sense of doubt and uncertainty in relation to my place in the scheme of things. It had to do with the fact that I considered myself to be living not in the house I was sharing with Satoru, but rather my parents' house. This was strange, no matter how you looked at it.

In order to solve my most pressing and urgent problems I took the easiest path available to me. The easiest and most convenient way forward for me was a continuation of the lifestyle I had when I was living in the apartment by myself. I ate at my parents' home virtually every night and even took my washing there to have it done. Since I wasn't working at the time it probably wasn't a matter of great consequence that I chose this approach to life. However, were I to get a job, I wouldn't be able to keep up this routine. After a day's work I would not have been physically up to making the trek to my parents' place to eat. Nor did I relish the prospect of eating in restaurants every day or relying on pre-packaged meals from the Seven Eleven supermarket chain. The difficulties I was having in coping with the tasks of everyday life were aggravated by the fact that I really didn't feel that I could do my laundry in Satoru's house. All this started to get on top of me and I started to panic. I simply wasn't able to find a satisfactory arrangement for organizing meals. I didn't have the foggiest idea of what to do to arrange things so that I could eat dinner in Satoru's house.

I remember that before I moved in with him he and I had discussed preparing a meal together once a week in an effort to extend our prowess in household management. After trying to implement this plan on a number of occasions, we found that it was just very awkward for us to use the kitchen for anything at all. Satoru's mother regarded the kitchen as her territory. And the fact that Satoru had never ventured into the kitchen and therefore didn't know where the various condiments and spices and what have you were kept just didn't help matters at all. I ended up having to ask Mrs Ito for help in finding things. I guess she wasn't very happy about the fact that the part of the house that she normally controlled was being taken over by us and that things were being taken from their usual places and not returned. We just didn't use the kitchen in the way she thought best. We were encroaching on her territory. Consequently Satoru and I virtually ended up making things under her direction. Thus, it wasn't long before we just dropped the idea of preparing meals together. Having abandoned that plan we never even once attempted to revive it.

I wanted to develop a sense of belonging to Satoru's household but in the process of developing a close relationship with his mother I got the feeling that she was saying to me 'looking after this house is my business and I'll thank you for not intruding'. Having identified this as the crux of the problem I decided to let things ride for the time being. I began to realize just how wishful our thinking had been regarding sharing the house and our lives with Satoru's mother. To escape from the isolation of my island room, I had gallantly played the role of the dutiful 'daughter-in-law', only to find myself unable to carry the burden of this role. Trying my best to be intimately involved in the life of the household, I had hoped to find a sense of place, a sense of belonging. But my efforts were in vain as Mrs Ito didn't welcome my intrusion into her territory. I could hardly achieve a sense of belonging in the household by staying in my own room, especially while there were no cooking facilities and I still felt very awkward about using the washing machine.

My life was full of contradictions – I was using Satoru's house only as a place to sleep while my life still centred on my parents' home. I was being torn apart by this. I gradually came to despise both Satoru and his mother. I blamed my being so unsettled and uncomfortable with our living arrangements on the fact that Satoru was totally ignorant of the forces at work in the household. I believed he and I could have been happy together if only it hadn't been for his meddling mother spoiling everything!

The New Year came and went. By about February my stress levels had once again reached the point where I was verbally lashing out at Satoru. I was barking things like 'How about doing all the washing yourself, just once in a while', 'You have no idea what I'm going through as you never lift a finger to help with the housework!' and 'If I'm going to be made to feel as out of place as this in your house I would be better off living by myself in a flat! How come it is always me that has to be put through the mill?' I was exploding from the pressure I was under and Satoru bore the brunt of it. At one stage I was in such a frenzy that Satoru started to really panic and get very emotional. He asked if I was threatening to leave and go and live in a flat. He begged me to stop making such threats. He said that he would die if I kept blaming him for everything every night. This emotional outburst was a cry for help in the face of my persistent and ferocious outbursts and accusations of ignorance about the facts surrounding the arrangements we were living under.

I was playing the role of the North Wind from Aesop's well known fable. But I was even more ferocious than the North Wind. It was more like a combination of a furious storm, tremendous thunder claps and an atomic blast all rolled into one! Satoru was playing the part of the traveler with one hundred leather coats weighing him down. Through this dynamic I lost touch with the one person it was most important for me to discuss things with. If at some earlier point I had been able to disentangle myself from the situation and discuss things in a detached manner, things might not have developed to the point they had. The level of stress I was experiencing was, however, of such a magnitude that it surprised even me when it was revealed in my outbursts.

Having reached a point where I could no longer confide in Satoru, I searched for someone new with whom to discuss what I was going through. I searched for someone who, like me, had the experience of going to live with someone new. And the person who fitted this bill was none other than my cooking teacher – my mom! On the evening that I visited her to discuss my problems, I found her laid up with a cold. I enquired how she was feeling and advised her to get some rest while I got straight into preparing the evening meal. My cooking skills had developed to the point where mom was comfortable giving me free rein in the kitchen. When I had the meal ready I woke her up and we ate together. Over dinner we conversed and mom offered me some advice:

'What's up then? Has anything happened between you and Mr Ito? You don't seem to be quite your usual self...'

I was getting used to hearing mom say this as she couldn't help but notice that I was becoming quite depressed from all the arguments with Satoru. She went on:

'If you are finding it such tough going you would be better off moving into a flat on your own you know. You shouldn't have to put up with being so unhappy. You only have one life and you shouldn't stay in that house if it's preventing you from enjoying it. I suppose things had to come to a head. At the very least you need to be able to cook in your own room'.

On this point mom and I were of the same mind.

Mom: 'Come to think of it I know someone who has a portable stove which sits on the table top. Have you ever thought of getting something like that?'

Me: 'I didn't know there were such stoves'.

Mom: 'It has a little gas cylinder attached to it which can be replaced when it runs out of fuel. Wouldn't that sort of thing do you?'

Me: 'I suppose I could give it a try...'

Mom: 'Yes, give it a go and see how you find it to cook with'.

Me: 'It's worth a try I suppose...'

Mom: 'You'll be alright, of course you will! As a matter of fact I was very impressed just now when you came to wake me'.

Me: 'Why was that?'

Mom: 'Well in the past you would have got mad and complained if you had come home hungry and there was nothing prepared and ready for you to eat. But today you made no complaints. Instead you went straight to the kitchen and prepared the meal without even being asked. I was very impressed to see how much you have matured. It is good that you have learned a little independence. I'm sure you're quite able to stand on your own two feet now. There is no reason at all why you shouldn't be able to be independent – you can certainly cook well enough...'

I hadn't thought about it until it was pointed out to me, but I could see that whereas in the past I probably would have flown off the handle if I had come home and found no meal ready for me, now it didn't even occur to me that mom should prepare the food. I reflected on the thought that perhaps I had grown up at least that much.

Anyway, with mom's words of encouragement ringing in my ears, I headed straight to the local Keiyō Home Centre[7] and bought myself the portable gas cooking ring that she had recommended. With this I was, at long last, able to start a life for myself where I had access to cooking facilities. This was six months after moving in with Satoru.

My first, and very successful, attempt at home cooking – using a tabletop gas ring. The outcome of this...

The first dish I made in my own room in the Ito household was one worthy of remembering. It was a weird sort of concoction, probably best described as 'sweet and sour chicken', which used chicken meat in a dish resembling sweet and sour pork. It was a dish I had been thinking I would like to try for a long time. I found the portable table top gas ring to be just the ticket and in no way inferior to a proper cooking stove in terms of what it could do. What was more, I got it at the very good price of 680 yen, with three replacement gas cylinders included in the price! Even if I were to use as many as six gas cylinders a month it would still come cheaper than the minimum monthly charge made by the gas company.

Just as I was congratulating myself on my new purchase, a new problem emerged. There was no exhaust fan in my room! Although the cooking itself was a great success the whole room filled with a greasy smell that permeated furnishings and would not clear of its own accord. Although I opened the windows before starting to cook, the smoke just didn't find its way out! I had never in my life contemplated the possibility of such an eventuality! Okay, now I know why every house is equipped with an extractor fan in the kitchen! That was not the time, however, to revel in such a discovery. My whole room had virtually turned into a kitchen. I learned the hard way that unless I opened all the windows fully before I started cooking there would be no chance of the air clearing and all of my clothes and furniture would smell of cooking. By the time I realized this though, it was a bit late. Even with all the windows fully open the smoke just sat there. A room would have to be positioned to catch a good breeze if the smoke were to clear away by itself.

I started to feel a bit sorry for myself sitting there, eating alone, knowing that on the other side of the partition wall Satoru and his mom were snug and carefree and enjoying some decent tucker. Curse them! They were able to prepare their food in a kitchen with an extractor fan and eat it with no worries. Meanwhile I had only a sink at one end of the room and a gas ring at the other and consequently faced all sorts of difficulties getting a meal together. To top it all off the entire room smelled of grease.

I ate my 'chicken *a la* sweet and sour pork' feeling very sorry for myself and shaking with anger. This was not a laughing matter. The fact that I didn't have an extractor fan was an immediate and pressing problem for me. Without one, dishes that gave off smoke, such as stir-fry meals, grilled fish and deep fried foods were out of the question. This enormously limited the number of dishes I could produce. I decided that if I couldn't cook then I couldn't live in this house and if I couldn't live in this house I would clearly have to move somewhere else. Again, I was rushing ahead of myself. All this for the sake of an extractor fan – a mere extractor fan!

That night I again had a vehement verbal confrontation with Satoru…well, perhaps I should actually say that it was more a case of my unilaterally lashing out at him. He couldn't understand my need for something so peripheral as 'an exhaust fan, a mere exhaust fan'. He seemed unable to grasp the gravity of the situation. I couldn't remain in the house if I was unable to do the things I needed to do. A vicious circle was set up. Just seeing Satoru put me on edge. If my memory serves me correctly we quarrelled right through the night, until daybreak. Satoru, quite worn down by my persistent attacks, finally said 'Look, I don't mind paying for it. Please just go out and get an extractor fan tomorrow'. This comment put an end to the argument.

The next day I wasted no time in heading off shopping for a fan and an electrician. I again found salvation in the Keiyō Home Centre.

However, I could not take advantage of Satoru's offer to pay for the fan. Immediately after he had produced the money I felt guilty for making him do so. With every debt I chalked up our relation-ship moved that much further away from being on an equal footing. I had been out of work for seven months at that stage and had managed to get by through dipping into the savings I had put aside when working as a carpenter. But these savings were being steadily depleted. To buy an extractor fan and have it installed would have cost tens of thousands of yen.[8] That would have left a big hole in my savings. Realizing this I had half given up on the idea that I would find anything suitable which I could afford. When I had a look in the Home Centre, though, they had just what I needed – a 'Kitchen Window Exhaust Fan'. Not only was it a great relief to find that the fan was far cheaper than I had anticipated, there was also no need to put a hole in the wall to install it! There would be no labour costs because I could fix it in place myself.

It took a mere thirty minutes to install, after which I went right to work, cooking something to test it. Well, what pure delight it was to witness this fan draw the smoke out of the room! After having been driven to despair by the lack of cooking facilities and then fighting over the lack of an exhaust fan, at long last I had the freedom to cook in my own room which meant that my everyday survival needs could be met.

My exhilaration, however, was short lived. In no time at all I was yet again feeling dissatisfied. This time it was borne of a realization that, with my cooking needs fulfilled, I would be cooking in this room by myself and for myself for the foreseeable future...

I goaded Satoru into arguments because I wanted him to understand my feelings.

It was only after a great deal of friction that my need for cooking facilities was resolved. I now knew that I had the facilities necessary to look after myself in my own room and yet I still felt a loneliness that I was at a loss to explain. I didn't know what the cause of this was – or indeed what I wanted beyond what I already had. I had thought that I would feel far more settled once I was able to cook for myself in my own room. But somehow that wasn't enough. My stress levels built up again as I struggled to identify just what it was that was niggling at me.

Satoru and I once again got into a most awful argument, during the course of which I experienced something unusual and inexplicable. We had probably been going at it for a couple of hours when I broke down in tears and, without realizing it, cried out to Nyāgo that I wanted to be able to have my meals with him. There was no mistake that I had cried this out, although quite involuntarily. It wasn't my conscious self that called it out. I must have presented a pitiful sight to Satoru that day. I was filled with a most unusual sensation as I realized that the cause of my frustration was simply that I was unable to have my meals with him. It was as though another 'me' was telling me what I actually wanted to know. Satoru and I locked ourselves in a long embrace as I confirmed in my own mind that what I really wanted was to belong in this household with Satoru.

Only after we had both cooled down and managed to approach things rationally and without emotions dictating our behaviour, did the arguments between us cease. We then found ourselves engaging in constructive dialogue. We took the opportunity to stand back and take stock of just what it meant for us to live together in the one house. First and foremost there was a need for both of us to become independent of other people. It was essential that we divorce ourselves from the socially defined image of what constitutes acceptable male behaviour which we had grown up with. In other words we needed to lead our own lives without any reliance on our mothers, and without following the normal and accepted pattern of behaviour of expecting a partner to assume the mother's role. It came down to a question of our acknowledging that divorcing ourselves from the normal and accepted path heterosexuals follow necessitated a breaking of the bond of dependence we had on our mothers.

We didn't both twig to this at the same time. I was quicker at appreciating it and moving towards achieving this goal than Satoru. Because of this I was very frustrated. Satoru just didn't understand the burden I was carrying. It wouldn't have been so bad if he had taken on some of the housework, but this wasn't the case. His mother did almost everything. He just didn't appreciate the fact that this made it difficult for me to use the washing machine or take a bath.

We discussed what we might do in order to alleviate the problems we faced.

Me: 'Why don't you try edging your way in and taking over some of the jobs your mother does? I know it won't be easy to become independent from your mother while sharing the same house, but you should give it a try…'

Satoru: 'I'll need to be careful not to move in and take over everything in one go. That would put her in an awkward position. She would be lost if she had nothing to do'.

Me: 'That's the difficult bit. Perhaps it's best not to make a big issue of it but rather to move in slowly. I reckon your mom would be quite thankful if you helped by hanging out the washing. That would save her from struggling upstairs with it for a start'.

Satoru: 'You've probably got a point there...'

Slowly a new lifestyle, accommodating the three of us in the one household, started to take shape. As far as housework was concerned, essentially I continued my self-contained lifestyle. I wanted it this way for several reasons. I wanted to extricate myself from anything that resembled the socially prescribed male role which I had been brought up with and which didn't accommodate a male being responsible for doing housework. I looked after the housework in my own domain. I also wanted to respect Satoru's mother's unexpressed wish that I shouldn't involve myself in the running of the Ito household. In addition I felt that I shouldn't be doing the jobs which, by rights, Satoru should be doing. Slowly but surely Satoru took on more jobs around the house, until finally he took charge of the overall running of the Ito household. To help me feel as though I was really a part of the household and sharing my life with him, we established the practice of cooking a dinner together in my room once a week. The resentment I had felt each time I had eaten alone in my room was actually a form of indignation directed towards Satoru's aged mother. It felt as though she, being unable to let her son go, had stolen my partner from me. Moreover, at her age, it took all her time and effort simply to maintain the lifestyle she was accustomed to. There was no point in hoping she would change.

Meanwhile, other than the meal we cooked and ate together once a week, our eating arrangements remained essentially unchanged. Satoru, continued to pay precious little attention to my plight – dining with his mom without a care in the world – while I was trying to get him to understand the frustrations I was experiencing. But then he told me that he had recently been giving it some thought and had come to realize that whereas I had managed to break away from my mother and come to live in his house, he had never managed to make the break from his mother. I had no words to respond to this. At last, I thought, he understood. He went on to say that he thought that it was probably too late to expect his mom to let go of the child she was used to living with and upon whom she had become dependent for company. He said:

'It's all up to me I guess, to make the move to break the bond of dependence I have on her. It's up to me to learn how to cook and to stop being reliant on mom's help'.

I responded with a simple 'Thank you'.

At this stage we had been living together for seven months and had had innumerable arguments. In hindsight, I think that we had so many arguments simply because I loved him. I goaded him into arguments because I wanted him to understand my feelings. It all boils down to the fact that, despite everything, I wanted to continue living in Satoru's house. At one stage I had very seriously considered moving to an apartment, but hoped against hope that somehow or other things would work out – simply because I wanted to live with Satoru, despite the difficulties we were having.

I want to take this opportunity to thank my partner, Satoru Ito, here and now for his patience, his understanding and for all he did for me and for us. If we hadn't been able to extricate ourselves from the belief system which heterosexuals embrace in relation to how men should act, should behave and should be, our future together would have been doomed to failure. I am indebted to Satoru for always tackling the persistent and obstinate arguments I caused, head on. And for refraining from forcing his own viewpoint and interpretation of things onto me. As a result we were both able to change for the sake of our relationship. For this I have nothing but heartfelt thanks for him.

3 Days of unholy clashes
by Ryuta Yanase

My screaming 'I'm leaving' and Satoru's tearful resistance.

I should not give the impression, however, that our relationship was all plain sailing from then on. On the contrary, it was yet again to be clouded by a sense of peril. I felt a cocktail of emotions relating to Satoru. These included hatred, jealousy and envy. I found myself using him as a means of stress management. I attempted to relieve my stress by taking it out on him. Yet I still had no idea whatsoever about where this stress was coming from. I made up my mind that the causes of my suffering were all to be found in Satoru's house and that he was to blame for them. I forced him to apologize and heaved a sigh of relief when he did, believing that the matter at hand had been settled. That was the easiest route for me to take, because it involved Satoru – not me – reflecting on things and taking stock of our situation. I felt there was absolutely no need for me to scrutinize my part in the scheme of things. Thus I was prepared to take him on in arguments of a grand scale and to threaten to find somewhere else to live. I took a cruel and selfish comfort in watching him tearfully apologize. But it remained inevitable that mountains of stress would continue to pile up on me until I faced up to my own shortcomings.

Certainly my stress could be traced back to many sources. There was the fact that we were living as a homosexual couple under one roof in an arrangement that society did not sanction in any shape or form. There was stress from the looks given by those in the neighbourhood. I could not escape worrying about this even though I knew in my heart that we weren't doing anything we should feel ashamed of. In addition, there was pressure arising from being unemployed and hanging around the house all day – a certain silent pressure resulting from the expectation of society that men should be gainfully employed. Then there was stress in the form of frustration at my inability to identify a direction in life. This was caused partly because I wasn't working and partly because I was quite unable to visualize what it was that I wanted to do for a living. I was totally bereft of the sense of worth which accompanies the feeling that one is leading one's own life. There was also the urge to drag Satoru down. I saw him as somebody who was streets ahead of me when it came to living his life with confidence as a homosexual. Furthermore, there was the real problem of having to learn how to cook. On top of all this there was the inevitable inconvenience that results from living under the same roof as someone else's mother. There was a plethora of problems arising from this. There were some which Satoru and I had to overcome together and some which I simply had to get over by myself.

I had been guilty of trying to put the responsibility for all these things onto him, even for the problems that I had to get over by myself. I simply didn't see myself as being responsible for anything. Rather, I fully believed that I was the victim, and since somebody must be responsible for the victimization, I blamed Satoru for every difficulty foisted upon me in the course of my everyday life. I was running away from my own failings and shortcomings.

Knowing full well that Satoru needed me to face life (if the truth is to be told, I needed him as much as he needed me), I threatened to move out. When he begged me to stay, saying how much he wanted to live with me, I used it against him to score a victory. I would come out with comments such as 'You'll excuse me if I take off once I've got enough money together. I'll be out of here quick smart. It's just like a prison here and that old hag of a mother of yours is the keeper. It is a prison with all the locals on guard duty keeping an eye on who is coming and going. I've got to get out of this jail cell pretty soon. You can't expect me to stay here, you'd have to be joking'.

As time went by the tenor of my threats to leave approached fever pitch, progressing to the point where my whole body would shake with rage. It was as though my whole being was being overtaken by a convulsion. I lost control of my emotions to such an extent that I pitied myself. When things were at their worst I found myself hopping mad and thumping the floor with my fists. It is no exaggeration to say that our relationship was teetering on the edge of a precipice. I felt I couldn't go on with Satoru, and I suspect that Satoru harboured similar thoughts about me.

Satoru even said that he found it depressing to come home, never knowing what sort of mood he would find me in. He dreaded coming home and finding me looking miserable because he knew that meant we would end up fighting again. This put him in a very depressed state of mind. He said he was unable to come up with a counter-argument when I blamed him for the predicament I was in. My response to this was that he would have to put up with me if he wanted me to continue living with him.

What was actually happening was that I was revelling in the knowledge that I held the trump card – I had the power to make him accept defeat. Yet whilst all this was happening I knew deep down that my behaviour was inexcusable and I felt sorry for him.

I drove him to the point where he could take no more. He cried as he shouted out 'I can't stand it, I'll go mad. I beg you not to leave me. If Nuta were to leave me I'd die'. His reaction was as vivid as the wild words and mannerisms I had threatened him with.

But he wasn't defeated. When I saw Satoru a broken man in front of my eyes, I relented and told him that I would stay. Thus I would ultimately find defeat at his hands. I would bring him to his knees with my threats only to be brought to my knees from seeing him reduced to tearful shouting. But I couldn't stand being on my knees and would feel compelled to turn the tables and, once again, would threaten to leave.

Looking at it objectively I can see that we went through many, many rounds of stupid arguments. We only got to see how meaningless and futile these arguments were through sitting down to sensible discussions. The fact of the matter was that the focus of our arguments had shifted from my threatening to leave and his begging me not to, to how one party might score a victory over the other. As things turned out, we both came to this realization at the same time. When Satoru said to me 'It's alright, you can leave anytime you want to', the feeling that I might do so disappeared immediately. Even I was surprised at how completely that feeling disappeared. I had reached a point where I started to lose sight of the fact that I wanted to be with him. I feel that it was probably because he harped on about how much he wanted me to stay and how much he wanted to be with me (I admit that I was probably the cause of his going on as he did) that I found myself in a position where I had to prepare an excuse to leave and thus try to convince myself that I didn't want to live with him. I never felt in my heart that I wanted to leave Satoru. Rather it was something I used as a means of humiliating him and thus scoring a victory over him.

Taking attention away from my own problems by rejecting Satoru and his positive attitude to life.

There was a stage when I tried furiously to totally reject everything Satoru Ito stood for. I did this in the hope that I might be able to justify to myself the position I was taking. He had gone out and made contact with those pursuing the idea of gay liberation – that is to say putting an end to the discrimination and prejudice directed towards homosexuals. He was very forward in his support of the activities of the Gay and Lesbian Action Association. He was leading what could be described as something akin to a fairytale life as a homosexual. Acknowledging that he was right and approving the course of action he chose to pursue would have been tantamount to acknowledging that the very negative life I was leading as a homosexual – exemplified by my having nothing to do with the gay liberation movement – represented quite the wrong approach, quite the opposite to the approach I should have been taking. Every single time he talked about Occur I would interpret what he said as a criticism of my personal lifestyle. This would inevitably trigger an incomparable level of resentment. The more I saw him being positive the more I felt I just had to drag him down to my own level.

Having quit my job as a carpenter, I had to start out again looking for both work and a purpose in life. Having to launch back into the wider society from zero level, as it were, was a terrifying prospect for me. The longer my isolation from society dragged on, the more I dreaded the thought of rejoining it, and this dread began to smother me. Thus it was that I avoided looking myself straight in the eye and facing up to my problems. I did my very best not to allow myself to acknowledge that I was shuddering with fear at the thought of going back out into society. I did my level best to refuse to acknowledge myself as the homosexual I was, someone still so very lacking in self-confidence and personal esteem.

Thus it was that I searched for an escape route. It wasn't a conscious search for an escape route as such. In fact I quite unconsciously chose the easiest way forward for myself, a path which involved putting blame on Satoru. In doing so I justified my own position to myself, interpreting the way I viewed things and my behaviour as being right. I was simply shutting my eyes to the problems which I, myself, had to come to terms with. Perhaps my thinking was a bit extreme, preventing me from viewing things in a detached manner. I convinced myself that I had to be a wonderful person who was absolutely correct in all he did. When I fell short of that mark I would go to the opposite extreme and conclude that I was quite a hopeless case.

With time, the fact that I was a homosexual came to be an excuse for my life being such a mess. I told myself that I was unhappy because I was a homosexual. I would be no good at anything because I was a homosexual. I couldn't show my face in society because I was a homosexual. Because I was a homosexual I had to suffer in my relationship with my partner, even though we might be living together. It is certainly a fact that homosexuals need an extraordinary level of inner strength and resources to find their way through life, living as they do in an overwhelmingly heterosexual society. In my case, however, I was strangling myself before any heterosexuals did it for me. Because rejecting myself had come to be such a part of my everyday life, I had not even realized that I was doing it. On one hand, I became extremely intolerant of myself and, on the other, extremely lenient – being willing to accept a life of self-rejection. In other words, I had decided not to fight by choosing defeat for myself. I was at the same time both intolerant of myself as a homosexual and willing to accept that intolerance in my life.

From my point of view the man called Satoru Ito was quite phenomenal. Although he was a homosexual like me, he was doing what he could to make a future for himself that would allow him to live as a homosexual. The excuses I used to justify my lifestyle were now invalid and could no longer be employed. For this reason I did all in my power to try to drag him down.

Though I was tormenting Satoru, in him I saw myself being tormented as a child.

In recent times I have given some thought to the question of why it is that I need a partner. Before meeting Satoru I was without an identity of my own. I had never had the experience of properly clashing with another person. I had never interacted in a meaningful way with anyone, nor had I interacted with myself.

Through my association with Satoru I was forced to confront several aspects of my being which I hitherto hadn't even been aware existed. In order for me to interact with my true self it was essential that I clash with my partner. Eventually, through these clashes I came to know the part of me which hated and held a grudge against Satoru. I came to confront that part of me which couldn't tolerate my gutlessness and that part of me which revelled in identifying Satoru's every weakness.

When he cowered after an attack I would get even more angry at the sight he presented. I almost wanted to shout out 'Anyone would think I was the scoundrel to be blamed, looking at the way you cower and cry! Why don't you stand up to me on equal terms?' But when I think of it, his cowering and crying were exactly the same as the cowering and crying I had been reduced to as a young child when my father punched me. In Satoru I could see myself as a young child. When my father saw me crying he would come over to me and hit me about the head, telling me off all the more. He would say 'Be a man and stop crying. What sort of an *otoko* are you?'

The fact that I was unable to accept myself as a cry baby and had come to loathe that aspect of my personal history was the reason why the sight of Satoru emotionally cowering before my eyes made my blood boil. Every time I witnessed him reduced to tears my heart would murmur the exact words that my father had used when denouncing me. I had been through that with my father and the situation I was now in represented my chance to stand up to him, to get my own back. This was my way of equalizing the score with my father.

In my heart of hearts, however, I wanted Satoru to win this one. I wanted Satoru to fight back in a way I hadn't been able to. While I was the one initiating the arguments, I actually supported Satoru and wanted him to win! He was acting on my behalf, was he not? He was me as a young child and I had come to play the role of my father. When I thought of it in these terms I was led to the inescapable conclusion that my father had actually been a very weak, cowardly person who had always acted high and mighty in the house and thrown his weight around. And now here I was, a coward just as my dad had been. I was able to throw my weight around only with Satoru. He was the only one I could boss around.

Even now I fear being called a coward. When people call me this I am simply not able to defend myself. I have my father's words indelibly branded on my psyche: 'You weak, lily-livered cry baby. You disgust me. You're like a woman, an embarrassment to the men of this world'.

Was I not now struggling to shake off these words, to expunge them from my experience? I was taking my frustrations out on Satoru, finding satisfaction in the knowledge that I had won a victory and was not a weak victor. I saw myself as a child, though, in the person of the defeated Satoru. Thus, the more victories I scored, the more wretched I felt. There was a great inconsistency in what I was doing.

In my deepest recesses I harboured a memory of myself as a child, totally cowed by the attacks made on me by my father. I was apt to compare myself with Satoru, who appeared to me as a homosexual who sought to actively get involved in movements aimed at achieving the liberation of gays; as someone who was streets ahead of me in terms of getting through life with a positive outlook. He appeared to me to have a far, far greater capacity to survive than I did. A part of me felt great pride in having a partner as strong as he was, yet another part of me sought to drag him down and make him cower. These two conflicting attitudes towards Satoru co-existed within me.

Having been made to cower myself I searched for some way to experience a sense of superiority over him. The first thing I found was his ineptitude at housework. So I thoroughly took him to task over it. In fact I overdid it. After taking up residence with him – no, even before that – I was guilty of excessively provoking him. There was an unquenchable anger burning in my soul which was directed towards those who had hurt me in the past. I had no love for myself, and in time came to loathe myself. I now believe that, in most cases, the anger I felt was not really directed towards Satoru. In fact I believe that the anger I felt was actually directed at myself. All the pent up anger and frustration that had found a permanent home in the inner-sanctum of my heart poured out onto Satoru immediately after he came into my life. For me he was a receptacle into which I furiously proceeded to pour my wrath. And he, in turn, allowed himself to be a receptacle for the rage of this person so burdened with problems.

The relationship which allowed me to clash with my partner. No longer was I able to run away from myself.

It would have been futile for me to just stay by myself in my room and try to turn myself into the person nature dictated I should be. I wouldn't have been able to get to know myself under those conditions. If it had been possible for me to do this by myself there would have been no need to have been concerned at having been born into the world of homosexuality in the first place. However, you can only expose your soul to yourself and truly get to know yourself through relating to other people.

Before meeting Satoru I had virtually never interacted in a meaningful way with anyone. I had never been lucky in love or in friendship. Saying that you've never had a deep and meaningful association with another person is tantamount to saying that you've never had a deep and meaningful association with yourself. The more I got to know Satoru and the deeper our association became, the more I was obliged to get to know myself. Mr Satoru Ito was the person who allowed me to be myself. Without him I never would have been able to know myself or to be myself. For this very reason he is indispensable in my life. This is why I refer to him as my partner.

The most important thing for us at the present time is to develop a relationship in which we can each reassess ourselves through the interactions, including the clashes, we have with each other. Why do I get so annoyed with him? Why do I provoke him into clashing with me? Surely these are questions I must find answers for through my relationship with him. Satoru is the one person with whom I can build a relationship through which I can discover the answers to such questions. He is the person whom I consider constitutes my personal 'family'.

I reject the suggestion that the typically portrayed happy family unit is the only sort of family that can exist. In our case it is because we can have confrontations with each other and clash with each other that we are able to lay bare our souls and put ourselves in situations where we are forced to come to terms with ourselves whether we want to or not. This leads to an inevitable acceptance of the other party.

As far as living under the same roof as Satoru's mom was concerned, I had to jettison the fantasy that I created regarding the type of association we would have. I must admit – reluctantly – that I now believe it will never be possible for me to fit into a family arrangement with her. That is not to say that I won't learn to get on with her. We will, of course, be on good terms. Our relationship may well fit society's image of 'belonging to the same family', but it does not go beyond the superficial. There is no depth to the relationship. If I were to attempt to interact with her or engage with her in what I consider to be a meaningful way, it would most likely destroy the relationship we do have. Certainly the sort of serious interaction I engage in with Satoru would be quite out of the question for his mom and me. As far as I am concerned, the only person in this house that I feel I could refer to as being a 'family member' is Satoru.

In fact the whole question of who you can call 'family' is quite a tricky and problematic one really, because although the existence or otherwise of blood ties is the most important aspect of the family as defined by society, the question of how individuals within the family interact with one another is simply not addressed at all. As long as there are blood ties there you can get acceptance as a family and society's seal of approval. Perhaps I should say that, rather, all are *forced* into belonging to a family. This goes for daughters-in-law, mothers-in-law, fathers-in-law, whoever. All are dragged into the one classification. Those people whose lives don't fit the standard 'family mould', however, simply never will be accepted as having formed a family relationship – and thus deserving of recognition as belonging to a family – no matter how they might try.

I personally am not able to consider Satoru's mother as a family member. Regardless of how well we might get on with each other, she will always remain an outsider as far as I am concerned. In fact the problems that cropped up since moving in with Satoru may well have been caused by my trying to force my way into the existing family arrangement. Accepting that we are not kindred souls, but that we are nonetheless on good terms, is probably the best arrangement we can hope for. I now really do believe this.

It would not be reasonable to expect that someone who has been emotionally scarred, as I have, could seriously and meaningfully engage with anyone other than his own chosen partner in life. This is because in order to bring about a healing, such people are bound – at least once – to use the words that caused their emotional scarring in arguments they have with their partners. It is also because it is necessary to be able to feel that you can allow your emotions to show, indeed allow yourself to be reduced to tears if the emotional need arises. These things are really only possible with one's partner in life. In my opinion, it is an unfortunate reality that the need to share one's emotions is part and parcel of human nature. Who on God's earth would be prepared to accept such a tremendous burden as providing for another's emotional needs unless the person in question was one's own partner?

Until very recently I felt both jealousy and resentment towards both Mrs Ito and Satoru, neither of whom was able to break the parent-child bond. Once I came round to thinking that there was no need for me to be anything other than an outsider on good terms with Mrs Ito, the jealousy I felt towards Satoru and his mom, and particularly the level of resentment I felt towards Mrs Ito, receded dramatically. When this happened I was able to develop a completely new approach to my relationship with Mrs Ito and smile at her with a feeling in my heart which was markedly different to that which I had felt before.

I feel, at long last, that in the near future things are going to crystallize with regards to the position that I occupy in this household, how I should interact with Satoru from here on in and what the best way for me to interact with his mother is. One thing I am certain of is that I am not going to rush in my search for answers. After all, my life with Satoru has only just begun.

When I was in high school the thought that I might be able to find a partner in life was the sort of dream one has in a dream! After I had found my partner, our living together in the same house was again the sort of dream one has in a dream! One by one, dreams I hardly even dared to dream were coming true. The road leading to that point, however, had been a perilous one, fraught with uncertainty. It is probably a hackneyed expression to use but I do now hold tremendous hope for the future. I feel in my bones that something is growing as a result of new developments in our lives together. I have a real sense that something new is going to be born out of the relationship Satoru and I have fostered. And I am hoping to graduate very soon from the practice of running away from myself. I realize also that I must be kinder to myself from now on. I must become much better at loving myself. The challenge is now before me to live my life with a confidence I have never known as I recognize that I am the only one who can lead my life and that no-one else can lead it for me.

4 Indications of a relationship with open communication
by Satoru Ito

An end is brought to the repeated arguments by my uttering the simple words 'You can leave if you want to'.

April proved to be a difficult month. There were very many occasions on which I simply did not know what to do or which way to turn as I witnessed my partner struggling and suffering. What on earth could I do to help him? To be brutally honest I must admit that on at least one occasion the thought crossed my mind that if our relationship was going to be as troublesome as it was, then perhaps we should just call it a day. At that time I even thought that just perhaps I was incapable of properly understanding the pain others go through and incapable of giving my all to the partnership.

When I had finished penning the first part of this chapter I felt that as a couple which had already cleared quite a few hurdles, we should have reached a stage in our relationship where we could catch our breath for a little while. The conflicts which had visited us earlier in our relationship, however, were soon to return. Indeed they returned with a vengeance, escalating to such a level of intensity that on one occasion Ryuta's bed was a victim and on another a light sliding *fusuma*⁹ door bore the brunt of his rage. This happened late at night, with the noise waking my mom, who came to investigate what was going on. Such incidents as these were common at that stage of our relationship..

I freely acknowledge that the stress Ryuta was experiencing had to do with our living arrangements. His living area was by no means ideally appointed. It certainly didn't lend itself to unwinding. It was by no means a spacious room. If a fold-away bed was used the fridge door couldn't be opened fully. There wasn't any room to stretch out or properly relax. He wasn't free to make use of the washing machine or to bathe when he wanted. Furthermore, he felt a great reluctance to open the door of his room, as that led directly into the room my mom would be in (the kitchen-cum-dining room was a common area that my mother and I shared the use of) and he thus felt he was invading her privacy. He possesses enough tact to prevent him from just barging through as he liked.

In addition the conversations locals had in the street carried with surprising clarity into the room from the window facing the road. It wasn't as though anyone was talking about 'these two men living together', but the fact that voices from the street carried as well as they did meant that Ryuta felt a certain reluctance to open the window. The pressures on him built up to a point where it took him courage just to go outside. The disparaging way he referred to his room as 'a prison' wasn't really that far off the mark. It was only a matter of course that stress would periodically build up within him, in much the same way as magma builds up in a live volcano, and then vent itself – which it did on me.

An even greater problem for Ryuta was what I might refer to as a 'need for surrender' mentality. This manifested itself as a cause of tremendous exasperation in our relationship. It affected our relationship by turning it into a succession of situations in which one of us would take on the role of absolute despot while the other would be forced into a submissive role. Ryuta would make all sorts of complaints and requests about his living environment and how we managed our lives together. Although I was keen for him to stay with me in the house, it was only after I twigged to the real difficulties he was facing that I was able to respond unconditionally to the demands he made.

Ironically, as far as Ryuta was concerned my capitulation was a source of discontent in itself. Despite the fact that I had my own opinions on various things, I kept these to myself. When Ryuta suspected that I was just placating him he would get very angry and frustrated. Ryuta, by the way, reports that he didn't know himself why he got so angry. When his magma reached a certain pressure he would explode in anger and declare that he was moving out. Then it was my turn to become half crazed. I would work myself into a state of tears and cry out 'I'll never make it alone. If you leave me I won't survive'. I used to walk around as if in a trance. I even caught myself punching my pillow on at least one occasion. I experienced real anxiety and mental anguish worrying about my future without him.

Later, when Ryuta cooled down, he would 'submit' to me. He

would then apologize and announce that I didn't need to worry, he wouldn't be leaving me. After a while, though, he would start wondering why he should have to surrender on all counts. He was in a room by himself, hardly ever going out and not speaking with anyone. Consequently he was enveloped by loneliness and isolation and it would all be a bit too much for him. He felt that he would end up quite incapable of carrying out any task if the situation were allowed to continue. He was bereft of hope and couldn't face the future. Having reached the point where he simply didn't know which way to turn, he was back at square one. This aspect of his life remained unchanged. The situation at hand seemed set to continue *ad infinitum*. A pattern of events had been established and was being repeated over and over.

I said something that finally put an end to the seemingly interminable cycle of arguments that characterized our relationship. I must not, however, give the impression that anything I did was grand or deserving of recognition. In fact the whole episode only goes to prove how inept I was at handling such situations. With considerable despair and in the belief that it would perhaps be in the long term interests of our relationship, I turned to Ryuta and told him that he was free to pack up and go anytime he wanted to.

I said this knowing that he couldn't go until he had some money in his pocket and that even if he did go it would be to a flat that would only be a few minutes walk away. When he replied that he wasn't saying that he wanted to break up with me, he only wanted to move out of the Ito household, I knew that I had read the situation correctly. I reiterated that he could leave the house if he so desired. By this stage Ryuta had tears in his eyes and he said 'Thank you for saying that. It was just what I needed to hear'. Opening the door for Ryuta to go if he wanted proved to be a watershed in our relationship. After that the two of us were able to discuss things together.

We agreed that in order to put an end to the situation where one of us acted like a tyrant while the other had to accept whatever was dished up, we would definitely never use the word 'definitely' again. We came to the conclusion that hard and fast expressions such as 'I've definitely made up my mind that I am leaving' or 'You definitely can't go and leave me' failed to take into account changes that might come about in our circumstances. We also agreed that the use of such expressions imposed powerful restrictions on the behaviour of both of us. This lack of flexibility, we concluded, had contributed to the stress we had suffered.

Once we decided that we should keep our minds more open about how our relationship might develop, the stormy times we had been experiencing abated unbelievably quickly. We got on with our lives in peace, with Ryuta and I continuing to eat separately and living independently of each other.

Then one day I felt an awful sadness and loneliness come over me and, without warning, *my* magma erupted. Why was it that Ryuta and I couldn't arrange things so that we got to eat together? We were, after all, living under the same roof, were we not? The feeling that enveloped me caused me to pick all sorts of quarrels with my mother and rendered me quite incapable of controlling my emotions. As a consequence of this I soon found myself crying in Ryuta's arms.

This whole matter, however, proved to be disarmingly easily solved – by adopting an approach that we hadn't hitherto considered. Surely there was nothing wrong with my mom eating dinner on her own! I acknowledged that she was always glad to have my company at mealtimes, but I wanted to eat with Ryuta. This was a clear conflict of interest which simply called for a compromise to be struck. No sooner did I approach my mom and explain my predicament – in the nicest possible way – than she agreed to our eating dinner separately every day. And apologized into the bargain for not having been able to read the situation herself earlier on.

I seem to have been guilty of presuming that because my mom was elderly her capacity to comprehend things had dropped to the level where there was no point in trying to explain anything to her. But I now realize that I had seriously underestimated her.

Another factor that came into play relates to an aspect of my reliance on my mom. Ours was a typical case of the child being unable to break the parental bond. I continued to make demands on her and act in a self-centred and inconsiderate way whilst ever she failed to understand the position I was in and see that my personal needs had changed. I was convinced that mothers intrinsically understand certain things, even without being told.

When she failed to do this of her own accord it was up to me to take her aside and explain, in a way which was easy for her to follow, that it was only natural that I should seek to become independent of her and set up my own life. The end result of all this was that the household resolved the question of how we should organize our evening meals.

Ryuta and I gave up the idea of preparing meals together. There were subtle differences in our approaches to cooking. Accordingly we found the greatest efficiency, both in the use of the kitchen and more importantly in terms of preserving our sanity, was to be achieved by our not getting under each other's feet. So we took turns preparing meals. One party was in charge of the operation while the other acted in a 'supporting capacity' on the sidelines. In all likelihood we will continue with this approach to preparing meals even after mom has left us.

We have now organized the seven dinners for the week along the following lines: two nights a week Ryuta goes back to his family home and polishes up his culinary skills. On these days I join my mother for dinner and either one of us might do the cooking, depending on how we feel and how the day's events have unfolded. For another two nights 'Nuta's Kitchen' is open and Ryuta looks after the dinner preparations in his room. I go there to eat and pay my share. On these nights my mom cooks and eats by herself. For another two nights my work and other commitments mean that I eat out, leaving Ryuta and mom to each look after themselves. The arrangement for the remaining day is that I do the cooking and invite Ryuta to eat with my mom and me. Alternatively, on the days on which Ryuta and I go out on a date, the three of us eat take away meals which I bring home. With these arrangements in place we were able to say goodbye to the experience of lonely meals in separate rooms. It took quite a bit of working out but eventually we hit on this solution and managed to please everyone.

Only when told me of his emotional scars did I get to know Ryuta fully.

Things settled down nicely for a while. After a number of days, however, quite out of the blue Ryuta told me something that drained the blood from my cheeks and left me quite unable to speak. In the next chapter he refers to this himself, but by way of introduction I should mention that during his early years at primary school he had been called a hermaphrodite and suffered dreadful harassment as a result. To make matters worse, he had no-one to turn to for comfort at home. He kept quiet about the harassment because he didn't want to add to his mother's burden; she was herself a victim of abuse – at the hands of his father.

He kept this locked away inside him all these years. He reported to me that merely recalling that period of his life was such an ordeal for him that he was powerless to prevent tears from welling up in his eyes. Indeed this was what happened both when he told me about it and as he wrote about it for this book. All that I could do was take him in my arms and hold him tightly.

It was a shock to learn of this episode in his life. Clearly it was not a matter to be dealt with lightly. Indeed it was a matter of such ponderous substance that Ryuta had never broached the subject with me in the eight years we had been together. I was taken aback by the fact that he had such an experience in his past and also that he had been harbouring this dark secret for so long. He had never been able to share it, not even with me, his soul mate and partner in life. For the first time ever the only thing I could do was take him in my arms and hug him gently.

When he told me about this aspect of his past I understood instinctively that there was no room for argument, no place for trying to advance any selfish interest, in fact no scope for even attempting to tactfully engage in a deeper discussion of this subject with him. It was clear that, emotionally, he was terribly scarred.

The way he treated me when I snapped at him during his bouts of moody silence and the awful self-deprecation that regularly took control of him could now be explained. Their root cause lay in this emotional scarring which he was simply incapable of healing by himself. The scars were so deep that he was left irritated and exasperated. He blamed himself for the position he was in. The only way he knew to express his emotional state was through bouts of numbing silence and emotional cringing. After eight years of associating with Ryuta the way I viewed him changed overnight, as dramatically as the way in which the dark, threatening skies disappear and are replaced by a piercing blue azure with the passage of a typhoon.

Why was it that this man repeatedly attacked the most vulnerable of my emotions and made such a concerted attempt to taunt me and hurt me by arguing and fighting in the dreadful way he did? Why was he never able to command a measure of self-confidence or hold his head up high and approach life with a positive attitude? Why did he always interpret his own actions so negatively? Why did he always remain in his shell, unable to reveal his soul to others? I had always wondered about these things to myself and on occasions confronted him directly with such questions, but I had never been given a reply which explained things satisfactorily. I had even at times thought of him as being a terribly troublesome figure to deal with. Any difficulties, misgivings or ill-feelings I had experienced in relation to him in the past, however, disappeared in an instant. All could be explained by the background this man had.

Soon after Ryuta's revelation my heart started to fill with anger. I was imbued with a sense of there being an immediate need to change the heteronormative society which was responsible for what it had done to my Ryuta. Never mind homosexuals hoping to find happiness in life, everything was organized to prevent us from even surviving in society. An anger grew within me as I wondered just what I could do to help Ryuta out of the problems ensnaring him. But think about it as I might, I was at a total loss; I simply didn't know what could be done. Ryuta though, said that he felt immeasurably better just from opening up to me.

When the emotion of the moment passed I started thinking it was arrogant of me to presume that I could be of assistance in relieving his burden. Yet, with each step we had taken during our eight years together, he had been gradually releasing himself from the past that ensnared him.

I had only very recently started living my life in a way which was both natural and comfortable for me. The way forward, it seemed, was to take each day as it came and support each other as we did. We should continue talking things through with each other and tackling the hurdles we came across as we came across them. Ryuta – let's work together to successfully negotiate each and every hurdle put between us and our happiness!

We had no major arguments in May. Today we went to collect our passports. We're going to America where we plan to take part in the Gay Pride parade together.

6 Homosexual Notebook

The Happiness We Seek.

1 The fight to overcome my feeling of self-rejection
by Ryuta Yanase

Violence meted out by my father. Being called a hermaphrodite and being picked on at school.

Thirty-two years have passed since the February day on which I was born in a Tokyo hospital. As a young child I was shy and very quiet. As far as my parents were concerned I was a good child who didn't cause them any trouble.

As a child, for some reason or other, I always felt more comfortable in the company of girls than I did with boys. Even now I remember I found the rough boys intimidating. The desire to play with the girls was, for me, a very natural and unforced thing. It came from within. The fact that I was a lad playing with the girls was, however, pointed out with a measure of disapproval and intolerance by the people around me.

As far as I can remember, the first time I displayed any interest in relation to matters of a sexual nature, was in the year before I started primary school. There was a children's book entitled 'The Origins of the Human Race' that contained pictures of primitive man. Of course, being primitive man, the pictures showed the subjects without a stitch of clothing. Yet despite the fact that they were all stark naked, for some reason or other the males were drawn without any genitals. I was greatly frustrated by this. I remember asking my dad why it was that these males didn't have willies!

Jumping ahead slightly to the time I was in my second year of primary school (if my memory serves me correctly), I remember that there was a group called the Monkees which enjoyed tremendous popularity in Japan, appearing on the small screen in a show called 'The Monkees' TV Show'. My sister liked Davey and would make a great scene every time he appeared on the screen. When she asked me who I liked I answered 'I like Davey too' because I wanted her to like me, but actually I was infatuated with Peter and unable to take my eyes off him. My sister saw through my lie and said 'Liar! You really like Peter, don't you!'

Having my sister see through my lie and identify my real feelings was a shock for me. I remember very clearly feeling that I had been caught out and was quite unable to respond to her accusation. As far as I can recall this was the first experience to prompt a self-realization of my sexuality, the first spark of an awakening to the fact that I was homosexual. Of course, it goes without saying that at the time I had never even heard the word 'homosexual'.

Later, during my formative years, my dad worked in a place where his presence was not welcome. He was employed at the local government offices but was given the cold shoulder by his colleagues there because in that workplace the union members, who belonged to the Communist Party of Japan, wielded great influence and he was alone in being a supporter of the Liberal Democratic Party[1]. Dad had to bear the brunt of all the workplace politics by himself. When he got home he would express his feelings about his work colleagues and the Communist Party.

'That Communist Party is a real pack of bloody ratbags' he declared. His comments were unbridled as he gave free vent to his emotions. 'A whole bunch of maggots who wouldn't realize their bums stank unless they pulled their fingers out and had a good smell. Can't stand the lot of them. They are a real bunch of wankers!' If mom were to remind him that such expressions were inappropriate in front of me the physical and verbal abuse would start. He would come back with 'Who the hell do you think you are? If you don't like what I say then get out! You cuss! You're a wretched parasite'. He would strike her while shouting at her. 'You're a hopeless case. If you've got any regrets for having married me, leave – get out! Get out if you're going to speak to me that way'.

Mom and I were at the mercy of dad's moods. We had to tread very carefully in order not to set him off. In our household, domestic violence was part of the daily routine. At that stage there was no way I could have envisaged the stress my father was under at work. My main concern from day to day was to avoid being punched by him.

In my third year of primary school I was given the nickname 'Herm' (short for 'hermaphrodite') and made fun of virtually every day. Both the boys and the girls joined in this sport. My primary school years were agonizing. I was tormented at school and suffered awfully. I never understood why they called me a hermaphrodite. I used to wonder if my mannerisms were on the feminine side. I saw myself as a boy…but why didn't they accept me as such?

I was by nature a quiet boy, unable to stand up to the bullies. In the end I submitted to them, accepting that I was to be their target. Virtually every day I copped it. Classmates would punch me and kick me regularly. I was too timid to stand up to them or even respond to their insults. It was a one-way street. I was the victim.

The trouble was that my dad would have beaten me if I had wagged school and stayed home. And he would have blamed my mom for it, shouting at her that she hadn't brought me up properly. Because I was determined to avoid this eventuality at all costs, I felt duty bound to continue turning up to school every day, despite the predictable consequences.

The words 'I don't want to go to school because I'm always picked on by others' nearly escaped from my lips on one occasion when I was with my mother. But I didn't want her to know that I was being called a hermaphrodite, so I had to handle that crisis by myself without anyone to share the burden. What I wanted, and needed, at that time was someone who would accept me un- conditionally, for what I was. Someone who would say that it didn't matter if I didn't exhibit all the traits generally associated with maleness. Someone who was prepared to accept me as the person I was. My life was a succession of being bullied at school and then being punched up by my father at home.

In my fourth year of primary school I set about making myself impervious to it all. I decided that nothing would ever hurt me; I would become a person without feelings. I made up my mind to become like a robot – impervious to all emotions. I swore to myself that I would do this. I reckoned that it was only because I had feelings that the bullying at school hurt me, so if I didn't have feelings I would never feel sorry for myself. I told myself that having feelings was also why I felt angry. I figured that if I had no emotions and no feelings I would not have to suffer anymore. I convinced myself of this, determined to get over my crisis by readily accepting the blows sent my way. When they would say 'Let's slap him on both cheeks' I put my face forward to accept it. I chased anger, fear and sadness out of my heart. I whispered to myself 'Go ahead, bully me all you like. I have no feelings'. In this way I lost any feelings I had. And with them went the last vestige of pride I had in myself.

Doing away with my true self and acting as a man 'should', in order to protect myself.

When I was in year five things took a turn for the better. My father decided to buy an apartment. This meant two things. Firstly, that the family would leave the public service housing behind; and secondly, that I would be going to a new school. While I believed that I would be saying goodbye to those guys who had humiliated me, I harboured a fear that I might still be called a hermaphrodite at my new school. I recall mustering all my mental faculties to ponder the question of just how to behave in order to appear more masculine. I was under pressure from my social environment to fit the mould for 'boys'. Before long I discovered that playing with boys could be enjoyable. At the same time, though, I realized that while I felt a certain envy of classmates who displayed the typical traits of male behaviour, I also felt a certain aversion towards them. I carried a sense of impending intimidation, fearing I would once again be the target of bullying attacks. I felt compelled to do everything I could to appear no different from the other boys in the school. I had to do everything in my power to appear ordinary, just like the other boys around me.

I now realize, of course, that to acquire the attitudes and behavioural patterns displayed by the other boys I would have had to discard the attitudes and behavioural patterns that were normal and natural for me. These represented a priceless treasure for me, irrespective of whether they fitted the parameters of the prescribed male model, or the proscribed female model, of behaviour as stipulated by society. In the end I was defeated by the unwritten rule that states that unless a boy acts in accordance with the accepted parameters of male behaviour he will be picked on. As a means of protecting myself, I discarded the mannerisms, attitudes and patterns of behaviour which came naturally to me and took to acting as the other boys did. Such a change was not my preferred option, but seemed the only choice for survival.

There are those in society who claim that there is no discrimination against homosexuals in Japan. If this is so, what would you call the bullying I was subjected to in primary school? I accept that after changing schools and forcing myself to fit the mould boys are supposed to fit, the incidents of harassment ceased, but this was simply and solely because I had blended myself into the surrounds.

In this country the terms 'hermaphrodite', 'poofter' and 'homo' are reserved for use as insults, expressions of contempt to be used in reference to men who don't fit the prescribed male model as defined by society. The latter two are used synonymously with the term 'homosexual'. In other words, in the public mind the term 'homosexual' equates with the terms 'poofter' and 'homo'. These terms are used to refer to any male who doesn't fit the masculine image as stipulated by society.

I would suggest that the contempt the Japanese people exhibit towards homosexuals is in fact essentially a contempt directed towards men who don't fit the conventional masculine image – in other words effeminate men – rather than something directed specifically towards homosexuals as such. This would explain why I was given such a terrible time at primary school even before I realized that I was homosexual, and thus before I could possibly have come out and disclosed my sexuality.

They bullied me because I wasn't 'masculine' enough, because I wasn't a 'manly' boy and for no other reason. Thus, unless we can get rid of the discrimination mentality directed towards 'unmanly' men we will not get rid of the discrimination mentality directed towards homosexuals. If we accept this as being a reasonable argument we can then reasonably surmise that even if all male homosexuals were to acquire the external behavioural attributes that society dictates they should display, they would still be considered unmanly because 'they have sex with men' or because 'they don't have sex with women'. In other words they would still be targets for discrimination because they differ from the majority and this is not what society wants. Men with feminine mannerisms are deemed not to be 'manly' because of their social behaviour. Homosexuals are deemed not to be 'manly' because of their sexual preference. Society has no room for either category of 'unmanly' men.

The excitement experienced as a result of my happening upon a gay magazine. Wondering if I might be a *'homo'*.

My awakening to the fact that I was homosexual accompanied my acquiring an understanding of the term 'homosexual'. This occurred soon after I entered junior high school. It is the usual thing for everyone to fall in love when they are in junior high school, but in my case those I felt attracted to were all male classmates, without exception. Initially I didn't question this; I just accepted it as a natural thing. I figured that because I was a boy myself it was natural enough that I should like other boys. The love I felt for my male classmates seemed a perfectly natural thing.

Junior high school was also when I came to learn about masturbation. In my case when I masturbated I would visualize well-built male bodies. This was also entirely natural for me. This most natural of desires, however, would later prove to be something I was unable to accept.

As I developed and experienced feelings of love and attraction to others, my sexual appetite grew to the point where I was unable to control it. My classmates, too, were experiencing the same sort of thing. The awakening of their carnal desires put the topics of masturbation and love high on the list of things to talk about. It was as plain as the nose on your face, however, that girls were the object of their carnal desires. Clearly they were attracted to members of the fairer sex and equally clearly they fully utilized sexual fantasies involving girls when masturbating. I couldn't escape the conclusion that I was different from the rest of them and intuitively felt that I should keep the words 'I prefer boys' to myself.

The realization that being different from all the others meant that my position was perilous, was something which was deeply ingrained in my psyche. This realization was accompanied by a sense of foreboding. I knew that a personal disclosure of the fact that I was different would not be in my interests. Furthermore, a feeling that I was the only one who was different grew, eventually reaching the point where I could no longer deny it.

It was at that stage in my life that a gay magazine called *Barazoku* caught my eye one day as I happened to be browsing in a bookshop. No matter how long I live, I will never, ever forget the shock – and the excitement – of seeing a picture of a male nude adorning the front page of this magazine. It was both a tremendous joy and surprise to find evidence of the existence of that which excited and attracted me. Nowadays pictures of male nudes may not be so exceedingly rare, but at that time such a photograph was unheard of as far as I was concerned. I will never forget how excited that picture made me. I *had* to have that magazine. I wanted to feast my eyes on that picture whilst indulging in self stimulation. This desire was mightily powerful.

I was very tense as I took that publication to the cash register and made my purchase. When I arrived home I voraciously devoured every page. I remember coming across the word 'homo' many times, which prompted me to wonder what it meant. I wondered if it, perhaps, applied to me. I felt an intense curiosity about it and went straight to a dictionary to look it up. The dictionary entry referred to 'abnormal sexual love'. It defined the word 'homo' as 'a sexual pervert' and went on to say 'generally used in reference to male homosexuals'. Needless to say, I was left with a dark and gloomy image of the people fitting this description.

I remember thinking that I must be a 'homo', but wondering if it was really something abnormal. If it were, then there was no way I was going to let myself be one! The discovery that homos were 'abnormal' and 'sexual perverts' came as a tremendous shock to me, a young lad in the second year of junior high school. I hoped against hope that there might be some mistake. In fact there had to be! I consoled myself with the idea that there simply had to be some mistake. Of course one day I would wake up and find myself with an interest in girls! What I was experiencing was transitory – transitory emotions and nothing more! The fact of the matter, however, was contrary to what I hoped for – I found myself attracted more and more to other guys. And yet, because of the contemptuous nuance of the dictionary definition I felt a loathing for the word 'homo' ever since the day I looked it up, despite the fact that it seemed as though I belonged to the category of people it described. Hence, instead of the disparaging term 'homo', I immediately elected to use the term 'homosexual' in reference to a person with my sexual orientation.

If I were a homosexual, the question of marriage would pose enormous difficulties for me. Performing sex would be an awful trial because girls did not arouse me at all. If I were to take a wife, I would simply have to clamp my eyes shut and fantasize about good looking men in order to perform. But even as a second year junior high school student I could see that such an arrangement was unfeasible – it just wouldn't work out. I was also aware that if I acknowledged my homosexuality I would lose my ticket to becoming a respected member of society. I told myself that I could never afford that. I would definitely marry a woman. And have kids. And be accepted. And get ahead in the world and be financially successful!

There is nothing at all strange about the fact that instantaneously my mind should turn to thoughts of a sham marriage. Although I knew nothing at all about the ways of the world, I felt quite comfortable with the idea of being party to a sham marriage, having already adopted a 'normal' boyish mode of behaviour which reflected the value system that boys were supposed to embrace. At that time I believed that the way for me to find happiness in life was to conform – to get married, as everyone does, and to do the same things as everyone else.

As I pursued my desperate attempts to adopt the mannerisms of a boy, I witnessed an aversion to the so-called 'hermaphrodites', the men who exhibited feminine mannerisms, germinating within me. In those days the only homosexuals appearing on TV were the likes of Carousel Maki and Akihiro Miwa[2] who dressed in drag. I would experience a sense of revulsion every time I saw them. They could hardly have been considered to portray a positive image of homosexuals. But in the absence of information or evidence to the contrary I decided that they represented 'homos' as a group and I was dead-set against joining that band.

My tortuous high school years were marked by a sense of alienation, isolation and self-loathing. I spent them acting out the role of a heterosexual.

After reaching senior high school my zest for life nearly expired. A numbing sense of isolation gripped me. I hated myself for having an interest in men and I suffered an inferiority complex on account of not being able to identify with the interests and thought patterns typical of my gender. I was simply unable to accept my homosexuality. I became overly self-conscious, always dreading the possibility that my friends might learn of my sexual orientation. So I pretended to be heterosexual, perennially feigning an interest in women.

It was not possible for me to admit that I alone was different. I felt that if it became known that I was homosexual everyone would shun me. In high school I could see that homosexuals were treated with disdain. They were laughed at. They were the target of scorn. They were considered to be unacceptable as members of society and were therefore deserving of contempt and ridicule.

Even today, more than ten years later, the situation has changed very little. Homosexuals are still the butt of jokes on TV comedies. We even have gays ridiculing themselves on TV, referring to themselves as 'homos' and 'poofters' and ingratiating themselves with the audience by playing the role of a jackass who deserves nothing more than to be treated as less than human. Thus they provide the sort of entertainment our heteronormative society has come to expect.

It is a fact of life that in Japan today, homosexuals are openly and publicly ridiculed. It is no wonder, then, that I feared I would become the laughing stock of the whole school if it became known that I was a homosexual. To ensure that this didn't happen I had to be prepared at all times to fit into the smutty conversations that friends would have. When the topic of conversation turned to women, however, I invariably felt as though I was putting on a false front. The 'real me' kept having feelings for male classmates, just as I always had. I was clearly and unquestionably a homosexual.

It goes without saying that the romantic attraction I felt for the boys around me was something I had to keep to myself. It could never be revealed nor would it ever be reciprocated. It never crossed my mind to reveal it. In a nutshell, the student I was in high school might be described as the personification of an inferiority complex. I never felt part of the scene. I always felt alone, even in a crowd. I was bereft of any sort of emotional support, even when all around me were friends – 'normal' heterosexual friends.

In those days I used to entertain a transient hope that perhaps one day I would be able to turn heterosexual. Accepting my homosexuality was out of the question. I piled wasted effort upon wasted effort in a futile attempt to become the heterosexual I should have been. Yet in my private life there was no room for doubt. I knew deep down that I was homosexual. It was something beyond my control. No matter how much I might try to deny it, no amount of determination on my behalf was able to change the reality of my orientation.

Your sexual orientation is not something you have any hand in determining. If it had been within my power to choose my sexuality I would have absolutely and definitely chosen heterosexuality when I was in high school. Life would have been so very much easier that way. I was totally powerless, however, to alter my sexual orientation. It was beyond my control.

Some heterosexuals ask me very openly 'When did you turn homosexual?' and in the past I have even come across people who suspected that I must have had some problem with women which led to my becoming homosexual. I can only speak for myself in this regard, but certainly I was only ever interested in guys, even before I experienced sex. I was only ever attracted to guys and I felt this attraction many years before I got to the age where it would have been possible for me to experience any difficulties with women. I would actually like to turn the tables and ask heterosexuals when they turned heterosexual! Could they answer why it is they are only attracted to the opposite sex? Are they able to change their sexual orientation by dint of their own volition?

Wanting to escape from the suffering experienced as a result of being different. Deciding not to make friends.

I graduated from high school but failed in my first attempt to get an offer of a place at a university, so I had to wait a year until the next round of university entrance exams was conducted to try again. On my second attempt I did manage somehow or other to scrape over the line and was offered a place at a technical college. When there, I took a completely new tack in my approach to associating with other people. I decided to have nothing to do with anyone and to avoid all contact with others. In hindsight I know that it was a terribly sad choice to have had to make, but at the time

I hoped that this decision might allow me to be myself, albeit in isolation from all others. I couldn't bear to think of the pain I would suffer as a result of being made to acknowledge that in fact I was, as suspected, different from the others. I was aware that any differences were likely to become increasingly apparent the closer I got to new friends. Hence, I chose to create a world of my own in which I could isolate myself.

Yet despite this determination, I found myself with some new friends. In the normal way one would welcome the formation of new friendships in an unfamiliar environment. Although it wasn't what I aspired to, I must confess that, in a sense, I was pleased with this development. I was, after all, a human being. And no matter how brave a face you might put on, there is nothing harder to contend with than social isolation. I was happy to have made new friends and yet, at the same time, I was sad. I once again felt that I just wasn't one of them. I felt a barrier between us, a distance which I found hard to manage. As before, I felt this distance the minute I got to know them. The following is typical of my friends' conversations and reinforced my sense of being separate from them.

Mr C: 'Hell, aren't there any nice girls anywhere? It's hard to find a chick at the college you study at, eh?!'

Mr D: 'We've got no chance. They've no interest in meeting guys from this college. To be honest, I reckon they are snobby. They think the guys at this college are below them, silly bloody women they are!'

It would have been quite beyond them to comprehend just how this sort of conversation affected me. It broke me up to realize that I would never be able to be close friends with these guys; the gulf between our worlds was just too great. I was interested in men, not women. I had already had enough of trying to fit into the world of heterosexual friends. Indeed, I had exhausted myself in my attempts to do so and I couldn't find the enthusiasm to try yet again. Thus, I consciously started to keep a distance from this new group of friends. I had no choice. It was the only path open to me if I was not to end up being belittled and laughed at and if I was to avoid living a lie. I had no alternative but to choose to set myself apart. I could see no other way for a homosexual to survive on that campus.

I purposely avoided friends, but this resulted in people considering me to be an odd sort. It takes quite a bit of effort to try to put an end to a relationship you have with others once it has been established. I had been on the point of saying 'I'm gay so just leave me alone' on at least one occasion. I really wanted to shout it out. But at that stage of my life such a thing was quite impossible. I simple didn't have the confidence in myself to come out and admit it. I was carrying a dreadful sense of guilt and inferiority about being homosexual. I carried this burden all alone. There was no-one but no-one with whom I could have shared it. On my own, I had no idea what I might do to build a little self-confidence. I thoroughly detested the homosexual I was. Since I had no confidence in myself, and could not possibly accept myself, you can imagine the utter impossibility of me confronting people with a comment like 'What's wrong with someone being a homosexual?' if they were making fun of my sexuality. In fact I am quite sure that if such a situation had eventuated I would have suffered an emotional blow from which I may never have recovered.

However, as things turned out, those friends eventually came to place a distance between themselves and me. Initially they couldn't understand why I tried to distance myself from them. This resulted in my feeling really, truly and dreadfully alone. I was always by myself when on campus. Even when I bumped into them they would ignore me. I tried hard to convince myself that it was best this way, that indeed, this was the only way forward.

However, I found the loneliness I was suffering to be a far greater cross to bear than I had ever imagined. I yearned to have a friend, someone to end the loneliness and isolation which was my world. I was sitting alone at the college, while all around me were groups of heterosexual classmates, laughing and enjoying themselves. I thought to myself that perhaps I would never belong to a group where I could join in and laugh with everyone. I thought that perhaps I would never find a friend. The sense of loneliness was far more acute when I was alone in a crowd at the college than when I was by myself at home.

With time I found myself unable to stand the isolation from the world around me, an isolation that was self-imposed, and I found it increasingly difficult to make myself go to the college. Eventually, about six months after enrolling, I reached the point where I hardly attended the technical college at all. However, in order to avoid having my parents ask troublesome questions as to why I wasn't attending classes, I pretended that I was. To this end I would catch the Yamanote Circular Line train[3] and stay on it for several circuits to pass the time. This charade continued for nearly a year.

Paying visits to a church seeking salvation only to be told that homosexuals would go to hell.

In those days I hated my homosexuality. I thought of myself as human trash. I believed that my sexuality was why no-one liked me and I was bereft of friends. I always blamed myself for the situation I was in, while at the same time I came to resent the society around me. I wondered why I had been given such a wretched lot in life. Why was it I had to suffer so? Curse society for having so many people with closed minds! This way of thinking provided me with just the pretext I needed to rationalize the loneliness I was experiencing. In retrospect I would say that, whether or not I knew it at the time, what I wanted, what I sought, what I yearned for, was an end to my suffering, my loneliness and my social isolation. I was calling out for help.

Day after day I spoke with no-one from the time I left the house in the morning until I arrived back home in the evening. On one such day when I was wandering aimlessly outside Shibuya Station[4] I was approached by a Mormon missionary who spoke to me. How many days had it been since someone had spoken to me? I was delighted with this development and found myself being taken to the Mormon Church in Shibuya by this very presentable and well-groomed American missionary from Utah.

In his broken Japanese he started explaining the doctrine of the Mormon Church to me. It had been many days since I had spoken to anyone and I felt overcome with emotion. We spoke together for a while and as we were about to part he said 'Please do come again'. What a delight it was to be made welcome like that! The welcome he extended to me marked the beginning of a period in which I attended his church.

When I got home that day I avidly read the Bible I had bought on his recommendation, together with a book outlining the Mormon Doctrine. These made reference to the teachings of Christ which said that the love of God was accessible to all. With my heart heavy with sadness and a desire to be rescued, I turned to the Mormon Church in the hope of salvation.

This, however, wasn't to be. I had been attending the church for about a month when one of the more highly placed missionaries started explaining the church's doctrine on homosexuality. He explained that 'People commit all manner of sins. God tells us that men who love other men, in the way that men love women, defile themselves and deserve to be despised. They don't realize the depth of the sin they are committing. That path leads to the burning fires of hell'. He went on to say that 'In recent times we even witness people openly and publicly displaying behaviour of that sort. This is something very disturbing, indeed it is frightening!'

At that I wondered if I also would be rejected and tossed aside by God. I was in no position to engage this missionary in any form of debate, being so very lacking in confidence and unsure of where I stood, having never received any positive reinforcement for my sexuality from any quarter. Consequently I bade farewell to my association with that church. But the guilt I felt on account of my homosexuality had only been made worse. Nothing could save me after that. Moreover, my exposure to the Mormon teachings left me seriously worried about the possibility of going to hell if I had sex with another man.

At night I used to make a point of confessing to God. I remembered that the Mormon missionaries had said that if you were to ask God for something earnestly he would be sure to answer your prayers. That being the case there was something I wanted to ask God about – whether or not homosexuality really was a sin. I asked this day in, day out believing I wouldn't be saved unless I got an answer. I wanted to hear the answer from God's mouth directly, not from the mouth of another human being. Was my being a homosexual really a sin? Practically every day I made the following prayer to God: 'Please God, I ask your help. I am a homosexual. Would it be better for people like me to die? When I do die will I go to hell? I can't bear the pain I am going through. Do you also hate me? I beg you to tell me the truth!'

Then one day God really did reply to me. To be honest I don't know whether God replied to me directly, whether I was guided to the answer or indeed whether I discovered the answer for myself.

But on the day in question, soon after I had started to pray, tears rolled from my eyes and I was powerless to stop them. This took me quite by surprise and presently my heart filled with joy as it cried out to me 'I am loved by God. He has blessed me! It's OK for me to lead my life as a homosexual!' This revelation was a most eerie experience. It released me from the dreaded fear that I would be banished to hell upon my death. Although this was certainly a great relief, it only returned me to the point I was at before getting involved with the Mormon Church. Still, having been released from the sense of sin I had learned from the Mormons, I made up my mind to look for a homosexual partner.

Meeting with my first homosexual friend, a Mr A, and later with my partner.

I turned twenty-one after withdrawing from the technical college. I had no fixed employment, no steady job. I remained unable to see any future in associating with heterosexuals. I spent three years in and out of different jobs before I settled into the carpentry trade. As had always happened in the past, the better I came to know my heterosexual workmates, the more I felt stifled by the fact that I was homosexual.

About this time there was a development, although very slight, towards my coming into contact with other homosexuals. Having finally succeeded in extricating myself from the sense of guilt the Mormons had introduced me to, I made contact with and started meeting a number of guys through the personal columns of a gay magazine. My liaisons were of a sexual nature. None of these contacts, however, developed into a romance.

In hindsight, perhaps the reason for this was that my expect- ations were too high. I was idealistic, not at all practical. You must remember that I had never in my life experienced anything vaguely approaching a romance with another homosexual. The only romantic attachment I had ever made was to the proverbial 'prince on a white horse'. He was someone who had perfect features and whose personality could not be criticized in any way. He was a handsome guy who kept me feeling wonderful the whole time. He would suddenly appear before me and say just what it was that I wanted to hear: 'Stay with me forever!' That was the hope I always held in my heart! Needless to say, this was a far cry from the real world.

In real life the other homosexuals I met were like me, insomuch as a total lack of positive homosexual imagery had rendered them unable to feel any vestige of self-esteem or sense of respect in themselves. And because they lacked confidence in themselves they were unable to position themselves to say things like 'I really hope you will continue seeing me'.

As far as looks went they were only the same as your average heterosexual guys and I quickly came to realize that it was time for me to discard the idealistic, utopian fantasies which I clung onto.

As it turned out, I wasn't able to form friendships with these guys either. I once again found myself enveloped by that familiar feeling of isolation and loneliness. For a while I gave up on hoping to find a friend and partner. Indeed the image I had of a partner was just too grand, quite idealistic. I could have spent my whole life in a vain search for such a person.

Meanwhile, through a series of liaisons that were unsuccessful (if their sole purpose was to meet a potential partner in life) I did finally end up with some homosexual friends. The first such friend I ever had was a guy I shall refer to as Mr 'A'. We were both members of a particular gay circle at that time. The circle itself folded about six months after its formation, but my association with Mr 'A' continued on beyond that. He was the first homosexual friend I ever had. Unlike me, however, he was familiar with the gay scene in the Ni-chōme district and had even made himself a regular at one of the bars there. Perhaps you wouldn't describe him as living life in the fast lane as such, but to someone like me, who was still not comfortable with the idea of accepting myself as a homosexual, he appeared to think nothing at all about making the most of his life as a gay man.

I viewed his lifestyle with envy. For some reason, though, I never developed an affinity with the Ni-chōme area. In most of the bars, both the customers and the *mama-sans*[5] spoke in drag queen tones. Although there was some difference between the various establishments in this regard, I was always the only one speaking straight Japanese – only to be told not to act so high and mighty! I started to wonder if the sort of speech they employed was their passport to successfully making a go of it in that part of the city.

Having been made fun of, called a hermaphrodite and bullied during my impressionable years, I had never in my wildest dreams thought that I would meet other 'hermaphrodites' under such circumstances. In these men I could see the poignancy of my youth, a life I had tried to keep the lid on and block out of my memory. To put those memories behind me I did everything in my power to adopt the behaviour, mannerisms and attitudes that society attributes to the stronger sex. I was prepared to protect this veneer of masculinity at all costs. Thus I rejected these gays who spoke like drag queens. The image I had built up in my mind of the Ni-chōme district of Shinjuku, an image that would have made it a paradise for homosexuals, was quickly demolished. The only people to be found there were hermaphrodites – half-way houses between those who associated themselves with the masculine gender and those who associated themselves with the feminine gender. They were much the same as I had been when called a hermaphrodite, and I thoroughly hated that person. The sight of these drag queens openly acting in ways I had convinced myself I never would, made me beat a hasty exit and head for home. This was so that I could once again put the lid on my former self, keep it contained and leave it behind me.

Looking back at it now, it seems to me that the homosexuals who, at that time appeared to be free to roam around the Ni-chōme district and enjoy it as they pleased, were in fact only able to cast aside the mores and social dictates of the wider society in that particular setting, one which was set aside from the rest of society. And then only at nighttime. This was only to be expected; society was a long, long way from accepting males who didn't speak in the conventional masculine way. The wider heterosexual society was the world in which these guys lived and worked every day. As long as they had to meet society's dictates in terms of adopting a conventional image, virtually all homosexuals, other than those who actually worked in the Ni-chōme area, would continue to be forced to live lives of suppression and bow to conformity. This was the real world.

Nevertheless, my association with 'A' had a big impact on my life. I felt a real sense of reassurance, knowing that I was not alone in being homosexual. It was uplifting to have a friend who didn't hide the fact that he was homosexual. It was also wonderful for me to be able to discuss the sorts of guys and entertainers who really appealed to me. This was something I hadn't been able to do until after I turned twenty. By way of comparison, for most hetero-sexuals, discussing the type of guys or girls that take your fancy and talking about sex, were things people did in junior high school. With 'A' I was finally able to discuss things in a way that I had never been able to do with anyone before. The following will serve to provide an insight into what I am talking about:

Me: 'I rather fancy Hiroyuki Watanabe, but I like Burt Reynolds, too. Ikkō Furuya is nice too, but then so is Morohoshi!'

'A': 'Better make up your mind! With so many different sorts of guys appealing to you it's very hard for me to form a picture of the sort of guy you are attracted to!'

'A' would always be surprised at how different the guys that appealed to him and those that appealed to me were. Even so, just being able to have such an unguarded conversation with someone was a wonderful thing for me. When talking with him I felt as though I was regaining some of my lost youth.

Through my association with 'A' I gradually developed a measure of confidence in myself and this proved to be what I needed to recommence writing letters to the personal columns of gay magazines. It was thanks to this that in the spring of my twenty-fourth year I eventually met Mr Satoru Ito – the man who was to change the course of my life.

My meeting with Satoru was, in a sense, a meeting with myself. He had something which no-one else I had ever met had. It would be fair to say that he simultaneously exhibited a strictness which rendered me incapable of making excuses about myself and a gentleness by which he accepted me as the person I was, un-conditionally and without qualification.

It was through my association with Satoru that I came to meet my other self, the one I had always attempted to suppress and keep contained. Thus in a sense my meeting with Satoru was also a meeting with a third person, if you like, the 'other me' who was always there watching me.

Supported by my partner I fight the 'other me' which was rejecting my homosexuality.

There is another person existing within me. This 'other me' is always there observing what I do. He continually calls me to task for being a homosexual. When I first started going out with Satoru this 'other me' tried to destroy our romance by telling me over and over that, being a homosexual, I had no right to be happy. My desire for happiness was so great it was beyond endurance, yet I feared it, and this led to my always getting into futile fights with Satoru. These were arguments which achieved nothing.

When I made the decision to live under the same roof as Satoru, this 'other me' caused me to waver and ask myself if I intended to set myself up as a laughing stock in the eyes of society. Whenever I tried to lead my life as honestly as I could – being as true to my feelings as possible – this 'other me' would, almost invariably, attack me for it. I was unable to come out to myself. I rejected myself. I was alienated from within. I simply wasn't able to love myself as a homosexual. Nor did I find it at all easy to love my life.

Is it possible for a person who can't love his own life to manage to fight on to the bitter end? Is it possible for a homosexual who doesn't love himself to stand up to the world all by himself? I hated myself for being homosexual and cursed the fact that I had been born. If I had allowed things to continue as they were I would have been totally crushed by this 'other me'. If things hadn't changed, I would have hated my homosexual self until the day I died. I was unable to avoid thinking about this 'other me'. What sort of person was this who continuously attacked and blamed me for being a homosexual? First of all I had to ask whether this 'other me' was really the same person as I was, or whether he was someone else.

What I can say with certainty after thirty-one years of living is that I am able to change this 'other me'. For example, ten years ago this 'other me' brandished values which very closely resembled those of the wider society, blaming and attacking me for being a homosexual. However, as I got to meet other homosexuals, acquired a partner in life and started gradually to accept myself as a homosexual, I became convinced that there was nothing wrong with me as such but that the problem lay in the value system of society itself. Realizing this, the 'other me' stopped denouncing me for being homosexual. Thus it is clear that this 'other me' changed as I changed.

Okay, so this 'other me' wasn't someone who was all pervasive and unchanging. Indeed I realized he was able to change as I changed. With this realization came an appreciation of the fact that this 'other me' was a party that I should be in control of, rather than the other way around. I concluded that he didn't intrinsically belong within me.

Having said that, I should point out that evidence of the stupidity of the human race can be found in the fact that, although you might conclude something and know it to be true, you often remain unable to capitalize on this knowledge and achieve control of the situation at hand. If someone is continually accused of things and blamed by the 'other person' within (who can be thought of as merely a 'passenger' so to speak), it precipitates a situation where he finds himself bereft of the self-confidence needed to overcome difficulties and meet challenges.

Recently I have started thinking that this 'other me' is perhaps just a fictitious being whom I myself have created, an outward manifestation of the internalized homophobic mores of the society around me. Even before I became aware that I was a homosexual I was exposed to the mainstream values that reject homosexuality. When you look it up in the dictionary 'homosexuality' is defined as being 'abnormal'. On TV homosexuals are invariably ridiculed. Male homosexuals are treated as a most unsavoury life form. The fact that I had to weather all of that by myself, the fact that during my impressionable years of sexual awakening there was no-one with whom I could broach the subject, proved to be a very significant factor in my self-development. I had no choice but to create this 'other me' who sycophantically adopted the value system of the wider, heteronormative society.

Although this was done as a means of protecting myself, I found myself continually dominated by the spectre I had created. Just trying to cope with life proved to be fraught with great difficulty because, although I was a homosexual, the 'other me' embraced the value system of the wider society. And this value system just couldn't accept the homosexual I was. It couldn't accept people for whom marriage and children were out of the question. In the end I was forced to query the values this 'other me' had embraced and work towards changing them. If I hadn't, it would have destroyed the real me, the homosexual.

People often say that homosexual love is short-lived and has no future. I am not going to argue that there isn't a tendency for homosexual relationships to be short-lived, but we should never forget that a very sad reality underscores this fact. That reality is that in today's society it is extraordinarily difficult for homosexuals to love themselves. Virtually all homosexuals, to a greater or lesser extent, abhor their homosexuality. The corollary of this is that they detest other homosexuals too. Without putting too fine a point on it, homosexuals find all homosexuals, including themselves, detestable. Are you able to imagine the likely consequences of two people who each hate themselves falling in love? Are you able to imagine the likely result of two people who each were unable to love themselves falling in love? You don't have to be a genius to predict that, for homosexuals, falling in love must be a very difficult process, something that presents tremendous obstacles to those concerned. Just imagine – your partner in romance is a hated homosexual!

Even if we homosexuals are to forget for a moment the problems we face on the inside, problems that we must somehow come to terms with by ourselves, we can never afford to relax our guard when in public. We must always be conscious of the prying eyes of society. Holding hands in public is out of the question. Couples must always do as I used to do – behave so as to attract no attention to themselves, to ensure that no-one suspects them of being a homosexual couple.

There must be many, many heterosexuals out there who lead their lives with never so much as a single thought in relation to questioning the value system underpinning society. Such people would be completely at the mercy of their 'other selves' – that is to say, influences in their lives that have totally absorbed the moral code and internalized the value system of mainstream society. It would never cross their minds to try to change their 'other selves'. Indeed, they probably don't even realize that they are being programmed by their 'other selves'.

If we pursue this a little further we might conclude that the whole set-up of Japanese society deprives those of the mainstream sexual persuasion of the chance to think about themselves as individuals. It deprives them of the chance to confront their 'other selves' head on. For this very reason they prove to be very awkward for people like me to deal with, even though they are not themselves guilty of any conscious wrongdoing.

People whose lives are dominated by their 'other selves' are unable to go against either the directives they are given or the rationality dictated by their 'other selves'. Being always guided and ruled by their 'other selves' – mindsets which reflect the value system of the wider society – they find it a simple process, one requiring no effort and no thought, to reject homosexuality. This rejection of homosexuality is in accordance with the dictates of the omnipresent value system which they unquestioningly accept. In other words, they are at one with the norms and mores of the prevailing social code and in fact cannot associate with the idea of accepting something which departs from this. They do not have the capacity to be independently minded individuals who can divorce themselves from the value system they grew up with. They are extremely fearful of the prospect of their familiar and comfortable value system being challenged or breaking down.

I am not, however, suggesting that each and every heterosexual is like this. These comments don't apply to those heterosexuals who are in control of their own lives and who control their 'other selves'. Such people are able to get their 'other selves' to accept challenges to their value system. They accept that by doing so they are maturing as people. They have the courage to discard old ways of thinking and embrace new ones. I know now that such people actually do exist. When I meet them I find it very easy to be myself.

I want to be able to love myself very much more than I do now. I want to be able to love my life. I was born into this world with the potential of loving myself, yet something prevents me from doing so. Why should it be that I despise myself? Whilst despising myself I have to cope with being unable to love others, too. I don't know how to love others. Will I be able to love others once I have learned to love myself? Some day I would like to properly understand what it really means to love somebody. But how am I meant to do this when I still harbour a hatred towards myself and a hatred towards others? I hate myself and I hate other homo-sexuals. I also hate the heterosexuals who cause me to suffer simply for being who I am. I want to learn to love myself and I want to learn to love others. I often think to myself how much it would have helped me when I was a high school student, if the book 'My Gay Pride Declaration' had been available. When I think that even today there are still many homosexuals being put through the same mill that I was put through and experiencing the same suffering as a result, I feel a terrible sadness and at the same time an incomparable anger. This anger is directed towards mainstream society.

I expect that amongst the readers of this book some will be, like me, homosexual. For the benefit of such readers I would like to share the fact that my ability to accept myself to the extent that I have is thanks to Satoru Ito and others who have accepted me as I am. They have enabled me to reinforce my identity as a homosexual. Yet there remains a part of me – deeply rooted within – that detests and tries to deny the homosexual that I am, although the hold it has on me is considerably weaker than it used to be. I still feel a great need for positive reinforcement from people around me. I need their support to divorce myself from that part of me which seeks to deny and reject the person I really am.

This is both a difficult aspect and a salient feature of my life – one which is by no means easy to come to terms with, no matter how much time I spend turning it over in my mind and pondering the implications. It remains a central feature of my life regardless of how much I philosophize about it or how much literature I read on the subject. It is very hard to overcome one's socialization into the dominant mores of society.

Consequently such strategies as thinking, pondering, philosophizing and so on virtually never lead directly to improved self-esteem. They are effective only in improving one's objectivity. One cannot, simply by dint of one's willpower, change the 'other self' which is part and parcel of one's being. It is not only important, but indeed essential, to have people around who unconditionally accept you as you are, because it is only through association with others who accept you as you are that you can learn to accept and love yourself. Yet to this very day many, many homosexuals remain unable to form associations with others as homosexuals, and suffer with their inability to love themselves as homosexuals as a result.

I must tell myself that the day will come when I am able to love myself as a homosexual. Being a homosexual is not abnormal nor is there anything wrong with it. I am fighting against the value system I have internalized which rejects the homosexual I am. But this struggle cannot be waged alone. The support and backup of others is essential. One cannot succeed in this struggle without the staunch support and positive reinforcement provided by others. In most cases this is to be found in others who are homosexual like you. The more such people there are and the deeper the relationship you can forge with them, the greater the boost to your self-esteem will be. If you want to love the homosexual you are, you must have contact with people who offer you positive reinforcement. If, in your heart, you always cherish the hope that you might one day be able to love yourself, you will most certainly be victorious in your struggle.

2 Feeling comfortable with Gay Pride
by Satoru Ito

As a child I forced myself to conform to societal expectations regarding 'prescribed masculinity' and 'proscribed femininity'.

Whilst there are certainly differences of degree to be observed between individuals, it is fair to say that every homosexual requires a tremendous amount of time, and must find tremendous inner resources, first to acknowledge his or her homosexuality and then to come to terms with it. In the heteronormative society we are in, 'discovering' our own sexuality, accepting it and learning to feel comfortable with it are by no means easy things to do.

Often homosexuals, even before their sexual consciousness takes a definite form, feel an unsettling discomfort from not identifying with the norms of behaviour and underlying thought patterns prevalent in the society around them. From my perspective as a male homosexual, I can say that this discomfort comes from a foresense that we simply are not on track to meet the patterns of behaviour, thought and speech so inflexibly prescribed by society. You may feel that there is some contradiction in this as male homosexuals, by definition, have their sexuality orientated towards other males and thus are likely to be highly influenced by them. The point here is that although we are highly influenced by other males we do not share the sexual orientation of the majority. Let me here briefly trace my own childhood experiences. I have only the vaguest memory of ever playing with friends during primary school. Until quite recently I believed that the cause of this lay in the fact that I changed schools four times. I no longer, however, accept that as the cause. I now think that I simply didn't have any interest in the sorts of games the boys played. When playtime came they dashed to the playing field and played rough games, despite warnings from parents and teachers. They were strong and never cried. They looked after and protected the girls. They tried to establish their leadership, getting others to follow and look up to them.

Ironically, playing in the mud is something I now almost long to do. But when I was a lad at school and it represented the symbol of a healthy boyhood, I couldn't bring myself to be a part of it. Fighting was another thing the boys did. It was an art form of the playground toughie. It demanded courage not to walk away. I just didn't identify with anything of that sort. I felt that none of these things were for me.

There was one incident in primary school that I remember as clearly as if it happened yesterday. The lunch provided by the school that day had a mandarin in it. Most of the boys, after peeling the fruit, threw whole segments, each in its own thin skin, into their mouths and gobbled them down, skin and all. I was struggling to keep pace with them because I was spitting out the skin of each segment as I went. I remember thinking that I wouldn't be regarded as 'one of the boys' unless I ate the mandarin segments complete with their skin, as the others were doing. An inexplicable unease arose within me and I made a point of changing the way I ate mandarins to bring myself in line with the other boys. I was able to manage this much, but I couldn't bring myself to join in the rough and tumble games which went on outside, games where the boys got all covered in mud. I just didn't want to do that.

The only exception to my not playing rough games was once, in year five, when I played a game of professional wrestling with a boy who dropped into my house from time to time. We both took the same route to school and he often spoke to me when he saw me. Now to this very day I don't have any interest in wrestling matches *per se*. Indeed on the occasion in question I wasn't wrestling with him because I was interested in the sport as such. What attracted my attention was the thrill I experienced when either of our hands or feet touched the other's private parts as we locked our bodies together in grappling poses. Yet despite the thrill and excitement of this I only ever did it once.

It wasn't that I was interested in the games the girls played either. Even if I had been I wouldn't have had the courage to approach a group of girls and join them all by myself. Consequently I spent almost every playtime in the classroom by myself – counting the minutes and wishing the time would pass quickly. And it was the same during class time. This continued until, in year 5, I learned that I was more comfortable at school if I scored top grades. I spent almost all my time at home by myself, too.

It wasn't a question of my developing a little earlier than the other boys and therefore not having much in common to talk about. It was rather that I didn't identify with the attributes and mannerisms that the other boys apparently felt comfortable with. Such attributes and mannerisms were simply not part of my physiological make up.

Learning how my partner, Ryuta, was bullied at school is what set me to reminiscing about this. He was bullied for being different and 'not fitting in'; for his failure to meet the conditions of membership of the boys' camp. When he told me of his experiences, eight years after we started going out together, it struck a chord with me. I realized that it paralleled the isolation I had known in primary school. It was something common to both our experiences.

We are now aware that the expected and socially sanctioned male behavioural attributes and mannerisms, which were embodied in the other boys in primary school, were internalized by us at a very young age. This internalization was especially deeply rooted in our consciousnesses, occurring at an age when we unconditionally accepted the influence of our parents, school and society. It never crossed our minds to question the stipulated male roles that were presented to us. The question of one's understanding of what constitutes appropriate male behaviour is subjected to a reviewed interpretation, however, as one reaches puberty and becomes sexually aware. It is also something which is viewed differently by different people, including those who have unconditionally accepted society's expectations in terms of the gender role ascribed to them.

This whole idea of 'acceptable male behaviour' has no claims to validity without the existence of the counterpart set of characteristics that constitute 'acceptable female behaviour'. Females are expected to be gentle and understanding, polite and ladylike and easily moved to tears. They should be prepared to display their weaker side, thereby rendering them needful of someone to take care of them. It is based on these culturally induced notions that the popular images of courting, romantic partnerships and establishing and maintaining households are constructed.

It is only natural for homosexuals to feel uncomfortable with society's narrow delineation of appropriate attitudes, mannerisms and types of behaviour. This delineation is always based on a presumption of heterosexuality. It is an omnipresent cause of the pressure that is exerted on us every day. However, there is no way a primary school student could appreciate this. Primary school students have a terrible cross to bear in trying to figure out just where they fit into society's scheme of things. They have a tremendously difficult time trying to cope with this question.

Faced with this quandary the path homosexuals follow divides into two. In both Ryuta's case and mine, we persisted in our attempts to make ourselves fit the masculine mould of behaviour, doing everything we could to assimilate into and identify with that world of masculinity. When we were not able to do so we did everything in our power to hide this fact and not allow our not belonging, our incompatibility with the role society defined for us, to be perceived by others. We continued to pretend and deceive. In the end we were powerless to stop feeling both admiration and yearning for those guys who fitted the mould and who displayed all the male attributes demanded by society. Sometimes this led to their becoming the object of our romantic desires. Since my late twenties, when I somehow began to come to terms with the culturally induced rejection of my homosexuality, I have been conscious of the fact that I am sexually attracted to rebel types – their build, the way they speak and the sorts of clothes they wear – in addition to the types I was attracted to at school.

The homosexual boys who choose the other path are those who realize that identifying with society's concept of masculinity and meeting society's expectations of masculine behaviour are not possible for them. They give up on trying to identify with this portrayal of masculinity and, whether consciously or otherwise, seek to find a place for themselves and a sense of belonging by assimilating the mode of behaviour stipulated for females. Often in these cases they just feel it is easier for them because they can get away without playing all the rough games and without growing up tough and strong themselves. Unless these boys find acceptance in a girls' group, taking on the attributes of female behaviour means they risk experiencing even greater social isolation, harassment and bullying. They then must find the strength to stand up and challenge the harassing party. This is a step that requires an absolutely incredible amount of personal conviction and tremendous inner strength.

Whether they identify with and seek to emulate socially defined 'masculine' or 'feminine' models of behaviour, homosexuals end up trying to fit a set of criteria which is quite different to the world they would mould for themselves if a choice were available. Accordingly, the process unavoidably results in emotional stress building up, especially since anything vaguely resembling a self-constituted homosexual culture is all but non-existent in Japan.

In fact, most homosexuals do not actually make a clear choice between the two paths described above. More often than not they face puberty wavering between the two paths, uncertain about choosing one path over the other – quite unsure about what to do. Lacking guidance, they find themselves terribly uncertain about choosing a road forward. It's a traumatic time. They are the butt of jokes and treated as a laughing stock. The emotional scarring that can occur when one's deviance from social norms is revealed – scars from bullying, humiliation and beatings – is not easily healed.

In fact this is what happened to Ryuta. He suffered a wound that he couldn't reveal to anyone – a wound whose pain no-one was able to assuage. It still prevents him from doing many things. For this reason, if for no other, I feel a strong sense of anger and resentment towards the heteronormative society in which we live.

Adolescent years spent worrying that I was abnormal.
Desperately trying to hide the fact that I was homosexual.

Dreadful as the prospect is for homosexuals, as they approach their adolescent years they must face the fact that their sexual consciousness is orientated towards the same sex. One after another the heterosexuals around them get love struck and invariably bring this up in conversation. For heterosexuals the usual course people follow in life – falling in love, love leading to marriage and this in turn leading to children and the setting up of a home – is seen as an attainable reality. It would be totally foreign to them to be uncomfortable with the gender based behavioural dictates of society. By contrast, the lack of positive reinforcement for any lifestyle that accommodates a homosexual orientation means that homosexuals are forced to label themselves 'eccentric', 'abnormal' and 'weird'.

Thanks to the commitment and hard work of 'Occur', many dictionaries and encyclopaedias have revised their entries for 'homosexuality'. Before Occur approached these publications, anyone searching for an understanding of who and what they were was confronted with clear-cut, abrupt and unyielding definitions such as 'abnormal', 'pervert' and 'deviant'. This discovery often delivered an almighty blow to them. Even today such derogatory terms can be found liberally used in reference to homosexuality in many books written about sex. By no means can the provision of misinformation be considered to be a thing of the past. Having said this, though, we must also recognize that the number of positive images being projected, while still exceedingly small, is on the increase.

All homosexuals, regardless of how they individually take the shock of learning of their sexuality, will at some stage experience a sense of self-rejection. They reject themselves because they see themselves as something that they believe should not exist – something that should not be allowed to exist. And some homosexuals can believe that they are alone in this world – that there are no others like them to be found anywhere. Their rejection of themselves can lead to despair and a feeling of being backed into a corner. They feel that there is no place for them in the world and no way forward for them in life.

When, in their impressionable years, they start to come to terms with their sexuality and begin to search for a way of life that will accommodate them, they confront a society which offers no place for them and they learn that they are 'not normal'. The angst experienced then is profound.

At this point almost all homosexuals decide they have to do everything in their power to hide their sexuality. This is a natural strategy to adopt. They seek to identify with the rest of society, thereby shielding and protecting themselves. They are alright in heterosexual company as long as they pretend to be heterosexual too.

The hardest situation for them, and this continues for their whole lives, is when the conversation turns to the question of who they are attracted to and they have to choose from amongst those members of the opposite sex they have dealings with in their everyday lives. This topic of conversation is tremendously popular amongst the heterosexual fraternity but one of the most wearing for homosexuals. The time spent discussing this with friends is really most unpleasant for homosexuals. Although we feel no attraction to the person at all, we have to choose someone from the opposite sex and carefully proceed to portray a fictional attraction in order to fit into the conversation and 'be one of the boys'. It is an experience which empties the soul, one which is devoid of the aspect of relaxation which presumably would accompany the experience if one felt the emotions being expressed. It serves only to strengthen the sense of alienation from the others that one feels. The harder you try to fit into the conversation the more acute this sense of 'being apart' becomes.

In every aspect of your daily life, including your dealings with your parents and siblings, you are conscious of the need to prevent people learning of your sexual orientation. Thus you are on guard twenty-four hours a day. There is no rest from the preoccupation of hiding your sexuality. It wears you down. You lose any self-esteem you might ever have had. You have real difficulties in demonstrating the talents and abilities you have and you find yourself depleted of the energy needed to battle on. I am not exaggerating here. Ryuta's description of his childhood experiences vividly portrays the difficult situation we homosexuals face.

It is easier to find people suffering neurosis amongst the homosexual people with whom you are acquainted than amongst heterosexuals. Undoubtedly one cause of the neurosis I have been battling for five years now is the tremendous stress of trying to forcibly adapt myself to fit the heterosexual environment in which I live. I tried to hide my true self all my waking hours, never finding release from the feelings of self-rejection. One aspect of living and working amongst heterosexuals is the barrage of questions such as 'How come you're still single?' and 'Isn't it about time you tied the knot?' I was on the receiving end of an almost constant stream of such questions since about my mid-twenties. In Japan the pressure society puts on people to get married, and on childless couples to have children, is a terrible, terrible thing. It is unrelenting, based on society's unbending formula that equates these goals with happiness.

After the publication of 'My Gay Pride Declaration' representatives of the mass media asked us for interviews on several occasions. The things we had most difficulty with were getting the interviewers (heterosexuals) to understand the omnipresent and all-pervading pressure placed on us to live out the lifestyle of the heterosexual majority; the deeply-rooted and inflexible rationality defined by the heterosexual majority and the constant battle involved in just trying to live our lives in a society where everything is oriented towards accommodating them. There was even one interviewer who imagined the greatest difficulty I would have had to deal with was the fact that I didn't have the chance to speak my native Osaka dialect after coming to Tokyo! How far off the planet can you get? Trying to maintain one's mental equilibrium in a situation where one's identity is continually being rejected and in which it will continue to be rejected for the rest of one's life (as I believed it would be at the time) is incredibly wearing. It cannot be compared to trying to get used to a new dialect!

As Makiko Ida points out in the book *Homosexuals* (published by Bungei Shunjū), you may never get to properly realize just how very trying it is to cope with life as a homosexual unless you keep company with a group of homosexual people for a long period of time – until you actually start believing you are abnormal and that there is no place for you in society. No matter how much I tried to emphasize the trauma that goes on inside a homosexual, it was merely referred to in passing – if at all – in the articles written about us. Upon reading the articles I felt a tremendous sense of wasted effort and a realization of how very far there is to go before a proper understanding of our position will be had by mainstream society. That is why I am again putting pen to paper.

But enough of that. Let me return to the main topic of discussion.

Naturally enough, not each and every homosexual will follow

exactly the same course or have the same experiences as they go through life. If one can grab the chance to love oneself and positively reinforce one's sense of identity as a homosexual, the course through life will be different than would otherwise be the case. In the 1990s we have witnessed the publication of books written by homosexuals, books which act to affirm homosexuality and portray it in a positive light. Such books encourage other homosexuals to lead their lives with greater confidence in themselves. Whilst the appearance of such books is welcome and, theoretically, it provides an opportunity for homosexuals to increase the level of self-esteem they have, the capacity for a person to move his reasoning from the theoretical realm to the realm of practical implementation remains an area fraught with intrinsic difficulties.

I was aware from quite early on that homosexuality was neither abnormal nor a mental sickness (not only the American Society of Mental Health but also the World Health Organization have removed homosexuality from their list of recognized mental illnesses) and that the human race has been programmed in such a way as to ensure that a certain proportion of homosexuals will always be found in its ranks. Of course, it has not yet been scientifically established that this has to do with genetics and the chromosomes one carries. Science has been completely unable to explain the process by which sexuality is determined. But, obstinately searching for 'the cause of homosexuality', or persistently asking homosexuals to furnish this information, is discriminatory by virtue of the fact that 'the cause of hetero-sexuality' is something that is never investigated. And yet, though I knew this, it wasn't enough to bolster my confidence in myself.

Meeting a homosexual with whom I felt at home was the first step on the road to self-emancipation.

The greatest chance there is for homosexuals to change their lot in life, indeed an indispensable step towards making this happen, involves meeting other homosexuals. The sense of emancipation which can be obtained simply by confirming that you are not alone, and knowing that you can relax your guard in conversation, is immeasurable. Let me cite a particular example relating to a high school student who was born a homosexual and who was quite unable to picture a way forward for himself through life. This young man had contemplated suicide. He happened to spot a copy of 'My Gay Pride Declaration' in a bookshop and, after some soul searching, made the purchase. Subsequently he wrote to me. We arranged to meet and eventually he got to know a number of members of the homosexual circle known as 'Taurus', a group I was co-ordinator of at that time. Simply by meeting these guys his outlook on life changed almost overnight. He took on a whole new lease of life.

The question of how someone who has sought to meet other homosexuals perceives himself when he has been successful in this quest, however, depends quite considerably on the circumstances under which the meeting takes place and the sort of homosexuals he meets. In my case I wasn't fortunate enough to come across any homosexuals either at school or at my place of work. Actually, I don't really know whether I came across any or not, as neither of us would have known since we kept our sexuality concealed at study and at work. Consequently my contact with the homosexual world started elsewhere – through the personal advertisements of gay magazines.

As discussed earlier, it wasn't always easy to attract replies to ads. When I did eventually get to meet someone face to face we often found that we were from very different worlds with nothing much in common. Hence there was no real chance of our becoming friends, never mind potential partners in life. When you experience this sort of thing several times over there is a tendency to develop something of a persecution complex. You begin to fear that you might be doomed to never meet a homosexual with whom you are compatible and with whom you feel comfortable. One thing I noticed was that all the homosexuals I met were desperate to keep their homosexuality hidden at all costs. That alone was enough to make me depressed, as it reinforced the belief I had that that was the only possible approach to life.

Okay then, if that was the case I decided I would at least have to somehow satisfy my sexual urges. And so it was that I found myself visiting premises which were popular as pick-up venues. I approached these places very timidly, not being at all sure of 'the ropes', as it were. I had never been one to express my feelings openly and honestly, but at these venues I found myself quite unable to initiate a conversation, and when I did speak I wasn't able to do so at all well. In fact I was less capable of holding a conversation at such pick-up joints than when talking with heterosexuals in the wider society. When someone spoke to me I found myself strangely servile. Nothing was coming together.

More than anything else the drag queen language they used grated on my ears. I just didn't feel comfortable in places where this manner of speaking was part and parcel of the scene. Perhaps I ought to add a word of explanation about this. One factor in my being so uncomfortable with this 'drag queen language' was that I lived in fear of losing the sense of place I had confirmed for myself in society. I had done my utmost to behave in accordance with society's dictates of what was acceptable masculine behaviour, and this included prescribed speech patterns. (Ryuta, by the way, reports having had similar fears).

Another factor is that failing to adopt a drag queen mode of speech meant that I felt the same sense of exclusion, the same not fitting in, that I felt when psychologically ostracised from heterosexual gatherings. It might also have had something to do with the fact that I was attracted to guys who displayed all the male mannerisms and attributes of behaviour and speech that society deems appropriate for members of the stronger sex. These guys were still the objects of my sexual desire, not the guys using drag queen speech and acting with feminine mannerisms.

Drag queen speech is distinct from female speech as such. It represents a culture in its own right. Whereas the register of speech one uses is fundamentally a matter of personal choice (this goes for heterosexuals too), when I was faced with the unfamiliar environment I was now in I found that I wasn't as yet in a position to calmly reflect on this issue of personal choice. Consequently my reaction was that I became very disheartened, thinking to myself that I would have to learn to use drag queen speech if I was to hope to lead my life as a homosexual. Perhaps I suffered from a distrust of men who didn't act like men and women who didn't act like women – the reaction which is at the very heart of homophobia.

I was finally to experience relief from this dilemma when I was invited to a meeting conducted by a homosexual group composed mostly of members who were in their teens. Here was a group of young men of the minority sexual persuasion who spoke about homosexuality as a serious subject, almost to the point where they appeared to be deliberately avoiding discussion of anything to do with sexual desires, as though in reaction to those adult homosexuals for whom seeking sexual gratification was of immediate importance and always foremost in their minds. As a group they were able to discuss their conviction that homosexuality is not abnormal and that sex isn't everything – there are other aspects to life and relationships. Of course they would also chat amongst themselves about which of the male TV personalities and singers they found attractive and about things like what sort of romance they hoped to find.

At such gatherings I was privy to information concerning the life experiences of others. Sometimes these were quite similar to my own, and sometimes quite unbelievable. I felt at home there. I felt like I fitted. I understood just what they were describing. I experienced delight, pure and simple! It was OK to talk about these things! I had never known before that there were these sorts of homosexuals in existence! There was even an eighteen year old youth who said he wanted to get involved in a movement which aimed to put an end to discrimination against homosexuals. He went on to become one of the founding members of 'Occur'. I found the possibility of such a dream to be stimulating. I felt as though it would be possible to embrace hope for the future.

It is probably best to have one's first contact with other homosexuals through a group like this where mental exchanges, not sexual encounters, are the object of the meeting. A very bad impression of the homosexual world could be obtained if one's first sexual experience were with an unscrupulous individual. (It is not inconceivable that one could be fleeced of one's money and possessions by a bad egg out there). When meeting a whole group of homosexuals in one go, one's loneliness and isolation can evaporate in an instant. You come to appreciate that homosexuals are a diverse group coming from all walks of life. The fetters are removed from one's stereotypical image of homosexuals. In such company it becomes easy to find other homosexuals with whom you have things in common.

Such homosexual groups and networks only came onto the scene, however, in the last ten years or so. I am heartened to learn that at the present time the number of members of the Occur group in their teens and early twenties who have never utilized the personal columns of gay magazines in order to make contact with other homosexuals is on the increase; some of these guys don't even know of any gay magazines! These are young guys who have never been to the popular pick-up venues and who first got to meet other homosexuals through gatherings organized by Occur. If only I had been able to access such a group – one which provided a follow up service to first timers and which gave thought to how homosexuals might chart a course through life! There is no doubt that the opportunities now existing for homosexuals to meet one another are more diverse and open than they ever used to be. There are homosexual groups that correspond on the net and there is an increase in the use of the telephone message dialing and recorded voicemail systems that allow love to germinate and friendships to form.

Finding a partner and grasping the opportunity to acknowledge who I am. Leading my life accordingly.

Although it might now be possible for young people to meet other homosexuals and perhaps find a lover, even perhaps join a homosexual circle, it is still necessary for homosexuals to have tremendous reserves of strength to ensure that their homosexuality will not be suspected by the heterosexuals with whom they associate in their daily lives. This is partly because there are still no businesses in Japan run by homosexuals. You still spend much more time denying and rejecting yourself than affirming and accepting yourself. Some homosexuals have become totally used to this situation and have even come to enjoy the double lives they lead.

But it is still a trial to have to laugh along with others when homosexuals are mocked and made the butt of jokes on TV. It is enough to give one a stomach ulcer. Comments such as 'This guy's a homo!' followed by retorts such as 'Can't stand pansy poofters!' are the usual fare the viewing public is served up. Homosexuals are simply unable to take a high profile and let their true work ability and level of talent manifest themselves. Homosexuals feel that they will never get any recognition for anything they do and, at the same time, fear that any successes they might record will be thoroughly deprecated if their sexual persuasion ever became known. This underlying belief puts the brakes on whatever enthusiasm they might otherwise have to strive and achieve. It tends to make homosexuals very negative. Homosexuals are probably the only remaining minority group to be targeted for ridicule and derision in TV programmes for the general viewing public. This is despite the limitless possibilities that abound for the disabled, the Koreans and other minority groups to be used as potential sources of humour.

Eventually we reach an age when we must face that most inflexible of behaviour defining institutions: marriage. Perhaps it reflects a natural expression of social change, but considerable differences can be seen in the way homosexuals of different generations deal with this issue. The older generation often went through with loveless marriages to a member of the opposite sex whilst maintaining a double life. The middle generation frequently proclaimed that they believed in remaining single while hiding their homosexuality from their parents. There is a growing trend for the younger generation to announce their sexuality to their parents, rather than risk them finding out from another source. The younger the generation the less time they need to develop self-confidence and feel comfortable with themselves.

In my case, it was thanks to my partner, Ryuta Yanase, and from my involvement with the Fuchū Youth House court case that I was able to develop confidence in myself as a homosexual. Before I go into some of the details about this court case, let me first mention an interesting co-incidence between the timing of my getting to know Ryuta and the establishment of Occur. It so happened that in the same year that I met Ryuta through the correspondence columns of a gay magazine (1986), the Gay and Lesbian Action Association was formed to create a network of support for homosexuals and to fight prejudice and discrimination against them. At that stage I had no interest whatsoever in the pursuits of the Occur group, although I was acquainted with some of its members. All I could think of was being with Ryuta and never leaving him. There was a period when I built my whole life around him.

I told myself that it was too early for me to get involved in what Occur was trying to achieve; I wasn't yet ready for any of that. I guess my way of thinking boiled down to the fact that I feared the prospect of my mother or anyone from work finding out about me. It was all I could do to produce a discussion type magazine (this died a natural death two years later) as a forum for homosexuals to talk about whatever was on their minds in the knowledge that they would be taken seriously. Although this seemed a modest goal in comparison to what Occur set out to achieve, I felt a certain satisfaction when the goal was realized.

In 1990 Ryuta and I entered a period of stability in our relationship, having learned to thoroughly talk things through with each other. This was in itself a very pleasing development for us and it proved to be a very appealing aspect of our relationship. We would each let the other have his say and explain his point of view until we could see where he was coming from. This wasn't to say, however, that we didn't have differences of opinion throughout this period. We did. However, the knowledge that I had a partner who would continue to love me, despite there being differences of opinion on various matters, served in no small way to sustain me. It prevented me from suffering a persecution complex and seeing myself as playing the lead role in a pathos play.

My getting involved in the Fuchū Youth House legal case opens my eyes to an awareness of Gay Pride.

I have already made reference to the treatment received by the Occur members who held a study camp at the Fuchū Youth House in 1990. When they requested that the House administration convene a special Leaders' Meeting to discuss the issue, believing they shouldn't have to tolerate such discriminatory behaviour, the person in charge, a Mr Tanaka, only organized a vague sort of informal session at which he took sides with the other groups staying there. It failed to produce any meaningful discussion about the complaint.

After the incident the Occur members requested the opportunity to discuss their grievances with the chief administrator of the House, a Mr Segawa, only to have their request turned down. To top it off they had their application to stay there the following May rejected.

Occur approached a lawyer on this issue to see if they had any grounds to consider legal action. Further, they presented a petition to the City of Tokyo's Committee on Education, a municipal body which comes under the jurisdiction of the Ministry of Education and which is responsible for setting the direction of educational policy in the Tokyo metropolis. They found that they ran into a brick wall in their dealings with the said Committee in exactly the same way as they had when they had tried to deal with the House administration.

The Occur members reported that they were indignant at being run rough shod over and felt the matter could not be left to rest as it was. The question was what could they do to stand up to this unfair treatment? Over and over they discussed their situation with great circumspection, investigating any options they could come up with.

After one year, and with the support and co-operation of two lawyers whom they knew they could trust, a Mr Nakagawa and a Mr Morino, it was decided that Occur's response to the treatment they had received would take the form of instigating legal proceedings against the City of Tokyo. They would allege discrimination against homosexuals and seek compensation through the courts.

While all this was happening, I wondered if I had been there when the Leaders' Meeting had been called, would I have agreed to openly divulge the fact that it was a homosexual group that I was a member of? Three of the Occur members, Mr Takashi Kazama, Mr Masashi Nagata and Mr Masanori Kanda were required to disclose their identities and reveal their faces to the world while representing the plaintiffs and pleading their case that the treatment they had received at the hands of the municipal authorities in the City of Tokyo represented discrimination. Would I have been able to take that stand?

The answer to both questions was 'no'. I would not have agreed to divulging the true nature of the Occur group at the Leaders' Meeting nor would I have been prepared to reveal my identity to the world in order to act as a representative of the plaintiffs in the court case. The Occur members suddenly seemed very distant from me. They were streets ahead of me in terms of having courage and the willingness to act upon their convictions. Though I felt I should be doing something to help, and to that end tried to galvanize myself into action, I was sent into a bout of depression brought on by a combination of my gutlessness and a sense of envy that was tinged with jealousy.

News of the progress of the court case couldn't escape my attention. I couldn't help but get angry when I heard the argument put forward by the City of Tokyo that homosexuals should not be allowed to use the accommodation facilities because they might engage in sexual activity if allowed to stay in the same room and that the reason mixed accommodation was not provided was to prevent that possibility. There was no doubt that this court case was an important one for homosexuals.

Reluctantly, I started to drag myself along to meetings relating to the court case. I was spurred on, however, by both the mass media proving itself incapable of properly reporting the importance of this court case (the question of homosexual rights was being brought up for the first time ever in Japan) and the fact that the number of supporters dropped as comments such as 'There's no point in taking on a battle you've no hope of winning', 'We're not ready for this yet' and 'In the long run life will be easier for you if you just keep a low profile and don't make waves' were batted around their ranks.

Through my association with Ryuta the difficulty faced by homosexuals trying to live in a heterosexually orientated world was fully brought home to me. We have already discussed our difficulties with going out in public.

Might it not be that what was holding back a healthy blossoming of the relationship between Ryuta and me was the same discrimination that the Occur people had faced at the Fuchū Youth House? I hadn't yet come out and wasn't yet able to join in their fight, but I did feel that if I couldn't join them I should at least try to show a measure of support for them in their struggle.

The members of Occur that I met at their meetings, although homosexuals, didn't stand out as being particularly special people in any sense. They had arrived at the point they were at through honesty and the developments that had taken place in their lives. There was no difference between them and me in terms of the worries that afflicted us or the uncertainties that we harboured on our way through life.

As I began to appreciate all of this, the distance between the

Occur group and me shrank, albeit slightly. But the closing of this gap was accelerated by the conference at which Mr Kazama's father expressed his whole-hearted support for his son and I had a heated debate with Mr 'A'.

I was saddened by the intolerance and narrow-mindedness that his comments reflected and by the jealousy directed towards those at the forefront of the movement to improve the lot of homosexuals – those who were brave enough to expose themselves to the public spotlight. I just couldn't allow him to get away with seeing Occur only from the pathetically narrow viewpoint that equates going to court with extremist radicalism. And this despite the fact that the Occur members had, in order to build up their legal case, painstakingly gathered evidence and assiduously done all the requisite groundwork behind the scenes! Yet though I felt disdain for this man, it struck me that his words and actions were but mirroring my own narrow-mindedness.

From that evening on the number of chances Ryuta and I found to talk about the court case increased dramatically. We went beyond merely discussing the court case to discussing how we, in the future, might carve out a life for ourselves. We both believed that unless we were to join in the fight against discrimination (although we didn't know at that stage just what form this might take) we would not see our lot in life improve nor would we see the difficulties we were facing being tackled in any positive way.

With that belief as a galvanizing force, we decided we would lend our support to the court case – we decided to offer backing to the tears shed by Mr Kazama. The natural reaction of showing anger when you have suffered emotionally as a result of being made the target of malice because of a character trait you posses as an individual could be thought of as a form of 'pride', could it not? A pride that represents proof of the fact that you are living as a homosexual.

Victory in the courts!

With the publication of 'My Gay Pride Declaration' in 1993, I had 'outed' myself to the whole country. However, although the book was published I was deeply saddened by the fact that the main newspapers and magazines, without even reading the book themselves, assumed that it represented some kind of a 'vaudeville production' and refused to include mention of it in their publications. I was so concerned and troubled that I lost considerable sleep over it.

However, I was happy with myself. I knew that producing the book had been very worthwhile. This had been proven by the many letters I received reporting that, as a result of reading it, the correspondents had found the inner strength they needed to confirm their homosexuality and start leading their lives as homosexuals.

At that point I anticipated that the amount of work yet to be done to educate the public would decrease, but the fact of the matter is that there hasn't been much change in this regard. This is probably largely because I have kept myself at the forefront of developments ever since. Allow me now to introduce one such major development!

At a little past 10 am on 30th March 1994, eight months into our life together, I rang Ryuta's number (we place great importance on respecting each other's privacy and to that end maintain individual rooms, each with its own telephone) in great excitement and woke him with some astonishing news. I was unable to control the flow of speech that poured forth as I made this call from a public telephone outside the Tokyo District Court.

> 'We've won! The City of Tokyo has been ordered to pay Occur about 270,000 yen in compensation! The court ruling included specific reference to homosexuality and went as far as acknowledging that homosexuals are discriminated against!'

I no longer felt any distance existed between the members of Occur and me. Ryuta and I were so delighted with the outcome of the court case that we filled our glasses with beer, something we hardly ever drank, and toasted this success over and over late into the night. What a wonderful result! As we toasted this verdict we agreed with each other that it was just the first step, and that there was still a lot more to be done in order to improve the lot of the homosexual in society.

Reflecting on the implications of the court's ruling that 'Homosexuality is not abnormal and that discrimination is seen to exist'.

What was epoch-making and really exciting was the fact that the presiding judge, Mr Toshiaki Harada, departed from the usual court practice and included a preamble in the ruling he handed down, prior to acknowledging the facts of the case. This part of the ruling was entitled '*On Homosexuality and Homosexuals*'. In it he defined homosexuality in neutral, non-biased terms which were free from prejudice:

> 'Homosexuality is one of the sexual orientations known to the human race. It refers to one's sexual consciousness being directed to members of the same sex.
> Heterosexuality, on the other hand, refers to one's sexual consciousness being directed to members of the opposite sex'.

He recounted how homosexuality is neither treated as a sickness nor as a disability by either the American Psychiatric Association or the World Health Organization. He made reference to the fact that in San Francisco same sex domestic partners are given public recognition and that there is a support service in place for homosexual students in that city. He concluded that 'Under the conditions which have existed heretofore we are told that homosexuals were prone to suffer alienation and social isolation and that they worried and suffered in respect to their sexual orientation'. I would like to point out here that there is considerable significance in the terminology employed in this ruling, as selecting an appropriate Japanese translation for the term 'sexual orientation' is something which breaks new ground. The judge correctly chose to write characters which mean 'orientation of one's sexuality' as opposed to other possibilities which would suggest to the reader that one's sexuality is something that one adopts or has a hand in choosing.

Not only can this ruling be interpreted as proof of the existence of discrimination against homosexuals, it also offers a powerful weapon for us when we try to explain about homosexuals and homosexuality to those of the majority sexual persuasion. It establishes a legal point of reference for us. In acknowledging this, however, we bear in mind the need to be ever aware of the danger inherent in relying on official views as espoused by so called 'authorities'.

I very much doubt that the inclusion of such a preamble or the award of financial compensation would have been possible without the dogged work of the untiring members of Occur in the three year period following the instigation of legal proceedings. What amazing things Occur has achieved!

Through the close links they kept with homosexuals in the USA they managed to get a Mr Tom Ammiano, the Head of San Francisco's Committee on Education, to take the witness stand. The result of their efforts can be seen in the most splendid way in the court ruling which was handed down. My word!

The wording of the ruling, while expressed in cautious terms, is based on very reasonable logic. As can be determined from the synopsis provided below, the court's ruling was founded on common sense and delivered in terms that were simple and clear. This was in sharp contrast to the high-handed and coercive development of arguments presented in the case put forward by the City of Tokyo.

I take particular delight in the third point of the court's ruling. This point very nicely demolishes the case put up by the City of Tokyo – a case which paid no heed whatsoever to the position of minorities in society and which exposes the city's disregard for the question of discrimination. A defamation lawsuit was instigated at the same time as the other but was not upheld, on the grounds that at the time in question it would have been difficult for a proper understanding of the question of homosexuality to have been held. There can be no denying, however, the importance and value of the overall ruling.

The court's finding in favour of Occur and the order for financial compensation were made because the City of Tokyo broke the law when it refused homosexuals the right to use the accommodation facilities provided at the Fuchū Youth House. The ruling of the court represents nothing more than a resolute reflection on something that should be perfectly obvious. However, the fact that it took four long years of simply tremendous effort and painstaking work by Occur members and supporters to have this publicly acknowledged means that while considering the court ruling to be epoch-making, we should actually stand amazed that there was any need to have such a ruling made at all. This need is itself testament to just how deeply-rooted and tenacious prejudice has been in our society.

In Japan, for a citizens' group to take on the authorities, and *win,* is a phenomenally difficult task. Given that such a sweeping victory over the nation's capital is so extraordinarily rare I think it would be no exaggeration to say that the fact that the justice system, for the first time ever, delivered a ruling in relation to homosexuals' rights, and indeed affirmed these in quite strong terms, is something that will go down in the annals of legal history in this country. It is thus reasonable to describe the outcome of this court case as being nothing short of a legal landmark. Yet despite this the media coverage given to this outcome was very dry and detached. The reports that were run were very bland, giving the impression that phrases such as 'for the first time ever' and 'a victory was recorded' were included out of a sense of professionalism rather than interest. There were virtually no comments reported from the parties involved. The fact that the ruling legally acknowledged the existence of homosexuals and gave recognition to them for the first time ever, was totally ignored. All the news coverage was on a one-off basis and there was virtually no reporting which delved into the significance of the ruling or the implications involved therein. The fact that someone was taking a stand shouldn't have been treated as though it were inconsequential, not in Japanese society where the rights of minorities are so easily trampled underfoot, a society underpinned by a value system based on conformity at the expense of everything else. Meanwhile the nation's capital, the City of Tokyo, has learned nothing and is appealing the decision. The crucial battle still lies ahead.

I offer the following synopsis of the outcome of the court case for your perusal.

Assertion Made by the City of Tokyo
1) Allowing homosexuals to stay in the same room would give rise to the possibility of sexual activity occurring.
The Court's Adjudication
1) Whilst it is natural to consider whether or not sexual activity

would be likely to occur when giving permission to utilize the facilities, in order to refuse permission, a concrete possibility must be established, not a general one. As the City of Tokyo made absolutely no identifiable effort to investigate this they are in breach of the law with there being no evidence to establish that there was a concrete possibility of the members of Occur engaging in sexual activity. Even supposing there were, it would have been possible to reduce this likelihood by imposing certain conditions. Refusing homosexuals permission to stay overnight in the same room would render them unable to utilize the facility at all, in contravention of Article 20 of the Constitution relating to the right to access learning and Article 21 relating to freedom of association.

Assertion Made by the City of Tokyo

2) The healthy development of other youths could be marred as a result of their witnessing or imagining sexual activity taking place.

The Court's Adjudication

2) The likelihood of anyone witnessing sexual activity would be exceedingly small and even if someone were to imagine it, it would not be detrimental to a healthy upbringing.

Assertion Made by the City of Tokyo

3) There is the fear that other youths would bait and harass the homosexuals.

The Court's Adjudication

3) Harassment wouldn't come about as a result of people staying in the same room. It has its genesis in a disdain directed towards homosexuals. This can only be seen as a reason to refuse permission to use the facilities to those carrying out the harassment.

Assertion Made by the City of Tokyo

4) There is no consensus amongst the Japanese people in relation to the question of having a number of homosexuals staying together in one room.

The Court's Adjudication

4) It is not possible to think in terms of consensus in relation to this issue as the vast majority of Japanese people would never have given serious thought to the question of homosexuality.

I am a homosexual. I want to be comfortable with this, live my life in a way that is natural for me and be sure of my place in society.

Immediately after the court ruling one of the plaintiffs, Mr Masashi Nagata, stated that it was the first time anyone had acknowledged homosexuals when they 'cried out that they had been kicked'. I learned through this court case that we should show anger when discriminated against or when society closes doors on us or makes life hard for us. I learned that it was alright to get angry and that this was what 'having pride in yourself as a homosexual' meant. I used to be so servile and full of self-denial, ever ready to try to sycophantically fit the heterosexual mould society demanded I should.

But with support from my partnership with Ryuta I have come to know myself better, and at the age of forty I have at last come to terms with my inner feelings. I can now plant my feet firmly on the ground and do the things I want to do in life, getting angry when the situation demands that I should. I believe that I have thus commenced a new chapter in my life. I have spent much of my time recently trying to bring change to government policies and educational practices. I have been involved in all manner of movements, even forming various clubs and discussion groups to further this end. Notwithstanding this, deep down inside me I still feel a certain dissatisfaction about the 'uneven field' approach I have taken, taking it upon myself to fight the contradictions and discrimination I witness in society. I believed I had to conduct a 'guerilla campaign', as it were, within the school system and virtually broke my back doing so. I further believed that I had to fight discrimination and the contradictions of society single-handedly. I am now very comfortable believing that I would like to fight to make society a more homosexual-friendly place, recognizing that this can be done in many ways, including taking direct action when the occasion demands and expressing my thoughts in writing. I will follow this course of action from now on, ever mindful of the need to be flexible and yet not compromising on matters of principle. I can see a life for me and acknowledge that there is no need for haste or to run too far ahead of myself. I have enough on my plate struggling to get over the hurdles society keeps putting in my way simply because I am living with Ryuta.

What I have penned here is, of course, my personal journey. It is the journey that brought me to the point where I feel I have confidence in myself – indeed have pride in myself – and at last feel as though I am the equal of heterosexuals. It is the journey that brought me to the point where I could be honest with myself about my feelings, and not be a traitor to my true self. Certainly it is the journey that brought me to the point where I no longer feel awkward or guilty about myself. It is the journey I have taken to the point where I can boldly and resolutely adopt a positive outlook on life, something that was denied me as long as I remained servile and unable to accept myself for what I am.

I do believe that unless we make real efforts to bring about changes to the heteronormative *status quo*, homosexuals will never be emancipated and there will be no guarantee of our even being able to live our lives with a partner. The basis for my concern here lies in the fact that landlords and real estate agents display a dreadful aversion to two men taking up residence together. To slightly overstate the argument, I am saying that it is only by crying out 'We want to be treated as human beings' and 'We want to have our human rights acknowledged' that homosexuals will ever be able to identify ourselves as members of society who are of neither greater nor lesser importance than those of the majority sexual persuasion.

Let me repeat myself. I am a homosexual; a homosexual such as can be found anywhere one cares to look.

Postscript to Part Two

by Ryuta Yanase

After my partner produced 'My Gay Pride Declaration' in September last year (1993), there was quite a flurry of media interest in us for a while. Typical requests would be things like 'May we cover the sort of lifestyle you lead?' and 'We'd like to get a photo of you two at mealtime if we may'. In the initial stages neither of us was accustomed to being at the centre of attention of reporters and we obliged in any way we could, explaining in detail about our lifestyle as we went. We even obliged a TV reporter by having a meal together on film for him.

However, as we objectively looked at ourselves in the public eye, we started to feel that something was wrong. This feeling grew within us with every passing day. What people from the media hoped to gain from us was to report on a weird and unconventional partnership where a gay 'bride substitute' had been brought into a household and where the couple lived together with the mother-in-law. One would have hoped they had read our book, but this apparently was not the case. No interest whatsoever was shown in the ordeals we had been through to get where we were. We were portrayed as a queer and curious sort of couple, in the way they thought would best please their audience. They asked us to perform the roles that would make us a 'curious couple'.

By co-operating with their requests we were meeting their hopes and expectations and fulfilling their desires. It was clear that if we hadn't spoken out we would have been portrayed in the mass media exactly in accordance with their stereotypical image of homosexuals. In other words we would have been presented as oddities, objects suitable for scorn and derision, something to be giggled at. Once we realized this we felt a need to speak bluntly and repeatedly ask the reporters to ensure they reported our trials and tribulations seriously and in an appropriately sober manner. We had to repeatedly make the point that they should not report the subject matter in a flippant, comical or facetious way.

My aim for this book was to portray the difficulties faced by homosexuals in such a way that they could be appreciated by anyone and everyone, otherwise there was no point in producing it. It was by no means easy for me to put in writing the fact that my emotional scars have not yet healed. However, by doing so I feel I have come a long way towards putting many of my troubles behind me.

I know there are certain things in our first book which must have been very difficult for Satoru to write about, particularly some of the arguments between us. He was kind enough to respect my privacy and avoid mentioning certain things, even though these considerations compounded his difficulties as a writer. There were also other parts of the original manuscript which Satoru would have included in that book, but which I requested he not include. Because of this it wasn't possible for him to fully describe all the difficulties we faced in our life together. In retrospect I must accept that I bear some responsibility for this. In fact this might be the very reason for my greater than usual enthusiasm in penning what I have in this book.

After writing this book there was yet another development in our relationship. Satoru and I together set up an organization called 'Sukotan Planning' and made the decision to use this to try to raise public awareness of the difficulties we face in life as homosexuals. Specifically we hope to combat society's ingrained homophobia, prejudice and discrimination through Satoru's public lectures and his activities as a writer. To this end we seek to enlist the support and co-operation of those people who are able to offer first hand accounts of the difficulties they have faced as a result of their homosexuality.

For nearly a full year I led a life of virtually cloistered isolation after coming to live in the Ito household. During that period there were times when I thought to myself that I would probably never be able to venture into the world outside. I felt that the hetero-sexually oriented world around me presented too many hurdles for me to cope with in trying to lead my life openly and honestly as a homosexual. If workplaces had not been structured around suppression there wouldn't have been any need for me to hide away as I did for a year in Satoru's house. Ideally, we should have a society that accepts heterosexuals and homosexuals openly working side by side.

What I need now is to learn to love the homosexual that I am very much more than I do and to come to terms with the homophobia I have internalized as a result of growing up in this society. In order for this to be possible I need the support and backing of other homosexuals. These aspirations, and the aim of boosting the level of confidence I have in myself as a homosexual, have come together in one, with the resulting invigoration I feel allowing me to apply myself more fully to whatever work I take on. That dreaded room where I battled in my attempts to produce some meals has now been turned into the Sukotan Planning Office. In the early stages it doubled as a living area for us, but in acknowledging that the combination of difficulties encountered in moving ahead with work and those encountered in moving ahead with life is a recipe for stress and emotional outbursts, I am seeking refuge in my parents' house for the time being. Yet, virtually all of my things other than my clothes are still housed in the room which has become the Sukotan Planning Office. It is quite an unusual living arrangement that I have at the moment, but I have no intention of continuing with it forever. Satoru and I are looking at various possibilities by which we can arrange to lead our lives together whilst accommodating his mother in the same household.

In closing I would like to take this opportunity to register my heartfelt thanks to my partner, Satoru Ito, and also to my parents who have made what some might consider to be a vast financial contribution to Sukotan Planning in support of its activities. I am also indebted to Mr Mitsuru Asakawa, Ms Riko Kitayama and Mr Hiroshi Kihara of the Tarō Jirō Publishing Co. for their constructive comments and feedback which sometimes delighted me and at other times depressed me, but which I now recognize were consistently based on fact and truth, something I only came to appreciate 'after the fact' as it were. I would also like to record here how useful certain books were to me. These are books which taught me what it means to put down in writing details of one's thoughts and to record the agony and suffering one goes through. In this regard I would like to mention *Homosexual People* by Makiko Ida (published by Bungei Shunjū), *Children With Magic Hands* by

Akiko Nobe (by Tarō Jirōsha), and *Control of the Name Love* by Yōko Tajima (by Tarō Jirōsha).

One final word. I intend to face the future, joining hands with my partner, Satoru Ito, and rise to the challenges that will present themselves to us.

October 7th 1994
The Sukotan Planning Office

About the Authors

Satoru Ito was born in 1953 and attended Kaisei Junior and Senior High Schools before proceeding to the Education Faculty of Tokyo University. He had misgivings about the elite course he was following in life and during the eight years of his university studies he was active in starting up various clubs, all the while searching for a path he might follow through life. He has worked as a teacher at a private high school and presently holds a position as an instructor at a preparatory school in Kashiwa. Whilst in this position he has been involved in a wide range of pursuits, including working as a freelance writer, a music critic and a disc jockey. In addition, he has been instrumental in the publication of the forum discussion magazines *Match* and *Nyāgo Tsūshin*. He holds the position of president of the Hyōtan Island Fan Club.

Amongst Mr Ito's publications which focus on the theme of education are *Pursuing English Practice Junior High School 1, Pursuing English Practice Junior High School 2* (published by Zōshinkai), *Essential English Grammar* (Asahi Shuppansha), *The Teacher's Ears are Donkey's Ears* (Jiji Tsūshin), *Rap in High School*, which is based on accounts of real life incidents provided by high school students (Shōbunsha), *Direct into Tokyo University, Sir! Being Slapped is Offensive* (in which students recount incidents of their rights being flouted at school) and *Vogue Studies of High School Students* (published by San'ichi Shobō). He was a tremendous fan of the television program *Hyokkori Hyōtan Island* in his youth and kept a written record of nearly the entire series. He chronicled his experiences in relation to being instrumental in the revival of this program in *A Notebook on Hyokkori Hyōtan Island Zeal* (Jitsugyō no Nihonsha). In addition he wrote *An Account of the Drifting of Hyōtan Island* (Asuka Shinsha).

Ryuta Yanase was born in 1962. After withdrawing from technical college he acquired work experience in several jobs, initially as a carpenter. In *My Gay Pride Declaration* (published by

Tarō Jirōsha) he publicly declared his homosexuality along with his partner, Satoru Ito. In September 1994 he established the Sukotan Planning Office. He provides a comprehensive backup service for Satoru Ito's public lecturing and writing activities that centre on the question of public education in relation to homosexuality.

Notes

Notes to Part One

Chapter 1

1   The title of this section, 'The courage to admit that I like what I like', is an adaptation of the message contained in Noriyuki Makihara's song '*At All Times*' which was a major hit on the Japanese charts in the early 1990s, selling over a million copies nationally. In a folksy way it expressed the sentiment that people should be able to live their lives true to themselves.
2   A teaching philosophy formulated by Mr Hiraku Toyama, a mathematician who looked at mathematical problems from the viewpoint of the student, simplifying things accordingly. Initially this teaching methodology met with opposition from the Japanese Ministry of Education but eventually it came to be accepted and its philosophical basis was incorporated into mathematics textbooks.
3   An epoch-making science teaching methodology devised by a Mr Kiyonobu Itakura.
4   Magazines of a discussion-forum genre directed towards a specific interest market were common in the 1970s and 1980s. They represented a forum for counter-culture thinking and a means of networking for citizens' movements, some going on to become major publications.
5   A monthly women's magazine which was tremendously popular at the time.
6   A game developed by adolescent boys based on the military practice of inspecting the private parts of new recruits.
7   Kaisei schools were elite and offered very bright students the opportunity to compete for positions in respected universities.

8   *Barazoku* was an early gay magazine of a very soft genre, incorporating articles and artistic drawings.

9   'That's Another College' was something of a unique circle. It was established by the author to encourage people to come to know the real world, the world outside academia, by gaining first hand knowledge of same. It encouraged people to reflect on their way of living.

10 The *buraku* are villages in Japan which house the descendants of criminals convicted in the Edo Period of Japanese history (1630-1868). Even now people from these villages are discriminated against in terms of employment and areas of social contact – particularly marriage with those from mainstream society. In effect they form a distrusted and despised sub-culture within Japanese society.

11 Ashio is the site of a copper mine which, since the beginning of its operations during the Meiji period (1868–1911), disposed of the waste produced in the copper refinement process in the local river, thus destroying farmland downstream. The airborne soot and smoke from its operations destroyed surrounding forests.

12 Kichijōji is a sub-centre of Tokyo.

13 Shinji Harada: A rock singer-songwriter known for his songs about love and peace, still active in the music industry today.

14 Hitotsubashi University is a prestigious university in Tokyo.

15 Sleeping arrangements where members of the same sex share rooms (and sometimes beds) are not unusual in Japan. Of itself such an arrangement carries no sexual connotations.

16 Ni-chōme: A seedy area on the fringe of the nightlife and entertainment area of Shinjuku in Tokyo.

17 The biggest sub-centre in the City of Tokyo and a major hub of the entertainment industry.

18 Ryokan: A traditional Japanese inn.

19 Hundreds of Australian dollars.

20 *Adon*: A gay magazine which rivalled its predecessor, *Barazoku*.

21 The Sōbu Line runs between Tokyo and neighbouring Chiba Prefecture.

22 TBS: The Tokyo Broadcasting Service, one of the 4 major television broadcasting stations in Japan.

23 Cram schools are part and parcel of the Japanese education system. After hours and weekend classes are held for the specific purpose of training students to prepare for university entrance examinations.

24 NHK: the *Nihon Hōsō Kyōkai*, the Japan Broadcasting Corporation, the national broadcaster.

25 A puppet play which was first broadcast by NHK from 1964 to 1969 and which recorded record ratings. A remake of this program was produced in 1991. With TV in its infancy in Japan in the 1950s and 1960s television stations operated on very low budgets. Because of this, when producing shows in the early days the practice was to record over existing shows, thus allowing the expensive video tapes to be used again and again until they were worn out. Thus it was that there were virtually no archives of programs aired in the 1960s that could be referred back to by the TV station management. Nor were copies of scripts properly kept in those days, resulting in only 3/4 of the scripts and scenarios being available from records. It happened that, through contacts both parties had with a local puppet theatre, NHK learned that the author had been an avid fan of this program and thus, when it was decided to do a remake of the show, the director of the TV station made contact with Mr Ito.

26 In relation to this, I would like to refer readers to a publication entitled '*A Report on Gays*' which was published by Asuka Shinsha and edited by Occur. The author was personally involved in the writing and editing of this report which contains some basic information about homosexuality, an outline of his personal history and the results of a questionnaire, which was given to some 50 homosexuals, on the issue of having confidence in oneself.

Chapter 2

1 *Hattemba:* Gay beats, that is meeting places such as gay saunas and hotels at which homosexuals pass information by word of mouth on issues of interest to those who seek such venues. *Hattemba* are also places where contacts are made and 'developments' occur.

2 Often a small and intimate shop with customers facing the counter behind which the chef works. *Sushi* is a popular traditional dish consisting of various seafood toppings on individual serves of vinegared rice. It is served with ginger and soya sauce.

3 Obtaining a driver's licence in Japan is a difficult, time consuming and costly exercise. There are several different sorts of tests which the applicant must sit and the costs incurred run into thousands of dollars. The considerable expense involved is one of the factors involved in ensuring that it is certainly not the case that all people eligible to apply for a licence do so.

4 *Orikon*: A weekly magazine aimed at the market provided by young music fans.

5 The Japanese title is *Katteni shiro shirokuma*, and represents a play on words.

6 A play on words, the Japanese word for badger being *tanuki*.

7 This name represents the onomatopoeic rendition of a cat's cry, *nya*.

8 A married couple with a high public profile in the entertainment industry.

9 The most prestigious academic institution in Japan. Winning a place at Tokyo University virtually ensures a successful career. It reserves its places for the *crème de la crème* of the intelligentsia.

10 In Japan sharing rooms to sleep is a common practice amongst students and in itself carries no sexual connotations.

11 The Edo period ran from 1630-1868.

12 In Japanese the terms are *danshoku* and *joshoku*

13 Saikaku Ihara: A novelist of the Edo period, popular with the masses; his subject matter incorporated large elements of the sex lives and customs of that time.

14 The Meiji period of Japanese history ran from 1868 to 1911.

15 *Karaoke*: A popular activity at bars. Patrons get the chance to entertain by taking the stage and singing to taped musical accompaniment.

16 'Johnny's' was a hugely successful enterprise which pooled the talents of many good-looking singers and high profile male entertainers. It was named after one Johnny Kitagawa,

a manager of the company.

17 Ōkubo: A station two minutes from Shinjuku on the Chuō Line.

18 ¥1000, approximately $A14.

19 The *urisen* was a particular kind of bar where selling (*uri*) the body was the house specialty (*sen*).

20 Manga: Comic strips and books hugely popular with adults in mainstream Japanese society.

21 The Japanese title is: *Otoko no tame no Boifurendo.*

Chapter 3

1 The terms *tachi* and *neko* are now hardly used in reference to human sexual activity.

2 Reference is made to an incident which occurred at Takatsuka High School in Hyogo Prefecture in July 1990. The school enforced a strict policy that the school gate must be rolled closed at the appointed time so that late-comers could only enter through the staff room where they would receive a penalty for being late. On the day in question an over zealous teacher slammed the school gate closed, crushing to death a girl who was desperately trying to beat the deadline. This incident was used as a point of reference for those arguing that the finer points of enforcing school rules were being taken too far in Japanese society.

3 Traditionally the Japanese father commands a position of fear and respect in the family. It is often said that one's father ranks with earthquakes, fire and thunder as being amongst the most feared things.

4 The Japanese terms are *dōseiaisha* and *iseiaisha* and the characters used to write these in Japanese contain 35 and 40 strokes respectively.

5 *Okama = poofter.*

6 ¥10,000 approximately $A140.

7 Osugi and Piko are two gay brothers who speak like drag queens and are well known to Japanese TV audiences. One is a fashion reviewer and the other a movie critic. They have been accepted in the Japanese TV world for their novelty value; they are a source of curiosity and amusement, and provide reinforcement for the stereotypical image of gays.

8 The *Ainu* were the original inhabitants of Japan. Neither the language nor culture of this aboriginal race is related to the people we think of as being Japanese today. The *Ainu* primarily inhabited Hokkaido and the northern part of Honshu.

9 Produced by the *Iwanami Shoten* Company, the *Kōjien* Dictionary is considered the most authoritative of all Japanese dictionaries.

10 Whilst the Japanese Constitution doesn't proscribe homosexuality it also doesn't proscribe discrimination based upon sexuality.

11 The Japanese Parliament.

12 An ornamental ceramic figurine of a cat characteristically portrayed sitting up with one paw beckoning good fortune. *Manekineko* are commonly found in shop windows where they are believed to entice customers.

13 The *burakumin* are the residents of the *buraku* or villages set aside exclusively for the undesirable class of people whose forebears were convicted criminals in the Edo period (1630–1868).

14 A monthly magazine focussing on teaching issues, considered a leader in the Japanese educational world in the 1970s and 1980s.

Notes to Part Two

Preamble to Part Two

1 The author includes a description of two Japanese terms which could be used to translate the expression 'sexual orientation'. One implies that sexuality is something that changes as one's likes and dislikes change and the other implies that it is something that you have a hand in choosing. Both are rejected, however, in favour of the expression *seiteki shikō* written with characters which imply neither of these things and which he thus concludes best corresponds to the English expression 'sexual orientation'.

2 An inexpensive and highly nutritious soup made from the soya bean. It is common in the Japanese diet.

Chapter 4

1 In this tale the North Wind and the Sun compete to see who can make a particular traveller remove his coat. For all its determination the North Wind was unsuccessful in its quest, succeeding only in making the traveller hold the coat on tighter and tighter. The moral of this fable is that sheer determination alone cannot be relied upon to achieve a set goal.
2 Osugi is the stage name of a well known gay television personality who flaunts his campness for the camera and who accepts that his role is to reinforce the popular image of *homos* by providing proof of the existence of the stereotypical gay man.
3 A week in late spring in which every second day is a holiday. It provides one of the few opportunities Japanese employees have to slow down during the working year.
4 The floors of traditional Japanese houses are made of stiff mats of tightly woven straw. One *tatami* mat measures approximately 1.8m x 0.9m.

Chapter 5

1 Approximately $A50,000
2 Japanese bedding. It is spread on the floor in the evening and removed and stored in a cupboard during the day.
3 The earthquake that struck the Kantō plain, on which Tokyo is situated, in 1923. It was the most destructive earthquake in Japanese history and is indelibly etched on the memories of those who survived it.
4 A traditional poem consisting of 3 lines and 17 syllables.
5 *Osōmen.*
6 The Japanese term *otoko* not only refers to membership of the male gender, it also implies a rigidly prescribed social role and fixed set of values and expectations in terms of behaviour, outlook and attitude.
7 A home handyman and appliance discount chain store.
8 Hundreds of Australian dollars.
9 An internal sliding room partition made of very light wood and paper.

Chapter 6

1 The biggest conservative political party in Japan. It enjoyed almost continuous power in post-war Japan and traditionally draws support from the strong rice farming lobby.
2 Akihiro Miwa is a gay actor and one of the first people with a public profile to come out in Japan. Carousel Maki was a homosexual stage personality.
3 A circular train line in Tokyo which connects most of the major city sub-centres. It takes approximately 1 hour to complete a loop.
4 Shibuya is one of the major sub-centres of the city of Tokyo. Its station is one of the biggest in Tokyo.
5 The usual term of reference for the proprietors of bars.
6 Approximately $A4000.